Luther, Ministry, and Ordination Rites in the Early Reformation Church

Renaissance and Baroque
Studies and Texts

Eckhard Bernstein
General Editor

Vol. 15

PETER LANG
New York • Washington, D.C./Baltimore
Bern • Frankfurt am Main • Berlin • Vienna • Paris

Ralph F. Smith

Luther, Ministry, and Ordination Rites in the Early Reformation Church

PETER LANG
New York • Washington, D.C./Baltimore
Bern • Frankfurt am Main • Berlin • Vienna • Paris

BV
830
.S65
1996

Library of Congress Cataloging-in-Publication Data
Smith, Ralph F.
Luther, ministry, and ordination rites
in the early Reformation church/ Ralph F. Smith.
p. cm. — (Renaissance and Baroque: studies and texts; vol. 15)
Includes bibliographical references.
1. Ordination—History—16th century. 2. Clergy—Office—History of
doctrines—16th century. 3. Luther, Martin, 1483–1546. 4. Lutheran
Church—Germany—Doctrines. I. Title. II. Series.
BV830.S65   264'.041084'09031—dc20   94-10287
ISBN 0-8204-2572-9
ISSN 0897-7836

Die Deutsche Bibliothek-CIP-Einheitsaufnahme
Smith, Ralph F.:
Luther, ministry, and ordination rites in the early reformation church/
Ralph F. Smith.–New York; Washington, D.C./Baltimore; Bern;
Frankfurt am Main; Berlin; Vienna; Paris: Lang.
(Renaissance and Baroque; Vol. 15)
ISBN 0-8204-2572-9
NE: GT

Cover design by James F. Brisson.

The paper in this book meets the guidelines for permanence and durability
of the Committee on Production Guidelines for Book Longevity
of the Council of Library Resources.

© 1996 Peter Lang Publishing, Inc., New York

All rights reserved.
Reprint or reproduction, even partially, in all forms such as microfilm,
xerography, microfiche, microcard, and offset strictly prohibited.

Printed in the United States of America.

Ave Atque Vale

Ralph lived his life in compassion and hopeful anticipation of justice and unity for all people. He embraced diversity as a gift of God's design, and knew the value of listening and learning from one another. Those characteristics, among others, made Ralph a Christ-like presence for many who knew him. This book is a reflection of Ralph's passion for unity in the midst of diversity. Ralph continues to be a gift to family, friends, colleagues, and the church.

M.F., M.R., and C.S.

In honor of
Robert W. Jenson
who taught me theology
and the centrality of Word and Sacrament

and

In memory of
Niels Krogh Rasmussen
who taught me to study liturgy

Acknowledgments

One of the difficulties in evaluating liturgical sources is not having texts available for comparing translations with the language in which the texts originally appeared. To facilitate such comparison quotations from primary sources used in this study are given in translation and in their original language. Published English translations are used wherever possible. When no published English translations are available or are not specifically cited the translations are mine. These are approximate and intended only as a means of assisting reading.

The format adopted for quotations from Luther's works is to cite the Weimar critical edition first (WA), followed in parentheses by the equivalent reference in the American edition (LW) when it is available. I am grateful for permission to reprint translations of Luther's writings from the following volumes of *Luther's Works*, used by permission of Augsburg Fortress Publishers: Volume 36, edited by Abdel Ross Wentz, copyright© 1959 Fortress Press; Volume 38, edited by Martin E. Lehmann, copyright© 1971 Fortress Press; Volume 39, edited by Eric Gritsch, copyright© 1970 Fortress Press; Volume 40, edited by Conrad Bergendorff, copyright© 1958 Fortress Press; Volume 44, edited by James Atkinson, copyright© 1966 Fortress Press, and Volume 53, edited by Ulrich Leupold, copyright© 1965 Fortress Press. I am also grateful for permission from Concordia Publishing House to reprint translations from Volumes 5, 28, 29, and 30 of *Luther's Works*. Most of the translations of Latin texts for ordination prayers in Chapter One and in Appendix I are by H. Boone Porter, *The Ordination Prayers of the Western Church* (SPCK, 1967), and are used by permission of the publishers.

This study depended on the encouragement and assistance of many. Faculty members of the Department of Theology of the University of Notre Dame who served as advisors and readers included James F. White, Paul Bradshaw, William Storey, Thomas O'Meara, and Niels Rasmussen. Special thanks are due to Paul Nelson and Thomas Schattauer, theological conversation partners who made this project lively and rewarding, to Julie Higgs, who retyped much of the manuscript, and to Mary Frohs for proofreading.

Contents

Introduction		1
Chapter 1	Ordination Rites Prior to the Sixteenth Century	17
Chapter 2	Luther's Liturgical Definition of Ordination	45
Chapter 3	A Decade of Transition: Rites From 1525–1535	87
Chapter 4	Emerging Consensus: Rites From 1535–1570	147
Chapter 5	The End of an Era: Conclusions	201
Appendix I	Texts of the Medieval Roman Rites	235
Appendix II	Text of the 1529 Hamburg Order	253
Appendix III	Texts of the Hesse Orders	257
Appendix IV	Text of the Württemberg Order	271
Bibliography		275
Index		289

INTRODUCTION

Ordination rites express and shape the theology of the communities that use them. The implications of this simple truth are often ignored. When the church ordains ministers its rites of ordination are the public statement of its thought and intent. Most important, ordination liturgies "alter the images we form of ourselves as church, and in particular of those whom the church ordains for ministerial priesthood. As the images change, a new theological understanding is called forth."[1] The sixteenth-century Reformation churches' thought and intent were made visible in the liturgical act of ordaining, and this ritually expressed thought and intent altered the images people formed of themselves as church.

Although new theological understanding was called forth by the various Reformation attempts at shaping an evangelical ordination rite, such efforts did not create a new theological datum. On the basis of the liturgical reforms one cannot argue that a clean break existed between the thought and intent of the church in the medieval rites and that in the early Lutheran Reformation rites. In both cases people were ordained. They were ordained for ministry within the Christian community. They were ordained by a public ritual act. Almost always this included laying on of hands and prayer. Almost always others ordained previously performed or participated in the ordaining.

This is not to imply that profoundly different images were not at work. It questions whether the sixteenth-century reformers abandoned what the inherited rites had intended, even if obscurely: to provide servant leaders for the Christian assembly by means of a liturgical act of that assembly. The ritual distinctions were of degree rather than of kind. To use a biological analogy, if one keeps in sight the focus of providing ministers for the Christian community, the distinction was one of species and not genus.

One can argue a theological distinction of kind at the point of the sacramentality of ordination, specifically in terms of indelible character. Yet nowhere in the medieval rites was the foundation for such a distinction of kind unambiguously articulated. It is possible to interpret the whole of the medieval liturgical action in ordination as equipping a person for service within the community. One can also interpret so as to create hierarchical distinctions of status among Christians. The reformers objected to the latter.

Does the evidence substantiate the view that in ordinations liturgical continuity existed between the medieval Catholic church and the early stages of the reform movement? If so, what are the significance and theological import of that continuity? More important, did the liturgical action of ordaining express and create Reformation theology, or was it only subject to secondary interpretation in the sense that the *lex orandi* had no meaning apart from the *lex credendi* that explained it?

Peter Fink reminds us that "once the act of ordination is recognized to be a liturgical act of the church in assembly, it becomes necessary to hold fast to a new way of imaging the Christ who is source and origin of orders in the church. It is not a Christ who stands over against the assembly. It is a Christ whose full and proper expression is the liturgical assembly itself."[2] The sixteenth-century Lutheran ordination rites reveal such a liturgical ecclesiology among the reformers in a richer way than has heretofore been recognized.

The following chapters consider the possibility that what united Lutheran Reformation churches in the sixteenth century in their understanding of ministry, and linked them with medieval Catholic tradition, was the liturgical act of ordaining. The evangelical movement, at least in its main branches, refocused the church's attention on a central ecclesial act—congregational and presidential prayer, usually with laying on of hands, for the gift of the Spirit for the work of pastoral ministry—as the defining characteristic of ordaining ministers. This act identified those properly called to and accepted in the office of the *ministerium verbi*.

Ordination was not understood narrowly as a ritual act, but rather as a liturgical act. In other words it was the church's work in the same sense that the church's work of word and sacrament is its *leitourgia*. The ritual means by which the *leitourgia* is accomplished, the way by which celebration of word and sacrament is brought to life in the assembly is not immaterial or unimportant. Liturgy cannot exist without rites. But, if one may mix the Latin and Greek, it is possible for the *ritum* to obscure the *leitourgia*.

Introduction

The attenuated liturgical act of the medieval Catholic church's ordination, ironically an attenuation created in part by ritual profusion, presented the problem. Luther and other reformers never abandoned a central liturgical definition of what it meant to be ordained. They altered its ritual embodiment. What they accomplished, as these various rites reveal, was to raise anew how to identify the unity of the church in the midst of its diversity. This tension emerged as a point of issue in the distinction intended by an act of ordaining considered as an unrepeatable act of the church universal in contrast to a locally repeatable installation or investiture in a specific congregation. The liturgical data serves to clarify the nature of the distinction.

Examining liturgical data serves to illuminate other points of controversy as well. A point of confusion throughout the period under discussion (1525-1580) was how broadly one should interpret the office of the *ministerium verbi*. Was it one office, namely that of pastor, so that presbyter and bishop were not different orders? Did it include deacons or the minor orders? Was there a place for elders, such as in the Hesse churches, and were they considered laity or clergy? One cannot answer these questions definitively because of the fluid way in which the various offices come and go as one moves from territory to territory. But if supposedly different rites were used to confirm people in these various offices the distinctions between them should find expression in the liturgical acts.

We undertake two comparative tasks. The first is to see the developing evangelical rites in comparison with the medieval rites. The second is to examine the interrelationship among the early evangelical rites. One can conclude that liturgical continuity as well as a measure of ritual continuity existed in both cases. We should not minimize the differences between the medieval Catholic ordination rites and the new images emerging in the critical, final three-quarters of the sixteenth century. The medieval Roman core of three prayers discussed in chapter one, for example, never appears in evangelical rites. Yet their *functions* as intercession, collect, and prayers of ordination were repeated. Similarly, although the content varies dramatically, the admonitions in the evangelical rites play a role similar to those which William Durandus edited and added to the medieval pontifical traditions, namely to instruct the candidates and community, and make them aware of the gravity of the office into which the ordinands were entering.

We cannot make the sixteenth century systematic. The rites discussed here, as well as the broader evidence compiled in comparative liturgical studies, make it clear that cultural-ritual dialogue is an ongoing process. Additional work can be done in exploring more fully the nature of this dialogue as the structural components of the ordination rites shifted in the Reformation's movement throughout western Europe, especially in light of that movement's commitment to the principle that *ecclesia semper reformanda est*.

Undertaking a study such as this can also provide a corrective for theological reflection on ministry. Since the sixteenth century Lutherans have used the doctrinal writings of Martin Luther and Philipp Melanchthon as the foundation for their understanding of ministerial office in the church.[3] A significant amount of research has accumulated in the past 450 years allowing one to trace various developments in the theological conceptions of ministry by Luther and in Lutheranism.[4] In spite of this wealth of material little analysis can be found of the actual rites for ordination used within sixteenth-century Lutheranism.[5]

The ordination rites in sixteenth-century Reformation churches clearly embody theologies of ministry.[6] To neglect what they tell us about the struggle to define the meaning of ordination and office in evangelical churches is to neglect a full and accurate picture of the way in which Lutherans in that period understood and practiced ministry as the break from medieval Roman Catholic traditions occurred.

Rites for ordination and installation of ministers appeared throughout sixteenth-century Germany in official Church Orders. These *Kirchenordnungen* were written for almost every imperial city and territory as each embraced the Reformation cause. Together with the theological treatises written by reformers concerning the priesthood of all believers and ministerial office this liturgical evidence provides information needed to understand how Lutheran Reformation communities defined the role of ministerial office.

The enduring question is this: What did sixteenth-century German Lutheran churches understand themselves to be doing when they ordained people? An answer to the question will be sought on the basis of what

Introduction

the rites themselves tell us about ministerial office and Lutheran congregations. Although it is beyond the scope of this study to trace the complex history of ordination rites in the Western church, it is helpful to remember what actually existed when Luther and other reformers sought to develop new rites for ordaining. A brief survey tracing the developments in liturgical structure and content is therefore in order. A natural restriction is provided by the fact that the Roman rite absorbed elements from other parts of the Western church's traditions and eventually supplanted them. Thus by the sixteenth century one finds a relatively fixed rite for ordaining bishops, presbyters, and deacons.[7]

In Chapter One we sort out the various ritual elements and briefly discuss their origins and purpose to make clear what rites for ordination Luther and others actually knew and used prior to their own efforts at liturgical reform. We then proceed to ask what was retained from these older rites, what was changed, what was added, and why. The Latin *ordo* helped to shape the reformers' personal understanding of office in the church, and it affected the substance and direction of their own reforms.

When Luther did finally produce a rite of his own it had lasting impact, along with his doctrinal writings on ministry, because of his place in the reform movement as a whole. Any discussion of the liturgical developments in this period must take account of his work. Hence Chapter Two provides a detailed analysis of the theological arguments made by Luther concerning ordination.

Luther was not the first person to produce a new ordination rite, even though he performed the first evangelical ordination of record when he ordained Georg Rörer deacon in 1525.[8] In fact the lateness of his own rite (written in 1535, printed in 1539) indicates in part Luther's sense that a new rite was not necessary. Nevertheless, new rites were being developed as early as 1526 (for Hesse) and 1529 (for Hamburg).[9] These initial attempts to produce a Reformation ordinal are important exactly because they are the first. They help to clarify the earliest tension between what existed and what it was the reformers were trying to bring into being. Furthermore, even if not officially adopted or used (as was the case with the first Hesse order) they anticipate the direction which later reform attempts took. Chapter Three traces chronologically the appearance of evangelical rites from the first in 1526 up to and including Luther's own rite in 1535.

An evaluation of the ordination and installation rites which sprang up subsequently throughout Germany as the Reformation cause was embraced throughout various territories constitutes the next step in developing a fuller picture of the shifts in ecclesiastical structure created by the reform movements. Although dozens of Church Orders containing these rites were written, they often simply copied ritual descriptions from one another. This makes it possible for what would otherwise be an unmanageable amount of material to be assessed in an intelligible manner. The focus of Chapter Four, therefore, is a comparative evaluation of rites used for presbyteral ordination and installation in the years during which the Reformation took hold (1535-1570). Few historians have examined this liturgical material in an inclusive way in order to see how it reveals the reformers' efforts to distinguish between lay, presbyteral, and episcopal ministry. The liturgical evidence is an invaluable resource for any attempt to discover what the issues of conflict were in the sixteenth century regarding pastoral office and to understand Reformation doctrines of ministry.

Much has been said in the history of Lutheran theology regarding Reformation concepts of ministry, but most of the theological interpretations and explanations have grown out of analyses of the doctrinal writings of the reformers (especially Luther and Melanchthon), or the Symbols (the *Augsburg Confession* and related documents in the *Book of Concord*). The difficulty is that few scholars have inquired into what the actual ordering was in the same period before proceeding to their interpretations of a doctrine of ministry. This raises the issue of the relationship captured in the phrase, *lex orandi, lex credendi*.[10]

No one can credibly deny that theological reflection (the *lex credendi*) concerning divine institution of the ministry, the biblical witness, and precedents for practice set in the early church (as the reformers understood them) influenced the shape of the new rites (the *lex orandi*). But liturgical theology has shown that theology as teaching is not directly translatable into worship just as worship (rite) is not reducible to texts or teaching.[11] What happens in worship cannot be turned into a functional equivalent in theological discourse. To study the rites in and

Introduction

of themselves allows us to uncover a primary experience of what it meant to be an ordained minister in sixteenth-century German evangelical churches.

The approach in Chapter Five of this study can be termed interpretive-synthetic. Having analyzed the ritual elements of the various rites for ordination and installation one can evaluate more fully the theologies of ministry expressed by them. Knowing what the ordering of ministry actually was in the sixteenth century can help us to make more balanced and accurate judgments concerning the doctrines of ministry advocated by the reformers.

As already noted, due to the ecclesiological and political upheaval occurring throughout the sixteenth century, Church Orders (*Kirchenordnungen*) were created in almost every territory and imperial city in Germany. These Orders explained the changes necessary to effect a transfer of power from ecclesial to secular authority as structural breaks with Rome solidified. The *Kirchenordnungen*, collected in a critical edition begun by Emil Sehling, provide the primary sources for investigating sixteenth and early seventeenth-century ordination rites.[12] Our investigation of Lutheran ordination rites is limited to the early period (1520-1580), to what can be called the first and second generations of Protestant reform. This puts the liturgical evidence in context and provides a broader and more integrated picture of the first stages of the historical development of an evangelical doctrine of ministry. We also focus on the ecclesiastical and political nature of the transition as the movement from the episcopal structure of the medieval Catholic church to a new, reformed structure for calling and ordaining pastors occurred.

A number of problems emerge in efforts to discover the meaning and significance of the liturgical sources for an evangelical doctrine of ministry in the sixteenth century. A difficulty shared by all disciplines addressing questions in early Reformation history is that of dealing with the polemics of the period, neglect of which can lead to distorted interpretations. Related to this is the provisional nature of much that was produced in response to emergencies or presumably temporary situations. So, for example, in the first quarter of the sixteenth century there was little need to address questions of ordination since most of the first evangelical pastors were already ordained priests, like Luther, and at least initially it was assumed that Catholic bishops would embrace the Reformation cause and continue to ordain. The evidence suggests that through the 1520's practical concerns about training, calling, electing and ordaining pastors did begin to emerge but were dealt with in somewhat makeshift fashion. What then is to be considered provisional and what permanent?

One can formulate an underlying question of this study as follows: What was the meaning, the content of *ordinatio* for the evangelical churches in sixteenth-century Germany? To answer the question we present a theological phenomenology of the early evangelical rites of ordination.[13] This includes honoring the distinction between the theology expressed by the rites and that which is the result of reflection on ordination. For example, we can learn from Luther's writings on ordination and ministry how theology might serve the ordering of the church's ministry, but only by examining the rites can we learn what that ordering actually was.[14]

This focus makes it necessary to refrain from asking questions that seek to locate ordination in a broader stream of theological concern such as, for example, the Jewish roots for ordination, its New Testament origins, or its relationship to patristic practices.[15] Employing the methods of comparative liturgy, we concentrate on sorting out of the common and particular elements of the various sixteenth-century rites while placing them within the context of the Roman Catholic liturgical tradition they sought to replace.

At stake in this discussion is taking liturgical evidence seriously as a source of theology, and using it to clarify how the church understands the distinction between clergy and laity. Despite considerable research concerning the theological formulations of Luther and Lutheranism regarding office (*Amt*), the liturgical witness provided by ordination rites has been neglected.[16] Few studies of this liturgical evidence have been undertaken.[17] The closest one gets to a liturgical analysis in English is an article by Ralph W. Quere published in 1975.[18] Quere's purpose was to provide a general historical survey of the evidence from the early church to the present in order to answer his specific question. Thus his treatment of sixteenth-century rites was understandably brief and

Introduction

focused. A dissertation by Richard Schoenleber discussed ordination in Luther's writing at length but devoted only a few pages to analysis of his rite.[19]

With regard to investigations of the history and theology of Lutheran doctrines of ministry the circumstances are quite different. A wealth of literature exists. Even in Luther's day fellow reformers were interpreting his dialectical explanation of ministry. In the *Augsburg Confession* (1530) and its *Apology* (1531), but already in his *Loci Communes* (1521) Philipp Melanchthon was beginning to alter Luther's views by emphasizing office at the expense of the concept of the universal priesthood. Other early Lutheran dogmaticians and theologians of Lutheran orthodoxy such as Martin Chemnitz (d.1586), Leonard Hutter (d.1616) and John Gerhard (d.1637), usually followed Melanchthon's lead rather than Luther's in their explanations of the office of ministry. Pietism, a reaction to orthodoxy, shifted the focus back to the common priesthood so that in the nineteenth century Lutheran theologians and historians began reassessing the relationship of two views in Luther's works.

The tension between two schools of thought in this period is evident in the work of J.W.F. Höfling and F.J. Stahl.[20] Höfling in his 1835 study argued that Luther "derived the authority of the minister from the divinely instituted means of grace rather than from the will of men, even though he regarded the ministry as given not to a special class within the church, but to the royal priesthood."[21] Yet this view leaned too much toward a potential subsuming of the minister's authority beneath the congregation's for Stahl who in 1862, representing the other side of the debate, emphasized that "the clergy are ministers of the Church, the divine institution, and not of the congregation, which comes into being through the will of men. The ministry does not issue from the common priesthood as though it derived its authorization from the congregation. For Luther, the exercise of the ministerial functions rests on divine authority, not on the will, commission, or consent of the people."[22]

Late in the nineteenth century Georg Rietschel sought to clarify the issue by reaffirming the tension and by examining the concept of ordination more carefully. He concluded that "ordination does not create a pastor, but in the name of the church and of the triune God and in the presence of a congregation it confirms the call by which somebody is summoned to the ministry of the word."[23] The difficulty was, according to Joachim Heubach, that Rietschel made ordination an ecclesiastical-legal matter when it was primarily a theological matter: "Ordination must be freed from the predominantly ecclesiastical-legal framework in which it has been customary to consider it in the Lutheran church and must be viewed in its theological significance and in the manifold relations which follow from this."[24] Heubach wrote this in 1956 and the freeing of which he spoke was already underway. Studies such as Vilmos Vajta's *Die Theologie des Gottesdienstes bei Luther* in 1952, and Hans Storck's *Das allgemeine Priestertum bei Luther* in 1953 kept the questions alive and broadened the theological framework in which they were being asked.[25] Yet by 1958 Klaus Tüchel was calling for a substantial monograph to serve as the basis for future research.[26]

Two major studies remedied this problem and provided the foundation for investigations in the second half of the twentieth century. Wilhelm Brunotte's *Das geistliche Amt bei Luther* appeared in 1959, and Hellmut Lieberg's *Amt und Ordination bei Luther und Melanchthon* was published in 1962.[27] Both men summarized previous research, reexamined the sources, and motivated further exploration and discussion—particularly since they had come to quite different conclusions. Much work has been carried on since the studies of Brunotte and Lieberg.[28] Most of these efforts have been to link ordination and office with other issues. Lutheran-Roman Catholic dialogues on the international level and in the United States during the 1970's also provided an impetus for careful study of the church's office of ministry.[29]

Despite this considerable body of literature, little use has been made of the liturgical evidence provided by ordination rites. A difficulty with much of the secondary source material is that it presupposes or reinforces a distinction between function and order in Luther's views on ordination and ministry, a distinction that may not be supportable. The views of Höfling and Stahl are characteristic of a position taken by scholars down to the present, namely that Luther understood the office of ministry in either functional terms or as divinely instituted. To be sure, Luther had varying conceptions of office, but the factors that have been termed functional or divinely instituted were always operative.

Introduction

Luther, for example, founded the common priesthood biblically on the command of Christ. It was divinely instituted just as the ministry of the word was instituted by God's gift in Christ and lived in his body the church through the power of the Spirit. Within that common priesthood the Spirit granted gifts, functions, vocations to each individual which served to build up the community. The office of ministry was one of these.

On the other hand when Luther argued for a particular gift of the Spirit in ordination somehow different from that given in baptism, the foundation for his view again contained both elements. The gift of the Spirit was given by Christ to the Apostles who in turn handed it on to their successors in the office of the word. It was divinely instituted. But this gift was operative only insofar as the person functioned in the office. It was not the personal possession of the individual believer, some individual, indelible gift of grace.

Lack of clarity in describing Luther's views, in part a problem of his often imprecise terminology, has plagued Lutheranism's attempts to come to grips with a workable definition of ordination and ministry that is true to Reformation insight and the broader catholic tradition. Analysis of the liturgical witnesses can help to clarify Reformation understanding of ministry and perhaps provide a means for overcoming the divisions which different interpretations of ministerial office in the church have reinforced.

Today it is necessary to develop a doctrine of ministry that does justice both to Reformation insights and catholic tradition. Criteria that can provide sound historical, theological, and pastoral reasons for making decisions along the way are needed. Investigation of the liturgical witnesses of the sixteenth century and their relationship to the broader theological concerns embodied in any doctrine of ministry can serve that purpose well. Furthermore, the present state of intra-Lutheran conversation and Lutheran dialogue with other Christian traditions heighten the need for clarification of Lutheran understandings of ministry, especially as revealed by the ordination rites.[30] The issue remains controverted, and continuing ecumenical commitment and involvement demand clarification of this matter if Lutherans are to provide any help in overcoming the barriers that divide Christians with regard to the ordering of ministries in the church.

NOTES

1 Peter E. Fink, "The Sacrament of Orders: Some Liturgical Reflections," *Worship* 56 (1982), 483.

2 Ibid., 486.

3 This is true of the official documents within Lutheranism such as the *Augsburg Confession*, as well as the secondary literature discussed below.

4 The secondary litrature listed in the bibliography is only a small sampling of this material. For a detalied listing of publications on the topic see, for example, the indices of the *Luther Jahrbuch*.

5 In the two most substantial monographs on ministry, Wilhelm Brunotte's *Das geistliche Amt bei Luther* (Berlin: Lutherisches Verlagshaus, 1959) and Hellmut Lieberg's *Amt und Ordination bei Luther und Melanchthon* (Göttingen: Vandenhoeck and Ruprecht, 1962), only a few pages are devoted to analysis of Luther's rite.

6 A wealth of literature exists on the relationship of liturgy and theology. See, for example, Geoffrey Wainwright, *Doxology. The Praise of God in Worship, Doctrine and Life*. (New York: Oxford University Press, 1980).

7 It is fixed most clearly by the work of William Durandus in his pontifical, widely used after its appearance in the fifteenth century. See Bruno Kleinheyer, *Die Priesterweihe im römischen Ritus: Eine liturgiehistorische Studie*. Trierer Theologischen Studien, Vol. 12 (Trier: Paulinus-Verlag, 1962), 189–216.

8 See the discussion of Rörer's ordination below, p. 87.

9 R. H. Grutzmacher, "Beiträge zur Geschichte der Ordination in der evangelischen Kirche," *Neue Kirchliche Zeitschrift* 23 (1912): 363ff., discussed Bugenhagen's 1529 Hamburg rite. For the text see Sehling, V, 502ff., (cited below, note 12). For the Hesse rite see Sehling, VIII/1, 58ff.

10 For a discussion of the history of this phrase and its implications for liturgical theology see Karl Lehmann, "Gottesdienst als Ausdruck des Glaubens," *Liturgisches Jahrbuch* 30 (1980): 197–214.

Introduction

11 Ibid., 208ff. Compare Geoffrey Wainwright, *Doxology*, 1-12, 182-283.

12 Emil Sehling, *Die evangelischen Kirchenordnungen des XVI. Jahrhunderts*, 15 vols. (Leipzig: O.R. Riesland, 1902ff., Vols. I-V; Tübingen: J.C.B. Mohr, 1955ff., Vols. VI-XV).

13 Wayne Arland Ewing, "What Is Ordination into the Ministry," *Lutheran Quarterly* 16 (1964): 211-221. The phrase is Ewing's, on whose analysis the following paragraph is based.

14 Ibid., 212.

15 Ewing, ibid., explained: "The positive thrust of a 'theological phenomenology' of the rite of ordination is thus twofold. First, it points us to the only place where we dare hope to say something meaningful about the evangelical intent of ordination, i.e. to the rite of ordination itself. This may keep us from immediately losing ourselves in the by-ways of exegesis, history, and dogmatic theology. Secondly, it will hopefully provide us with some sort of promising insight into how the presence and protection of the 'preaching of the Word' within congregations need not lead to intentions that lack either a theological dimension of good church order and need not lead to an unresolved, restless kind of doublemindedness (215)."

16 See the secondary literature listed in the bibliography.

17 Frieder Schulz, "Evangelische Ordination," *Jahrbuch für Liturgik und Hymnologie* 17 (1972): 1-54, is an exception, but the scope of his study was limited as he acknowledged. His purpose was to ascertain the basic elements of evangelical ordinations in the sixteenth century and then to trace subsequent historical developments in Germany in order to facilitate contemporary reforms of the ordinal there. The studies of Brunotte and Lieberg treat ordination more extensively but devote only a few pages to detailed analysis of the liturgical evidence.

18 Ralph W. Quere, "The Spirit and the Gift Are Ours: Imparting or Imploring the Spirit in Ordination Rites?", *Lutheran Quarterly* 27 (1975): 322-346.

19 Richard Walter Schoenleber, "The Sovereign Word: The Office of Ministry and Ordination in the Theology of Martin Luther" (Ph.D. Dissertation, University of Iowa, 1983).

20 Johann Wilhelm Friedrich Höfling, *Grundsätze evangelisch-lutherischer Kirchenverfassung* (Erlangen, 1835, third ed.); F.J. Stahl, *Die Kirchenverfassung nach Lehre und Recht der Protestanten* (Erlangen, 1862, second ed.). See also the analysis by

Holsten Fagerberg, *A New Look at the Lutheran Confessions (1529-1537)*, trans. Gene J. Lund (St. Loius: Concordia Publishing House, 1972).

21 As cited by Brian A. Gerrish, "Priesthood and Ministry in the Theology of Luther," *Church History* 34 (1965): 404-442; see page 408.

22 Ibid., 408-409.

23 Georg Rietschel, *Luther und die Ordination* (Wittenberg, 1889), 105: "...so schafft die Ordination nicht einen Pastor, sondern sie bestätigt im Namen der Kirche und des dreieinigen Gottes vor der Gemeinde die Vokation, wodurch jemand zum Dienst am Wort berufen ist... ."

24 Joachim Heubach, *Die Ordination zum Amt der Kirche: Arbeiten zur Geschichte und Theologie des Luthertums*, Vol.II (Berlin, 1956), 168; quoted by Ewing, "What Is Ordination," 213.

25 Vilmos Vajta, *Die Theologie des Gottesdienstes bei Luther* (Stockholm, 1952); English translation, *Luther on Worship* (Philadelphia: Fortress Press, 1958); Hans Storck, *Das allgemeine Priestertum bei Luther in theologischer Existenz Heute*, Neue Folge No. 37 (Munich, 1953).

26 Klaus Tüchel, "Luthers Auffassung vom geistlichen Amt," *Luther Jahrbuch* 25 (1958): 61-98.

27 Cited above, note 5.

28 Examples of such work are Heinz Schütte, *Amt, Ordination und Sukzession* (Düsseldorf: Patmos Verlag, 1974); Reinhard Mumm and Gerhard Krems, eds., *Ordination und kirchliches Amt* (Paderborn: Bonifacius-Druckerei, 1976); Johann-Adam-Möhler Institut, *Amt und Eucharistie*, (Paderborn: Bonifacius-Druckerei, 1973).

29 See, for example, the essays in Paul C. Empie and T. Austin Murphy, eds., *Eucharist and Ministry*, Lutherans and Roman Catholics in Dialogue IV, (Minnesota: Augsburg, 1979).

30 The United States Lutheran-Roman Catholic dialogues have been in progress since 1965, producing nine major documents exploring areas of agreement, convergence and divergence in matters doctrinal and liturgical. In January 1988 three major Lutheran groups in the United States, the Lutheran Church in America (LCA), the Amercian Lutheran Church (ALC), and the American Evangelical Lutheran Church (AELC)

Introduction 15

merged to form the third largest Protestant denomination in the United States. The new Evangelical Lutheran Church in America (ELCA) was mandated by the conventions of the predecessor bodies to do a six year study of the doctrine of ministry. The study phase was completed and a report adopted by the ELCA in Assembly in Kansas City, Missouri, August, 1993.

CHAPTER 1

ORDINATION RITES PRIOR TO THE SIXTEENTH CENTURY

Reform of a liturgical order is necessarily rooted in the history of the traditions which created and shaped that order. Even if earlier forms are repudiated they remain the starting point for understanding both the content of the new order and the reasons for its development. Sixteenth century German ordination rites emerged in the midst of controversies about issues such as the meaning of priesthood, the authority of ecclesiastical offices, the political and economic power of Rome, the nature of the church and the proclamation of the gospel. All of these were related to the question of how ministry in the church was understood. From a liturgical point of view, however, the German rites stand in the tradition of the Roman rites for ordination which developed from the fifth to the fifteenth century. These rites, rather than the larger controversies, provide the starting point for this study.

A sketch of the history of the ritual development of ordination in the Western church helps to put in focus what happened when reformers like Luther and Bugenhagen produced new rites. They were familiar with a liturgical order which had become relatively fixed in the fourteenth century with the publication and widespread use of William Durandus' pontifical.[1] His work, the interpretations made of it, and its actual use shaped their primary experience of what it was to be ordained in the church.

The details of the ritual history which found its conclusion in Durandus' rite have been thoroughly studied and documented.[2] The task here is to provide a description of that rite with commentary sufficient to establish in general terms what the ritual elements were and how they would have been understood. Only when one has clarified what the reformers experienced ordination to be liturgically can one proceed to an analysis of what they were trying to do when they produced their own rites of ordination.

In order to understand both the significance of Durandus' ordination rite and the retrieval of earlier patterns by Luther and others it is helpful to review the history and theology of ordination rites in the Western church. Hippolytus' *Apostolic Tradition* was the first source to describe ordination as an independent rite.[3] It also provided the first full text of an ordination prayer and was the only representative of an ordination liturgy in the West between the New Testament period and the appearance of the Roman sacramentaries.

The *Apostolic Tradition* began with a description of a bishop's ordination which included celebration of the eucharist. The ordination of presbyters and deacons followed this section. The comments on the presbyteral rite were brief: the bishop and other presbyters laid their hands on the candidate's head, the bishop said the prayer of ordination. The phrase "and let him say according to those things which were said before" indicated, however, that the action paralleled that described by Hippolytus for the ordination of a bishop in the sections preceding the presbyteral rite.

The earlier description stated that the bishop was chosen by the people. All then assembled on the Lord's day and gave their consent to the ordination. The bishops present laid hands on the candidates while the presbytery and all others stood by silently praying in their heart for the descent of the Spirit. Then one of the bishops present, at the request of the others, laid hands on the candidate and said the prayer of ordination. One can perhaps assume that the same pattern was used for the ordination of a presbyter.

Hippolytus also offered a hint at the theological significance of the laying on of hands when in describing the deacon's ordination he explained, "let the bishop alone make him a deacon; on a presbyter, however, the presbyters as well should also lay on their hands because of the common and like spirit of the clergy." From a ritual point of view it was clearly the focus of this austere rite.[4]

The presbyteral ordination prayer had three parts: 1) the opening invocation; 2) a petition for the sending of the Spirit for the work of a presbyter; and 3) a petition for preserving the Spirit of God's grace on those ordained.[5] As was the case for the bishop's ordination so here one may assume that the ordination took place within a eucharistic celebration, probably on a Sunday. There was no act of election mentioned explicitly for the presbyter (as for the bishop), but because this was well attested in the tradition one can presume that the community was directly involved.[6] Thus this was a simple rite consisting of laying on of hands and prayer in the context of a community's Sunday eucharist. If the description of the bishop's ordination can be used as a guide, the rite for presbyters occurred at the end of the liturgy of the word and was then followed immediately by the kiss of peace, the offering of bread and wine, and the *Sursum corda*.

After the evidence of Hippolytus several centuries pass before the appearance of texts and rubrics that enable us to describe and understand the liturgy of ordination as it developed at Rome and ultimately spread throughout the Latin patriarchate. The witnesses to this development and diffusion are the *Verona Sacramentary*,[7] Ordo XXXIV of the *Ordines Romani*,[8] and the so called *Gregorian Sacramentary*.[9] The old *Gelasian Sacramentary*[10] in its Frankish forms contained a Roman core of prayers and so is included in the analysis here. The *Verona Sacramentary* dates from the seventh century but its materials were authentically Roman and its ordination prayers may be those of the fifth century. The old *Gelasian Sacramentary* which survives in only one Frankish manuscript of the mid-eighth century also contained the Roman ordination prayers from an earlier era. The *Gregorian Sacramentary* (Hadrianum), a ninth century document, contained the same ordination prayers, while Ordo XXXIV in the *Ordines Romani* presented the directions and rubrics concerning the time, place and circumstances of their use.[11]

These ordination prayers were not direct descendents of those presented by Hippolytus, but rather were fresh compositions of the high patristic age. The same core of prayers appears in all three sacramentaries: 1) an invitatory (*Oremus, dilectissimi*); 2) a collect (*Exaudi nos*), and 3) a prayer of ordination (*Domine, sancte pater*).[12]

Using the material in these sources one can reconstruct the rite of presbyteral ordination as it was conducted in Rome during the sixth to ninth centuries. The arrangement of the ordination mass for presbyters and deacons was the normal mass for the Ember Saturday vigil.[13] Although the reasons for restricting ordinations to Ember Days is not entirely clear, the connection was fixed by the time of Pope Gelasius I (482–496 C.E.). The relationship was generated in part by the fasting required as preparation for ordination, and by the practicality of having ordinations a few times a year. The regular fasting of the Ember Day observances made the preparation of the ordinands part of a community fast. Also, the station day liturgies associated with Ember weeks fit well with the participation of the community in attesting the candidate's worthiness. The mass took place at the basilica of St. Peter, the stational church for the Ember Saturday vigil.[14]

At the singing of the introit the pope and his assistants made their entrance. The *Kyrie* which normally followed was displaced at this point since it appeared within the ordination rite. Hence the pope said the opening prayer upon arriving at the altar after the introit was concluded. The readings with responses and prayers then followed.[15] After the epistle reading and tract, before the singing of the Gospel, the ordination took place. In Hippolytus' *Apostolic Tradition* the ordination seems to have occurred at the end of the liturgy of the word just prior to the kiss of peace and celebration of the eucharist.[16] No evidence explains specifically why the rite in Rome at the later period being described here took place the midst of the readings.

Ordinations did not occur frequently in Rome (perhaps only every four or five years from the fifth through ninth centuries).[17] Thus the many readings, prayers and songs for the normal Ember Day liturgies did not make any specific reference to ordinations.[18] On those Ember Days when ordinations were to take place special readings were appointed. The *Ordines* gave such particular readings only for the ordination of deacons and bishops. For deacons the epistle reading I Timothy 3:8–13 was stipulated, for a bishop, I Timothy 3:1–7.[19]

An early lectionary, the *Comes of Würzburg*, which listed both of these epistle readings also designated the reading of Titus 1:1–9 for presbyteral ordination.[20] Kleinheyer contended that these ordination readings probably took the place of one of the six prescribed New Testament readings for the Ember Saturday on which the ordination occurred, rather than being an additional lesson.[21] For the gospel text, Matthew 24:42–47 was prescribed for the days on which presbyteral ordination took place, John 8:30–39 for the ordination of deacons.[22] No special sung texts were indicated in the antiphonaries of the period, and only in the *Hanc igitur* of the Ember Saturday of *Quadragesima* in the

Gelasian Sacramentary was there a specific reference to the act of ordaining in a mass formula.[23]

To begin the ordination the pope left his chair, took his place in the apse before the altar and read the *Breve advocationis*, that is, the names of the candidates, their assigned church, and their order.[24] The archdeacon went to the candidates and delivered their vestments to them.[25] He then led them to the pope.[26] The act of ordination was introduced by a prayer of the whole community. The pope first said the call to prayer (invitatory):

> Let us pray, dearly beloved, to God the Father Almighty that, upon these his servants, whom he has chosen for the office of presbyter, he may multiply heavenly gifts, with which, what they have begun by his favor they may accomplish by his aid; through....[27]

The prayer to which all were invited was accomplished in two parts. The community offered its prayer in a general form in the litany, then the pope concluded the prayer with a final oration. In the *Ordines* this first part of the prayer was called either the *Kyrieleison, letania*, or *Kryie eleison cum laetania*. In each case the same thing was intended, the old Roman Kyrie.[28] The schola sang the petitions and the community answered with *Kyrie eleison*. Both the pope and the candidates prostrated themselves before the altar during the *Kyrie*.[29] The collect said by the pope concluded the prayer of the community:

> Hear us, O God of our salvation, and pour forth the benediction of the Holy Spirit and the power of priestly grace upon these your servants, that you may accompany with the unfailing richness of your bounty these whom we have set before your merciful countenance to be consecrated; through....[30]

The ordination proper followed, although the directions for it were slight.[31] Using the description in the *Ordines* for the ordination of a deacon one can reconstruct the following steps for the presbyter's ordination: the pope returned to his chair; the candidates ascended the steps to him, one at a time and knelt; the pope, standing, laid hands on each candidate; after all had received the laying on of hands the prayer of ordination was said by the pope.[32] As in Hippolytus' rite, the ritual focus here was still clearly the laying on of hands with prayer. Concerning the content of the ordination prayer itself, Kleinheyer aptly summarized:

> The connections of this prayer to the presbyteral ordination prayer (as well as the episcopal ordination prayer) of the *Apostolic Tradition* of Hippolytus are noteworthy. In both cases there is a three-part structure to the prayer. First, there is the address to God with its narration of salvation history. As an Old Testament type along with the seventy elders (Numbers 11:16ff.) the bestowal of the office of presbyter on the sons of Aaron (Numbers 3:2-4) is mentioned. The petition for the sending of the Spirit indicates an emphasis on personal holiness. Also, in both cases there is the notion that the priests are assistants of the bishop in caring for the community and (as appended in the prayer) as *presbyteri doctores* in the proclamation of the word. Finally, in both cases the absence of a reference to the celebration of the eucharist as the exclusive responsibility of the priest reflects the old order where the bishop is surrounded by his community in the eucharistic celebration.[33]

At the conclusion of the rite the pope exchanged the peace with the newly ordained. The eucharist then continued as usual.

An outline of the rite produces the following structure:

[Ember Day Vigil Mass]
Introit
Collect
Readings (with responses)
Ordination Rite
    Breve advocationis
    Vesting
    Invitatory (*Oremus, dilectissimi*)
    Kyrie/Litany
    Collect (*Exaudi nos*)
    Laying on of Hands
Ordination Prayer (*Domine sancte pater*)
Tract or Alleluia
Gospel
[The mass then followed its normal course]

Although representing elaboration of the minimal ritual description of Hippolytus, the rite reveals that the core action and prayer of the

Apostolic Tradition was not obscured.

For the development of ordination outside Rome during the same period (pre-Carolingian) one must turn again to sacramentaries and rubrical books. Two sacramentaries help at this point, the *Missale Francorum* and the *Gelasianum*.[34] A Gallican church order, the *Statuta Ecclesiae Antiqua*, provided a short but important directive concerning the presbyteral rite.[35] The *Statuta* was a product of southern France, perhaps written by Gennadius of Marseilles around 490 C.E. The *Missale Francorum* came from the north of France (St. Denis?) around 830 C.E. The date and origin of the *Gelasian Sacramentary* were discussed above.

No extant sources reveal what shape the ordination rite may have taken in Gaul prior to the eighth century. When one examines the sources noted one finds a mixture of Roman and Gallican elements. The tendency during this period seems to have been to balance the Roman and Gallican liturgical formulas. The rubric concerning ordination in the *Statuta* stated simply that the bishop (consecrator) and presbyters joined in the laying on of hands. In this respect the *Statuta* followed the pattern rooted in Hippolytus' *Apostolic Tradition* (a source for the *Statuta*).[36] This rubric was reproduced in the *Gelasian Sacramentary* and the *Missale Francorum*.[37] An examination of the euchological texts reveals that the core of Roman prayers discussed above was retained while new, non-Roman prayers were added.[38]

The three non-Roman prayers of the *Missale Francorum* were an address to the community (*Allocutio*), an invitatory (*Consumatio*), and an ordination prayer (*Benedictio*). With regard to the latter two prayers, which also appear in the *Gelasian*, Kleinheyer commented: "The Roman consecration prayer is the actual consecration formula. The two non-Roman prayers become unimportant appendages. They have lost their proper function—a feature which in the presbyteral rite of consecration surfaces here for the first time and appears repeatedly in subsequent development."[39] Whether the candidates actually were acclaimed before the ordination as the allocution in the *Missale Francorum* indicated is questionable. The acclamation of the people in the *Gelasian* was included in the rubrics concerning the hindrances to ordination. One element appeared for the first time in the *Missale*

Francorum, the anointing of the hands. This will be considered in more detail in the analysis of its function in Durandus' pontifical below. The point here is to recognize it as part of the Gallican rite not found in the Roman sources already considered.[40]

The tendency to add the Gallican to the Roman elements continued in the second half of the eighth century, the first phase of the Carolingian reform. The Gelasians of the Eighth Century are the primary sources for this stage of development. There were two basic recensions of the eighth-century Gelasians: 1) an *Urtypus*, represented by the Gellone Sacramentary (ca. 770 C.E.); and 2) a larger group, the most important of which are the Sacramentary of Angouleme and the Phillips Sacramentary.[41]

With regard to the presbyteral ordination rite the two recensions were the same. After the introductory rubric, the same as in the *Gelasian* and the *Statuta*, the first six prayers of the *Missale Francorum* followed. One entirely new element appeared at this stage, the *traditio casulae* which followed the prayer of ordination.[42] The rite then concluded with the anointing of the hands. The two forms for participation of the people noted earlier, namely at the *Allocutio* (*Missale Francorum*) or at the point of recognizing any hindrances to the ordination (in earlier sacramentaries and *ordines*) were joined together.

The *ordines* related to the eighth-century Gelasians are in Andrieu's collection B.[43] These rubrics provide important additional information. The preferred time for ordination became *hora tertia*.[44] The Kyrie was sung after the Introit and was then repeated within the ordination rite. The candidates prostrated themselves for it while the ordinator knelt. Also, before the ordination, while the *Benedicite* was sung, the archdeacon vested the candidates with Orarium (stole) and Planeta (chasuble). A contradictory rubric then stated that after the ordination the archdeacon gave the stoles to the ordinator who placed them on the candidates. Hence there was again a conflation of Roman and Gallican elements, with no apparent attempt to reconcile differences.[45] The resulting hybrid rite had the following elements (based on the *Missale Francorum* and the *Gellone Sacramentary*):

Introit

Rites Prior to the Sixteenth Century

Kyrie
Ordination Rite
    Rubric: *Presbyter cum ordinatur*
    Allocution (Gallican: *Quoniam, dilectissimi*)
    Invitatory (Roman: *Oremus, dilectissimi*)
    Kyrie/Litany
    Collect (Roman: *Exaudi nos*)
    Ordination Prayer (Roman: *Domine sancte pater*)
    Invitatory (Gallican: *Sit nobis, fratres*)
    Ordination Prayer (Gallican: *Sanctificationum*)
    Traditio Casulae (Gellone: *Benedictio patris*)
    Anointing of Hands (Gallican: a. *Consecrantur manus*; b. *Unguantur manus*)
[The mass then continued in normal course]

This outline makes clear that the conflation of Roman and Gallican ritual elements was resulting in a rite filled with duplication as well as lack of clarity regarding the movement and purpose of its parts.

After Charlemagne's reforms were underway and the *Gregorian Sacramentary* was imported as a model the rite underwent a bit of retrenchment. Ordo XXXVIIA of Collection B, which provided the above information, was reworked.[46] The core of the rite was no longer the six prayers of the *Missale Francorum*, the *Gelasian*, and the eighth-century Gelasians but the three of the *Gregorian Sacramentary*.[47] The mixed ritual development was to continue. As Kleinheyer aptly concluded:

> When one compares the general form which the rite for consecration of priests took at the end of the steps of development described in this chapter—around 900—with the administration of priestly consecration in Rome about the same time, one observes a series of differences. Among the most conspicuous is a completely new element, the anointing of the hands. Some of the prayers of the Gallican rite are also strange to the Roman rite. Another difference is the placing of the handing over of the vestments after the laying on of hands and the prayer of consecration. On the other hand, there is no question that the essential core has survived. Indeed again and again the development of the rite of consecration in lands north of the Alps is fed by Roman sources.[48]

In the century after the period described above by Kleinheyer a new type of liturgical book appeared combining the contents of the earlier sacramentaries and *Ordines*, the *Pontificale Romano-Germanicum* (hereafter, PRG).[49] An analysis of its ordination rite reveals a combination of familiar items and new additions. For example, the preparatory rubrics of the PRG had two forms, a mixture of old and new elements in both. This is a clear sign of what was peculiar about this book—it was a compilation of material from a variety of sources.[50]

The presbyteral rite began with a long introductory rubric (*Post lectionem*) which appeared for the first time here in the PRG.[51] The rite was said to take place after the reading, tract, and litany, familiar ground in spite of the new rubric. The rubric described two new elements in the rite: 1) two deacons led the candidates to two priests who in turn led them to the bishop; the bishop and the priests (perhaps only the two, perhaps all the presbyterium) then engaged in a dialogue concerning the candidates' worthiness; the dialogue was repeated three times; the bishop concluded the interrogation with a blessing; all responded Amen; and 2) the bishop had a dialogue with the candidates concerning their acceptance of responsibility, including a demand for obedience.

This form of the dialogue for obedience was shown by Jungmann to be older than the PRG.[52] It was rooted in an old high German priestly oath which in turn had its roots in Carolingian vassal oaths.[53] This indicates the influence of Germanic feudal law on the developing rite. The PRG said nothing about the action which might accompany this promise of obedience. If it assumed the form of the vassal rites the candidate would kneel before the bishop and make the promise by laying his hands in the hands of the bishop.[54] Following this rite the familiar allocution (*Quoniam dilectissimi fratres*) was said by the bishop to the community; the community responded with its acclamation.

The bishop addressed the candidates (*Qui ordinandi*).[55] The laying on of hands by the bishop and presbyters followed as shown in the recasting of the familiar rubric from the *Statuta*.[56] The issue here, of course, is the place of this action. It was now dissociated from the ordination prayer. Kleinheyer explained that "the basis for this reshaping was the desire to relate this rubric organically to the description of ordination. But exactly because of this reshaping of the rubric the laying on of hands now decisively establishes its place here before all the prayers of ordination."[57]

After the laying on of hands the familiar core of three Roman prayers followed. The invitatory (*Oremus, dilectissimi*) received a new title, *Prefatio presbiterorum*, but the call of the deacon which followed reveals that the sense of its original function was not entirely lost.[58] The collect (*Exaudi nos*) concluded the litany as was the case in the preceding texts. The prayer of ordination then followed, although with a new opening line appended from the prayer for deacons.

Considering the nature of the PRG one might expect additional elements from past rites to appear, and indeed that is the case. The handing over of the vestments was more detailed, with prayer formulas for receiving the stole and chasuble.[59] The two prayers which appeared for the first time in the *Missale Francorum* (namely, a second invitatory and ordination prayer), as well as the anointing of hands, followed. The Gallican invitatory retained the title *Allocutio ad populum*, showing again that the original meaning and use may not have been lost. An additional note of interest is that in the Gallican prayer of ordination the phrase *corpus et sanguinem transformare* was altered to *panem et vinum in corpus et sanguinem transformare*. It reveals the effect of the theological debate underway in this period concerning the real presence of Christ in the eucharist and the developing perception of the role and power of the ordained to consecrate the elements.

In connection with this same issue another entirely new element made its appearance here, the handing over of the chalice and paten, the *traditio instrumentorum*.[60] More will be said about it later. It was an extremely important addition in light of subsequent developments where it led to a shift of focus in ordination from laying on of hands with prayer to the handing over of the instruments of office as the substance of the rite.[61] The ordination concluded with the kiss of peace.

The ordination rite continued to develop in Rome after this foundation laid by the PRG. Two pontificals are of interest in this regard, the *Pontificale Romanum Saeculi XII*,[62] and the *Pontificale Romanae Curiae* (PRC).[63] Kleinheyer provides an analysis of both.[64] The final form of medieval development in the rite as it came to expression in the *Pontificale G. Durandi* is of more immediate concern.[65] The importance of this work cannot be overestimated. As Kleinheyer observed: "In the years 1292–1295 a pontifical emerged in the small episcopal city of Mende in southern France which was to become as decisive in significance as the PRG for subsequent development of the pontifical liturgy, the pontifical of William Durandus."[66] This source helps one understand the ordination rite as it existed (with minor changes) until the reforms of Vatican II. In Durandus' pontifical one finds still another reworking of the material that had been gradually attaching itself to the original core of Roman prayers witnessed to in the earliest sacramentaries.[67]

By the time of Durandus the individual rites of ordination for the different grades of order were being placed at different points in the liturgy, although often occurring within the same Ember vigil ordination mass. Thus the first reference to presbyteral ordination came at the beginning of the rite for subdeacons when all the candidates for major orders were also called forward: "Let those approach who are to be ordained subdeacons, deacons and presbyters."[68] The litany was then sung and a threefold blessing said over the candidates. After the litany the candidates for deacon and presbyter returned to their seats as the ordination of subdeacons took place.

The ordination of presbyters began after the singing of the Tract or Alleluia, with the call: "Let those approach who are to be ordained into the office of presbyter" and the naming of each candidate.[69] The candidates, clothed in the vestments of a deacon and with a chasuble over their arm and a lighted candle in their hand, proceeded to their place before the bishop. The *Interdictum*, a formula threatening anathema for anyone attempting to receive ordination illicitly, was then read.[70] The dialogue *Postulat mater ecclesia catholica* followed, its placement here was taken over from the *Pontificale Romanae Curiae*.[71] It provided for the archdeacon's public attestation of the worthiness of the candidates. The familiar allocution, *Quoniam dilectissimi fratres*, also appeared here. Durandus recognized that it served the same purpose as the *Auxiliante* formula which the PRC had attached to the dialogue *Postulat mater*, thus he dropped the *Auxiliante*. But because he reshaped the *Quoniam*, especially in eliminating its concluding sentences, he recognized the need for an acclamation by the community. Thus he appended the concluding sentence of the *Auxiliante* to the *Quoniam*.[72]

Rites Prior to the Sixteenth Century

A long address to the candidates, *Consecrandi, fratres mei*, occurred at this point.[73] It was a new element which served to remind the ordinands about the responsibilities they were undertaking. The *Pontificale Romano-Germanicum* and *Pontificale Romanae Curiae* had a few words of explanation at this same place, but not an extended exhortation. Durandus combined here elements drawn from both the Roman and Gallican euchological tradition in order to provide a theological rationale for what was happening in the rite. The laying on of hands followed immediately. Each candidate went to the ordinator and knelt before him for this action. The bishop and presbyters (whether all or only some of the presbyters present is not clear) came forward then and extended their right hands over the candidates, at which point the bishop said the old Roman invitatory (*Oremus dilectissimi*).[74] The bishop then proceeded to the altar, said the old Roman collect (*Exaudi nos*) and sang the ordination prayer.

The handing over of vestments was retained after the prayer of ordination. In this case it was first a stole with the accompanying formula: "Receive the yoke of the Lord, for his yoke is easy and his burden is light. In the name of the Lord. Amen."[75] Then the chasuble was given with the words: "Receive the sacerdotal vestment through which charity is understood, for the Lord is able to increase charity for you and the work completed. Response: Thanks be to God."[76] After saying a prayer of blessing the bishop knelt at the altar and sang either the *Veni creator spiritus* or the *Veni sancte spiritus*.[77]

The anointing of the hands was done with the formula from the PRG but according to the rubrics of the PRC. It was stated specifically that oil of the catechumens, not chrism, was to be used (*non cum crismate, sed cum oleo cathecuminorum*).[78] As the hands were anointed the bishop said:

> May you deem it worthy to consecrate and sanctify these hands, O Lord, through your anointing and our blessing. So that they may consecrate anything rightly, let them be consecrated; that they may bless anything, let them be blessed, and let them be sanctified in the name of our Lord, Jesus Christ. Response: Amen.[79]

After the anointing the bishop folded closed the hands of the candidate. They remained closed until the conclusion of the mass.

Next the candidates received their chalice and paten as the bishop said: "Receive the power to sacrifice to God and to celebrate mass as much for the living as for the dead. In the name of the Father, and of the Son, and of the Holy Spirit. Amen."[80] Because their hands had been closed at the anointing the candidates touched the chalice and paten rather than actually holding them. The detailed formulation of this rubric communicated its importance.

The mass continued with the reading of the gospel by one of the newly ordained deacons. Instructions for the eucharist followed (it was noted specifically that all of the newly ordained were to commune), accompanied by an entirely new set of ritual elements which took place after the communion. Kleinheyer noted that these elements were not the work of Durandus, but they were clearly new and important additions in terms of altering in yet another way what had once been a simple and relatively unceremonious rite of presbyteral ordination in the West.[81]

The new set of post-communion rites was introduced by the ordinator intoning the responsory *Iam non dicam vos servos*, which the choir then concluded.[82] During the singing of the responsory the newly ordained prayed the creed, which had been displaced from earlier in the rite when the ordination began. The newly ordained then went one at a time to the bishop who laid on hands and said: "Receive the Holy Spirit, those whose sins you forgive are forgiven, those whose sins you retain are retained."[83]

The reason for this second laying on of hands and accompanying formula is difficult to trace based on the manuscript traditions.[84] It is important to note that it results in ritual confusion about the meaning of laying on hands. After this laying on of hands the bishop unfolded the chasuble for each with the words: "Let the Lord clothe you innocently with the stole."[85] After all had this done to them, the newly ordained individually made a vow of obedience to the bishop. Laying their hands in the hands of the bishop they answered his question, "Do you promise me and my successors obedience and reverence?", with a simple "I promise."[86] The bishop then gave the kiss of peace.

When all had returned to their places the bishop delivered a brief exhortation (*Quia res*), reminding them that they should learn from others how properly to celebrate mass.[87] The *Communio* and

Rites Prior to the Sixteenth Century

Post-Communio followed. Another short admonition to the new priests was given after the *Ite missa est*, again reminding the newly ordained of the responsibility of their order.[88] The rite then concluded with the benediction: "The blessing of Almighty God, the Father, Son and Holy Spirit descend upon you, that you might be blessed in the priestly order, and offer pleasing sacrifices for the sins and offenses of the people to Almighty God, to whom is honor and glory forever. Amen."[89]

An outline of the rite makes it clear how much it had been expanded:

[Alleluia or Tract]
Presentation of Candidates
Interdictum
Dialogue (*Postulat mater*)
Allocution (*Quoniam*)
Exhortation (*Consecrandi, fratres mei*)
Laying on of Hands (in silence)
Extending of Hands
Invitatory (*Oremus dilectissimi*)
Collect (*Exaudi nos*)
Ordination Prayer (PRG version of the Roman Prayer)
Handing Over of Vestments (with formulas)
Ordination Prayer (Gallican: *Sanctificationum*)
Veni Creator Spiritus
Anointing of the Hands
Handing Over of Chalice and Paten
[Gospel reading; normal continuation of the mass
 until the conclusion of the communion]
Responsory (*Iam non dicam*)
Creed
Laying on of Hands (with formula)
Vesting with Chasuble
Vow of Obedience
Exhortation
[Communion and Post-communion]
[Dismissal]
Admonition
Benediction

Because Durandus' pontifical assimilated material from a variety of disparate sources and was widely used, little substantive ritual development occurred in the ordination rite in succeeding versions of the pontificals.[90] This becomes clear when one examines early printed editions. The first appeared in 1485, edited by Agostino Patrizzi-Piccolomini, bishop of Pienza, and by the papal master of ceremonies, Johannes Burckhard. Patrizzi-Piccolomini relied heavily on the PGD. Few interesting points emerge in reviewing his shaping of the rite. The ordination still took place between the tract and gospel. It began with the Interdictum and followed the structure of Durandus' rite with only minor variations (such as binding the hands with a small cord after they had been anointed). The rubric concerning concelebration was expanded. Concelebrating was no longer optional as in the PGD. Here the newly ordained were to say the canon *tacite* and together (simultaneously was emphasized).[91]

In general the changes tended to be juridically motivated, that is, to dictate as accurately as possible exactly how each step was to be carried out. But apart from such clarification of directives Patrizzi-Piccolomini maintained the structure and substance of Durandus' rite.

Several key points emerge from this survey. First is the gathering of the whole local church during the Saturday to Sunday Vigil of Embertide for the ordination of men by the bishop to the minor and major orders. It was held in Rome at the shrine of St. Peter and in other cities in the cathedral. It involved the canons of the cathedral and the pastors of at least the neighboring parishes. Second is the stability of the Roman core of prayers with the laying on of hands by a bishop. Despite the ritual additions and even overlays of later centuries, these prayers are instantly recognizable in the ordinations to the major orders. They remained the patristic kernel around which subsequent elaboration grew. Thirdly, this fairly simple and direct rite was already culturally enriched by a more elaborate terminology than that found in Hippolytus.

From the first appearance of the *Veronense* there were now references to worthiness, rank and dignity which pointed to analogies between Christian ministry and Roman public office. The Gallican ordination prayers that were added to the Roman core drew their typology from the pastoral epistles rather than from the Mosaic tradition reflected in the Verona Sacramentary. Their emphasis was both on the personal moral and pastoral qualities of the presbyter and on his transforming role in the eucharist *per obsequium plebis tuae*. While one might prefer the simplicty of the ancient Roman core, this additional *consecratio seu benedictio* added an important specifying dimension to the role of the elder of the community. When the pontificals proper emerged (tenth to thirteenth centuries) additional ritual actions and accompanying verbal formulas, some quite old, were attached to the Roman and Gallican formulas to enhance what was taking place.

The work of Durandus provided the final step of the synthetic-interpretive development underway for more than five centuries. He maintained the structures of the earlier pontificals while reshaping some elements of the rite: 1) an expanded allocution, necessary in Durandus' mind because of the lack of education among the clergy; 2) the recitation of the creed, so that the one ordained "can acknowledge publicly the faith he is to preach"; and 3) a second imposition of hands connected with the power to forgive sins (done by the bishop alone). The priest's power here depended on his ecclesiastical status; that is, he needed jurisdiction. The issue of power given in ordination became a point of contention when reformers like Luther and Bugenhagen challenged the contemporary understanding of ordained ministry and produced new rites.

In the developments considered above the centuries-long interplay of *lex orandi, lex credendi* led to a rite for ordaining priests which was richly ceremonial and, perhaps it is fair to say, somewhat confusing ritually. The sixteenth-century reformers knew little if any of the detail of this ritual development. They did, however, know what it meant to be ordained in terms of the prevailing presbyteral rite for ordination represented by Durandus' pontifical. This analysis has been confined to the presbyteral rite, although at points ceremonial detail from the rites for other orders have influenced the investigation, in order to ascertain to what degree it functioned as a model for evangelical presbyteral rites. Given this historical perspective the task now is to investigate how and why the reformers in the sixteenth century responded to this liturgical witness.

NOTES

1 M. Andrieu, *Le Pontifical Romain au moyen-âge*, Tome III. "Le pontifical de Guillaume Durand," *Studi e Testi* 88 (1940).

2 For example, Bruno Kleinheyer, *Die Priesterweihe in römischen Ritus* (Trier: Paulinus-Verlag, 1962), offers the most extended treatment of the ritual development. The critical editions of the various pontificals with their introductions, and of the Roman *Ordines*, along with abundant secondary literature on various facets of the history and theology of ordination, provide a wealth of material for analysis.

3 For the text see Bernard Botte, *La tradition apostolique de saint Hippolyte* (Liturgiewissenschaftliche Quellen und Forschungen, Heft 39; Münster: 1966), chaps. 2-14.

4 Who laid hands on whom was clearly a theological issue of some import for Hippolytus. An analysis of it can be found in H.-J. Schulz, "Das liturgischsakramental übertragene Hirtenamt in seiner eucharistischen Selbstverwirklung nach dem Zeugnis der liturgischen Überlieferung," in *Amt und Eucharistie*, ed. by Peter Bläser (Paderborn: Bonifacius-Druckerei, 1973), 208-255; see especially 214-231. Cf. Kleinheyer, 171ff.

5 Kleinheyer, 18. See also, H. B. Porter, *The Ordination Prayers of the Ancient Western Churches* (London: SPCK, 1967), 7-11.

6 See Kleinheyer's argument, 22-24.

7 L. C. Mohlberg, *Sacramentarium Veronense*. Rerum Ecclesiasticarum Documenta, Series Maior, Fontes I (Rome: Herder, 1956), 121-122.

8 M. Andrieu, *Les Ordines Romani du haut moyen âge*, III, Spicilegium Sacrum Lovaniense, Fasc.24 (Louvain: 1951), 604-606.

9 J. Deshusses, *Le sacramentaire grégorien*, Vol. I, Spicilegium Friburgense, Vol. 16 (Fribourg: 1979), 95-96; 602-603.

10 L. C. Mohlberg, *Liber Sacramentorum Romanae Aeclesiae Ordinis Anni Circuli* (Sacramentarium Gelasianum). Rerum Ecclesiasticarum Documenta, Series Maior, Fontes IV (Rome: Herder, 1960), 24-26.

11 For a discussion of the dating, authorship, place of composition, etc., see the introductions provided in the works cited. See also Kleinheyer, 26-35.

Rites Prior to the Sixteenth Century 35

12 The relevant sections of the sacramentaries can be compared by reviewing the texts in Appendix I.

13 *Gelasian*: "Mensis primi, quarti, septimi et decimi sabbatorum die in XII lectiones ad sanctum Petrum, ubi Missas caelebrantur" (Mohlberg, *Liber Sacramentorum*, ch. xx, n. 140, 24); ORXXXIX, n. 12 (Andrieu, *Ordines* IV, 284): "Sabbato autem veniente in XII lectiones, statio ad beatum Petrum apostolum. Procedit pontifex hora VII et omnis clerus, tam presbiteri quam diaconi et electi"; ORXXXVI, n. 13 (ibid., 197): "Sabbato vero egreditur pontifex ad sanctum Petrum et universae regiones cum eo laetaniam canendo"; ORXXXV, n. 15 (ibid., 36): "Mensis primi, quarti vel septimi seu decimi, sabbatorum die, qualecumque placuerit pontifici infra ipso mense degentem, veniunt ad sanctum Petrum tam ipse electus vel omnis clerus seu populus, hora diei octava." See also John C. Reiss, *The Time and Place of Sacred Ordination* (Washington, D.C.: The Catholic University of America Press, 1953); J.A. Jungmann, "Die Dezemberordinationen des Papstbuches und ihr Messformular," *Zeitschrift für Katholische Theologie* 56 (1932), 599-604; T. Michels, "Beiträge zur Geschichte des Bischofsweihetages im christlichen Altertum und in Mittelalter," LF 10 (1927), 20-30; L. Fischer, *Die kirchlichen Quatember*. Ihre Entstehung, Entwicklung und Bedeutung in liturgischer, rechtlicher und kulturhistorischer Hinsicht. (München: Lentnerschen Buchhandlung, 1914); and Kleinheyer, 38-52.

14 *Veronense*: "Admonitio ieiunii mensis septimi et orationes et praeces; ...sabbatorum die hic sacras acturi vigilias; ut per observantiam competentem, domino purificatis mentibus supplicantes, beatissimo Petro apostolo suffragante, et praesentibus periculis exui mereamur pariter et futuris: per." (Mohlberg, *Sacramentarium Veronense*, n. 860, 108). *Gelasian*: "Denuntiato ieiuniorum quarti septimi et decimi minsis: ...die vero sabbati apud beatum Petrum, cuius nos intercessionibus credemus adiuvandos..." (Mohlberg, *Liber Sacramentorum*, 101-102).

15 The sources offer different forms of the directions for the ordination mass but do not vary in substance. For example: *Gelasian*: "...postquam antephonam ad introitum dixerint, data oratione adnuntiat pontifex in populo discens: Auxiliante..." (Mohlberg, *Liber Sacramentorum*, n. 140, 24); ORXXXIV, n. 5 (Andrieu, *Ordines* Vol.III, 605-606): "Non dicitur tunc Kyrieleison sed, completo introitu, dat orationem episcopus et legitur apostolum ad Timotheum: Fratres, diaconos esse opportet pudicos, non bilingues, usque in finem: quae est in Christo Jesu domino nostro. Et psallitur gradale. [Then after a brief description of ordination for deacon and priest, the Ordo continued, n. 13]: Et dicitur Alleluia vel tractus et evangelium et quod sequitur et completur missa ordine suo." See also Kleinheyer, 54, note 144.

16 The only textual evidence for this was the explanation given at the beginning of chapter four: "And when he has been made bishop, all shall offer the kiss of peace,

greeting him because he has been made worthy. Then the deacons shall present the offering to him."

17 Jungmann, "Die Dezemberordinationen," 601. Jungmann cited the work of A. Harnack, *Über die 'Ordinationes' im Papstbuch* (Sitzungsberichte der Berliner Akadamie, 1897), 761-778, in making the case that for small geographical areas with few candidates infrequent ordinations would be understandable.

18 For a discussion of the Ember Day readings and possible connections with ordinations see J. A. Jungmann, "Die Dezemberordinationen," 602-603, where he argues that ordination themes were reflected in the vigil readings, especially in the December Ember week.

19 ORXXXIV, n. 5 (Andrieu, *Ordines* III, 605) for the deacons, and ORXXXIV, n. 36 (ibid., 612) for the bishop.

20 G. Morin, "Le plus ancien comes ou lectionnaire de l'Eglise romaine," *Revue Benedictine* 27 (1910): 41-74; see 65.

21 Kleinheyer, 56, note 151.

22 See Kleinheyer, 56-57. When diaconal and presbyteral ordination occurred together the readings for each were probably substituted for some of the six normally prescribed.

23 See Kleinheyer, 57.

24 ORXXXV, n. 22 (Andrieu, *Ordines* IV, 37): "Quo expleto, descendit pontifex de sede et venit ante altare, vertitque se ad populum et dicit..."; ORXXIV says nothing about the place of the ordination; ORXXXVI, n. 18 (Andrieu, *Ordines*, Vol. IV, 198) has: "...stat pontifex in sede sua..."; and the *Gelasian Sacramentary*: "...ascendunt ipsi electi ad sedem pontifices..." (Mohlberg, *Liber Sacramentorum*, ch. xx, n. 142, 24). Concerning the *Breve* see ORXXXVI, n. 16 (Andrieu, *Ordines* IV, 197): "Deinde apostolicus legit ipse advocationis brevem coram populo..."; ORXXXIX, n. 19 (ibid., 284): "Et vocat pontifex vocae magna unumquemque per nomina ipsorum ad sedem et dicit: Talis presbiter, regionis tertiae, titulo tale, Ille." For a discussion of the reading of the *Breve* see Kleinheyer, 50-52. The *Ordines* indicated that the *Breve* was read by the lector at the Wednesday and Friday stational liturgies of Ember week. The *Gelasian Sacramentary* stated that it was read on Ember Saturday, and therefore within the ordination liturgy.

25 For a discussion of this see Kleinheyer, 74-82.

26 ORXXXIV, n. 11 (Andrieu, *Ordines* III, 606): "Si vero voluerit eum consecrare presbyterum, tenens eum archdiaconus ducit foras rugas altaris, exuit eum dalmatica et sic eum induit planeta et ducit iterum ad episcopum." See Kleinheyer, 59, note 160 for comparisons.

27 See Appendix I for Latin text. Translation here is from H. Boone Porter, *The Ordination Prayers of the Ancient Western Churches*, 25. See Kleinheyer's discussion, 59–60. He noted: 1) that the phrase "multiply heavenly gifts" indicated that the prayer was for an increase in the grace already received by the candidate for the office of presbyter, and 2) that a "per" appended revealed that although an invitation to prayer, the invitatory was understood as itself a prayer.

28 ORXXXIV, n. 8 (Andrieu, *Ordines* III, 605): "Et tunc scola initiat Kyrielesion. Et prosternit se episcopus ante altare et post eum ipse subdiaconus"; ORXXXV, n. 23 (Andrieu, *Ordines* IV, 37): "Et tunc incoat scola letaniam et prosternit se pontifex ante altare cum diaconibus vel ipso electo..."; ORXXXVI, n. 17 (ibid., 198): "...et prosternit se pontifex cum ipsis in orationibus, clero interim canente laetaniam"; *Gelasian Sacramentary*: "...incipiunt omnes Kyrie eleison cum laetania" (Mohlberg, *Liber Sacramentorum*, ch. xx, n. 142, 24). The old Roman form is that of the *Deprecatio Gelasii* (Kleinheyer, 61). For a discusssion of its development, see Kleinheyer 63–64, note 193.

29 ORXXXIV, n. 39 (Andrieu, *Ordines* III, 612–613) provided the rubric in the rite for the ordination of a bishop: "Deinde scola incipit Kyrieleison, cum laetania, prostrato domno apostolico cum sacerdotibus et ipso electo in terra ante altare."

30 See Appendix I for Latin texts. Translations by Porter, 25.

31 ORXXXIV, n. 12 (Andrieu, *Ordines* III, 606): "Et tunc alia illi dante orationem, consecrat illum presbiterum..."; ORXXXV, n. 27 (Andrieu, *Ordines* IV, 38): "...et dat illi benedictionem consecrationis solus per se"; ORXXXVI, n. 21 (ibid., 199): "...et conplentur benedictiones eorum qui presbiteri ordinantur"; ORXXXIX, n. 23 (ibid., n. 23, 285): "...et accipiunt orationem presbyterii ab ipso"; *Gelasian Sacramentary*: "...ascendunt ipsi electi ad sedem pontifices, et benedicit eos a quo vocati sunt, et discendunt" (Mohlberg, *Liber Sacramentorum*, ch. xx, n. 142, 24).

32 See Appendix I for Latin text and translation. Kleinheyer argued that the lack of specific reference to laying on of hands in some of the *Ordines* did not mean that this gesture was omitted. Also, when a bishop ordained presbyters all other presbyters present joined in the laying on of hands. But when the pope ordained bishops he alone laid on hands as a special papal privilege (66).

33 Kleinheyer, 69.

34 L. C. Mohlberg, *Missale Francorum*. Rerum Ecclesiasticarum Documenta, Series Maior, Fontes II (Rome: Herder, 1957), 8-10. For the *Gelasianum* see note 10. See also Bruno Kleinheyer, "Studien zur Nichtrömisch-Westlichen Ordinationsliturgie," *Archiv für Liturgiewissenschaft* 23 (1981): 313-366.

35 C. Munier, *Les Statuta Ecclesiae Antiqua* (Paris: Presses Universitaires de France, 1960), 95-96: "Presbyter cum ordinatur, episcopo eum benedicente et manum super caput ejus tenente, etiam omnes presbyteri, qui praesentes sunt, manus suas iuxta manum episcopi super caput illius teneant." For a discussion see 181ff.

36 See Munier, 105-106.

37 See Kleinheyer, 83-84. The text of the *Missale Francorum* is: "Presbyter cum ordinatur, episcopus ei benedicat, manum suam super caput eius teneat; etiam omnes presbyteri qui praesentes sunt, manus suas iuxta manum episcopi super caput illius teneant."

38 The chart below shows the relationships. It is based on Kleinheyer's, 94. The abbreviations are modified to key with the texts in the Appendix. See also the less abstract comparison in the chart in G. Ellard, *Ordination Anointings in the Western Church before 1000 A.D.* (Cambridge, Mass.: The Medieval Academy of America, 1933), 25.

$$GaF_1$$

$$RP_1 \, Ve - RP_1 \, Gr - RP_1 \, GeV_1 - RP_1 \, GaF_2$$

$$RP_2 \, Ve - RP_2 \, Gr - RP_2 \, GeV_2 - RP_2 \, GaF_3$$

$$RP_3 \, Ve - RP_3 \, Gr - RP_3 \, GeV_3 - RP_3 \, GaF_4$$

$$GeV_4 - \quad GaF_5$$

$$GeV_5 - \quad GaF_6$$

(Key: RP = Roman Prayer; Ve = Veronense; Gr = Gregorian; GeV = Gelasian; GaF = Missale Francorum; the numbers refer to the prayers as they appear in order in each sacramentary).

39 Kleinheyer, 101.

Rites Prior to the Sixteenth Century 39

40   For a discussion of this ritual act see Kleinheyer, 114-122. See also Ellard, *Ordination Anointings*. A variety of opinions exists concerning the origin of the anointing. It first appeared in the *Missale Francorum* and the *Gelasianum* (Vat.Reg.316). Ellard traced its origins to old Spanish influence. Klauser argued that the *Missale* was under British-Celtic influence and that the anointing entered the rite at the beginning of the eighth century in connection with developing understanding of the consecration of the eucharistic gifts, as well as with appropriation of Old Testament anointing themes. Of the two anointing prayers, the first appeared in the *Missale Francorum*, the *Gelasian*, and the Eighth-century Gelasians, while the second (the Samuel-David form) appeared only in the *Missale Francorum* (in later sources of the Eighth-century Gelasians it was transferred to the bishops' anointing). Sometimes one, sometimes both hands were anointed. Which form might be older is not clear.

41   A. Dumas and J. Deshusses, *Liber Sacramentorum Gellonensis*. Corpus Christianorum, Series Latina, CLIX (Turnhout: Typographi Brepolis Editores Pontificii, 1981); see also Bernard Moreton, *The Eighth-Century Gelasian Sacramentary* (Oxford: Oxford University Press, 1976); and Cyrille Vogel, *Medieval Liturgy: An Introduction to the Sources*, translated and revised by William G. Storey and Niels Krogh Rasmussen (Washington, D.C.: The Pastoral Press, 1986), 71, for a listing of the manuscripts and editions of these sacramentaries.

42   The *Gellone Sacramentary*, n. 2356, 391: "Hic vesti ei casula: Benedictio patris et fili et spiritus sanctus discendat super te et sis benedictus in ordine sacredotale et offeras placabiles hostias pro peccatis adque offensionibus populi omnipotentem deum, cui est honor et gloria in secula seculorum." See Kleinheyer, 123-131 for an analysis.

43   Kleinheyer, 105-107. The important Ordo here is XXXVIIA (Andrieu, *Ordines* Vol.IV, 233-238), dating from the years 800-813 C.E..

44   Reiss explained: "Pope Anacletus (76?-88?—i.e., Pope Cletus) is reported to have written to all bishops in Italy and to have determined precisely that the consecration of bishops was to take place on Sunday at the hour of Terce. It is now known that this letter is spurious.....Despite the fact that this epistle is not authentic, it was included in many canonical collections...(and) is of value in so far as it is quoted in any of these collections" (2-3). Reiss made it clear that subsequent legislation restricted presbyteral and diaconal ordination to the Ember Saturday vigils, and the vigils of Passion Saturday and Holy Saturday.

45   See Kleinheyer, 107.

46   For a discussion of the recensions, see Andrieu, *Ordines* Vol. IV.

47 Kleinheyer summarized the issue, 110.

48 Ibid., 141.

49 C. Vogel and R. Elze, "Le Pontifical romano-germanique du dixième siècle," Le Texte I, *Studi e Testi* 226 (Rome: 1963), 28-36. Cited hereafter as PRG.

50 Kleinheyer discussed these preparatory rites, 147-148.

51 PRG, n. 21 (Vogel and Elze, 28): "Post lectionem et tractum atque letaniam, parato electo qui presbiter ordinandus est diaconi more cum orario, presentantibus eum atque ducentibus duobus diaconibus usque ad presbiteros, duo presbiteri ducant ad sedem pontificis."

52 As cited by Kleinheyer, 149.

53 Ibid.

54 Ibid.

55 Taken from the PRG's text for minor orders. PRG, n. 25 (Vogel and Elze, 31-32): "Illis etiam profitentibus dicat episcopus his qui ad presbiterii gradum provehendi sunt: Qui ordinandi estis presbiteri offerre vos oportet et benedicere, preesse et predicare, baptizare et bonis operibus et Deo placitis undique redundare." See Kleinheyer, 151.

56 PRG, n. 26 (Vogel and Elze, 32): "Tunc eo inclinato, imponat manum super caput eius, et omnes presbiteri qui adsunt manus suas iuxta manum episcopi super caput illius teneant, et ille det orationem super eum."

57 Kleinheyer, 151.

58 PRG, n. 27, 28 (Vogel and Elze, 32).

59 PRG, n. 30 (Vogel and Elze, 34): "Hic reflectat orarium super humerum eorum dextrum, dicens ad eos per singulos: Accipe iugum domini, iugum enim eius suave est et onus eius leve." PRG, n. 31 (ibid.): "Hic vestiat eos casula, dicens ad unumquemque: Stola innocentiae induat te dominus. Accipe vestem sacerdotalem per quam caritas intellegitur; potens est enim Deus ut augeat tibi caritatem et opus perfectum. Qui vivit." PRG, n. 32 (ibid.): "Item alia. Induere vestibus praeclaris a cunctis commaculationum spurcitiis expurgatus, descendatque super te divinae trinitatis ante mundi constitutionem tibi benedictione data. Per omnia saecula saeculorum. Amen."

Rites Prior to the Sixteenth Century 41

60 PRG, n. 36 (Vogel and Elze, 35): "Hoc facto, accipiat patenam cum oblatis et calicem cum vino et det eis discens: Accipite potestatem offerre sacrificium Deo missamque celebrare tam pro vivis quam pro defunctis, in nomine domini. Resp. Amen." For a discussion of the transfer of vestments, anointing of the hands, and handing over of the chalice and paten, see Kleinheyer, 154–162. For a different point of view see J. Le Goff, "Les Gestes symboliques dans la vie sociale, les gestes de la vassalite," in *Simboli e simbologia nell'alto medioevo* (Settimane di Studio del Centro Italiano di Studi sull'alto Medioevo, Spoleto: 1976), 679–779.

61 As declared in the "Decretum pro Armeniis," (DS 1326) by the Council of Florence in 1439.

62 M. Andrieu, *Le pontifical romain au moyen-âge*. Tome I. "Le pontifical romain du XIIe siècle," *Studi e Testi* 86 (1938).

63 M. Andrieu, *Le pontifical romain au moyen-âge*. Tome II. "Le pontifical de la curie romaine au XIIIe siècle," *Studi e Testi* 87 (1940).

64 Kleinheyer, 167–188.

65 M. Andrieu, *Le pontifical romain au moyen-âge*. Tome III. "Le pontifical de Guillaume Durand," *Studi e Testi* 88 (1940). Hereafter cited as "PGD."

66 Kleinheyer, 189.

67 See text with translation in Appendix I.

68 PGD, ch. xi, n. 1 (Andrieu, *Pontifical* III, 349): "Accedant qui ordinandi sunt subdiaconi, diaconi et presbiteri."

69 PGD, ch. xiii, n. 2 (ibid., 364): "Accedant qui ordinandi sunt ad ordinem presbiterii." An alternative was given for it to occur between the Gospel and Creed. See Kleinheyer, 191, 205–208.

70 PGD, ch. xiii, n. 2 (ibid.): "Omnibus ergo hoc ordine dispositis, ponitur interdictum ut supra." The "ut supra" referred to the rubric in the ordination of porters. There the text for the *interdictum* read: "...interdict publice sub anathemate ne quis ad susceptionem ordinis illius se ingerere presumat, qui non fuerit canonice examinatus et approbatus, et ne, uno ordione suscepto, alium sine licentia recipere presumat" (PGD, ch. vi, n. 2 (ibid., 340)).

71 PGD, ch. xiii, n. 3 (ibid., 364–365). See Kleinheyer, 192.

72 Kleinheyer, 193, provided a comparative analysis of the PRG and PGD forms of the *Quoniam*.

73 PGD, ch. xiii, n. 5 (Andrieu, *Pontifical* III, 365-67).

74 For a discussion of the origins of the ritual gesture of extending the hands over the candidates see Kleinheyer, 197ff.

75 PGD, ch. XIII, n. 10 (Andrieu, *Pontifical* III, 368): "Accipe iugum domini, iugum enim eius suave est et onus eius leve. In nomine domini. Amen."

76 PGD, ch. XIII, n. 11 (ibid., 368): "Accipe vestem sacredotalem, per quam caritas intelligitur. Potens est enim dominus augere tibi caritatem et opus perfectum. Response: Deo gratias."

77 The prayer was the Gallican ordination prayer attested in the *Missale Francorum*: "Deus sanctificationum omnium auctor." See above, p. 25. The singing of *Veni Creator Spiritus* at this point was attested in all other pontificals. Only one, in Mainz, had the *Veni sancte spiritus*. In all of the pontificals before the PGD as well as in the PGD itself, the singing was not a prelude to the anointing of the hands as in the PRC. See Kleinheyer, 202-203.

78 PGD, ch. xiii, n. 14 (Andrieu, *Pontifical* III, 369).

79 PGD, ch. xiii, n. 14 (ibid.). The full formula was from the PRG, n. 35 (Vogel and Elze, Le Texte II, 35): "Consecrare et sanctificare digneris, domine, manus istas per istam unctionem et nostram benedictionem, ut quecumque recte consecraverint, consecrentur et quecumque benedixerint, benedicantur et sanctificentur in nomine domini nostri Iesu Christi. Resp. Amen."

80 PGD, ch. xiii, n. 17 (Ibid., 370): "Accipe potestatem offerre sacrificium Deo missaque celebrare tam pro vivis quam pro defunctis. In nomine Patris et filii et spirtus sancti. Response: Amen."

81 Kleinheyer, 204-205.

82 PGD, ch. xiii, n. 23 (Andrieu, Pontifical III, 371): "Iam non dicam vos servos, sed amicos meos, quia omnia cognovistis que operatus sum in medio vestri. Alleluia. Accipite spiritum sanctum in vobis paraclitum. Ille est quem pater mittet vobis. Alleluia. Vers. Vos amici mei estis, si feceritis que ego precipio vobis. Accipite. Gloria patri et filio et spiritui sancto. Ille." This use of the responsory was new in Durandus' pontifical although it was the responsory which followed the second lesson of

Rites Prior to the Sixteenth Century 43

Nocturn on the Saturday of Pentecost. Kleinheyer explained the connections, 211.

83 PGD, ch. XIII, n. 25 (Andrieu, Pontifical III, 372): "Accipe spiritum sanctum, quorum remiseris peccata remittuntur eis et quorum retinueris retenta erunt."

84 Kleinheyer argued that it was the result of a formula developing for the otherwise silent first laying on of hands being transferred to this concluding point in the rite in connection with a communion rubric. It was also related to the stretching out of the hands over the heads of the candidates rather than laying on hands at the earlier point in the rite. The significant fact is that Durandus joined these elements with the responsory and vow of obedience in an effort to create a coherent relationship among the elements he found in the manuscript traditions with which he worked (204-216).

85 PGD, ch. XIII, n. 26 (Andrieu, Pontifical III, 372): "Stola innocentie induat te dominus."

86 PGD, ch. xiii, n. 27, (ibid.): "Promittis michi et successoribus meis obedientiam et reverentiam? Et ille respondet: Promitto."

87 PGD, ch. XIII, n. 28 (ibid., 372-373).

88 PGD, ch. XIII, n. 30 (ibid., 373).

89 PGD, ch. xiii, n. 31 (ibid., 373): "Benedictio Dei omnipotentis, patris + et filii + et spiritus + sancti descendat super vos, ut sitis benedicti in ordine sacerdotali et offeratis placabiles hostias pro peccatis atque offensionibus populi omnipotenti Deo, cui est honor et gloria in secula seculorum. Resp.: Amen."

90 For an analysis of pontifical revisions produced in the 15th century see Marc Dykmans, *Le Pontifical romain* (*Studi e Testi* 311, Rome: 1985).

91 "Presbiteri vero ordinati retro pontificem vel hincinde ubi magis commodum erit in terra genuflexi habeant libros coram se super scabellis seu bancis ordinantes: dicentes tacite canonem et quecumque de missa dixerit pontifex, qui tamen bene advertat quod secretas morose dicat et aliquantulum alte ita ut ordinati sacerdotes possint secum omnia dicere: et presertim verba consecrationis que dici debent eodem momento": *Pontificalis Liber* 1485, f 28[v]; as cited by Kleinheyer, 220, note 24.

CHAPTER 2

LUTHER'S LITURGICAL DEFINITION OF ORDINATION

Luther influenced almost every facet of the Reformation in Germany, but that influence was perhaps nowhere more pervasive than in evangelical perspectives on ministry. The task here is straightforward: to explore how Luther's understanding of a specific event of worship, the celebration of ordination, provides both a context and means for interpreting what he believed ordained ministry in the church to be. Some preliminary remarks will help to put in context the reasons for a liturgical focus.

It is difficult if not impossible on the basis of his writings to argue that Luther had an unambiguous or single understanding of pastoral ministry in the church. A case can be made for contradictory positions if one simply picks and chooses evidence from among the many works that address this topic. Yet it is not sufficient to explain that Luther's various assessments of ordained pastoral ministry are only the result of different periods in his career when he found himself battling different opponents.[1] This can result in a situation ethic approach that leaves no room for continuity or integrity in Luther's understanding. Neither is it helpful to search for an underlying theme or thread of unity by subordinating the clearly divergent perspectives to an abstract theological concept.[2] It is the issue itself that provides the core around which specific questions revolve. That core has one center: ministry.

Attempts to evaluate Luther's views on ministry have usually focused on the various doctrinal treatises which directly or indirectly discuss it.[3] With a few exceptions, scholars have rarely included liturgical evidence, rites actually used for ordination, in their evaluation.[4] Such an omission may lead to consequences such as those noted—seeing no consistency in Luther's views over time or imposing on them an arbitrary principle of unity. The dilemma results from not recognizing a break between theory and practice which often characterizes research on Luther's understanding of ministry. Incorporating an assessment of the development and use of Reformation rites for ordaining may provide clues for interpreting the larger questions surrounding Luther's views while at the same time helping to overcome any implied theory/practice dichotomy.[5]

This also means that liturgical evidence cannot be isolated and interpreted apart from the larger doctrinal controversies. Vilmos Vajta was correct in asserting that it is "not enough to examine the actual liturgical reforms introduced by Luther and his collaborators. The inner motives for these reforms must be explored and set within the framework of his whole theology."[6] Although one must be cautious in expecting that inner motives can ever be understood, the focus on broader context is necessary. One need only remember that Luther's devastating commentary on the abomination of the mass on the one hand and his actual reforms of it in 1523 and 1526 on the other reveal a strange mix of radical reasoning in terms of doctrine with conservative changes in actual practice.[7] To base historical judgments of Luther's reforms of the mass solely on the 1520 treatises, for example, would result in a distorted perception of what was in fact a significant strain of pastoral, liturgical conservatism within him.

Frieder Schulz has offered an additional caution for those who focus on Luther's liturgical reforms, arguing that they were not all alike. He believes that the reforms of various rites can be understood as forming a continuum that ranges from continuity to innovation when compared with existing medieval rites.[8] He sees Luther's 1523 reform of the baptismal liturgy (*Taufbüchlein*) as an example of continuity with then current baptismal liturgies. The 1523 reform of the mass (*Formula Missae*) is an example of innovation occurring within a framework of continuity, while the 1535/39 ordination rite is viewed as a clear example of innovation. Schulz explains:

> Because Luther did not want to exchange the legalism of older rites for a new legalism of reformed rites, he could dispassionately allow the traditional orders and customs when the evangelical core of the event was not obscured, as he did in the *Taufbüchlein* of 1523 and in the *Formula Missae*. Also, he was hesitant about liturgical innovation for pastoral reasons. When the time was right, however, he did not hesitate to establish something new and do away with whatever diminished the proclamation of Christ or was no longer deemed appropriate, as the revised *Taufbüchlein* and *Deutsche Messe* show. . . .[This is the case] in the reform of the ordination liturgy. Here Luther saw it necessary

to work anew from the ground up without regard for precedent. That is why one can recognize in the ordination formula, more clearly than in Baptism and the Mass, how Luther proceeded with liturgical structure rooted in Reformation starting points. What earlier had been only partially operative is here impressed on the whole of the order.[9]

Schulz's assessment of the innovative nature of Luther's ordination rite was not new. Paul Drews had made the point in his introduction to the Weimar edition of the rite, and it was carried over in Ulrich Leopold's translation for the American edition of Luther's works.[10] Commenting on Leopold's evaluation, Bryan Spinks noted that Luther developed a new rite of ordination for two reasons:

> One factor for this radical departure from the Western Church's traditional liturgical forms may have been the Reformer's lack of attachment to and familiarity with the medieval rites. He would have been acquainted with them, from his own ordination and his presence at other ordinations. But the rites were contained in the *Pontifical*, the bishop's book, and as an Augustinian Friar, Luther himself would never have had the occasion to use them. Furthermore, unlike the Mass, they were not part of his regular liturgical life; the Reformer would have felt no personal attachment to them. However, the overriding factor for the lack of resemblance between the rites was Luther's theology of ministry; it is here that the absolute necessity for a new rite is to be found.[11]

It is true that Luther's library did not contain a copy of any *Pontifical*. The question is whether his presumed lack of familiarity with it and his lack of personal attachment are adequate criteria by which to judge his reforms.[12] Even Spinks' admission that a more important factor was Luther's theology of ministry is troublesome for it may presume the problematic break between theory and practice noted above. Was Luther so clearly committed to the position that *legem supplicandi lex statuat credendi* (to reverse Prosper of Aquitaine's dictum)? Why did it take so long for Luther to produce a rite for ordination when he was conscious of the need as early as 1525? Cannot the same argument about Luther's pastoral conservatism with regard to his reluctance to revise the mass be made here as well, even though the ordination rite was not part of the daily liturgical life of the reformer or the people?

To say that Luther created something completely new, having nothing in common with the medieval rites, is to assume that: 1) the medieval rites had no connection with the biblical foundations which Luther sought to recover, and the scriptural texts in Luther's rite had no relation to scriptural texts incorporated in the medieval rites; 2) the ritual acts in the medieval rites which Luther did abandon carried the whole intent of the rite; 3) the structure of the rite was immaterial; 4) the context for celebrating the rite had nothing to do with its interpretation.

If Luther had desired to do something completely new he could have abandoned a public rite altogether. Or, even if retaining a version of it, he could have refused to involve others who had been ordained previously in the laying on of hands. He could have demanded renunciation of ordination from those ordained by Roman Catholic bishops, or required reordination of those who embraced the Reformation cause but had been ordained previously. Luther did none of these things. Even in the early treatise on ministry to the church in Bohemia (1523), with its strong polemic against Roman Catholic consecration, Luther did not advocate that ordination be abandoned but rather argued that the church there make its action and theology consonant.

The task, therefore, is to reexamine the question of the relationship between Luther's developing doctrinal expressions of his understanding of ministry with the emerging Reformation practices for calling, ordaining and installing pastors in Reformation churches in Germany.

Priesthood and Ministry

Luther's personal experience of ordained ministry began soon after he entered the Augustinian monastery at Erfurt in July, 1505. His period of postulancy there would have been a few weeks, up to two months at the most, which means that his novitiate began in the fall of that year. Late in the summer of 1506 at the earliest Luther was admitted to profession. The minor and major orders followed in succession, although the dates are not certain: subdiaconate, September 19 or December 19, 1506; deaconate, February 27, 1507; priesthood, April 3, 1507. A dispensation was necessary since Luther was not yet twenty-five, the canonically prescribed age for ordination. The ordinations were done by the suffragan Johann Bonemilch who resided in Erfurt and was titular bishop of Laasphe.[13]

One can assume that Luther witnessed and perhaps participated in ordinations periodically between 1507 and 1520, but there is no evidence to support such an assumption or interpret its impact on his thinking. The first substantial material to reveal Luther's thinking on ordained ministry is that of the well-known 1520 treatises.[14] The intent of these works was to make a distinction between priesthood and the office of ministry, even though that distinction was often less than clear.

Luther's liturgical starting point was the issue of consecration. He wanted to eliminate any possibility of seeing clergy and laity as different kinds of Christians and so he argued that baptism was the true and only consecration of all Christians into Christ's priesthood:

> ...all Christians are truly of the spiritual estate, and there is no difference among them except that of office...The pope or bishop anoints, shaves heads, ordains, consecrates, and prescribes garb different from that of the laity, but he can never make a man into a Christian or into a spiritual man by so doing.[15]

Anointing was the focus of Luther's liturgical criticism because he believed that anointing in both baptism and ordination had created a confusion of the two, and resulted in the denigration of baptism:

> But what is most especially one of the real abominations opposing the dear and blessed baptism is that they boast that with their chrism and consecration they produce clerics in the holy church, that is, a far, far higher and holier estate than baptism bestows.[16]

Yet even at this early stage when he most vehemently attacked Roman Catholic practice the legitimacy of a rite for ordaining was not called into question. Luther's concern was the abuse and misinterpretation of the rite.

The point of contention for Luther was that the rite of ordination as practiced in the medieval church was consecration to a sacrificial priesthood rather than to the preaching office or administration of word and sacrament. Baptism and ordination as liturgical acts therefore become a key for interpreting Luther's understanding of the church.

Liturgy has inevitable ecclesiological implications, as he clearly recognized. One cannot separate the church's rites, its worship, from what it means to be the church. If the liturgical act of consecration to priesthood, for example, could be used to justify saying mass privately it was for Luther a false intention and false substance that had to be corrected. Similarly, if the rite could be understood as somehow divorced from the community, as was the case with absolute ordinations (those done without an accompanying call to a specific community) then it was in fact not ministry.[17]

The influence of the polemical cast of the 1520 treatises was apparent where Luther diminished the significance of the rite of ordination by comparing it to other less important acts. Of course the point of the argument here was that ordination was not a sacrament, and for a specific reason:

> ...ordination is a certain churchly rite, on a par with many others introduced by the church fathers, such as the consecration of vessels, houses, vestments, water, salt, candles, herbs, wine and the like. No one calls any of these a sacrament, nor is there in them any promise. In the same manner, to anoint a man's head with oil, or to shave his head and the like is not to administer a sacrament, since no promise is attached to them; they are simply being prepared for a certain office, like a vessel or an instrument.[18]

Luther made no mention of laying on of hands and prayer but rather explained the content of medieval ordination in terms of its secondary ritual elements. The ritual significance of ordination was not abandoned, although it was clear that at this point Luther held the opinion that the rite was *iure humano*, that is, introduced by the church fathers. One should admit the possibility, however, that only those elements he rejected as secondary and invalid were considered *iure humano* by him.

In light of the fact that he was at this time defining a sacrament partly in terms of whether it had a dominical command behind it this minimizing of ordination was understandable. A year earlier in a 1519 letter to Spalatin, Luther had expressed his doubts about the sacramental character of holy order.[19] Although never willing to concede that ordination was a sacrament like baptism and eucharist, Luther was ready to defend its efficacy as a liturgical act.[20] Writing in 1521 against

Emser, Luther acknowledged that if understood correctly Roman Catholic ordination did accomplish something: "Thus consecration does not make a cleric, but it does make servants out of clerics."[21]

The contrast Luther was drawing between priest (cleric) and minister/pastor (servant) merits more detailed analysis. The biblical foundation for his understanding of priesthood was I Peter 2:9.[22] In his 1522 sermons on I Peter he explained its implications.[23] It would be easy to eliminate the confusion about what ministry is among Lutherans if Luther had made a sharp distinction between the tasks of priesthood and the pastoral office of ministry. We are all priests through baptism, but not all are pastors. Luther had said this even in the 1520 work "To the Christian Nobility."[24] Thus, if the functions of each are clearly distinguishable, one can arrive at a clear differentiation, albeit juridically, of the two roles. Such differentiated definition is not accessible in Luther's explanations because it is in the overlapping of his descriptions of the roles that the confusion is generated.

In the sermon on I Peter 2:9 Luther first made it clear that the text was not supporting any clergy-laity distinction. It was not presenting a case for a twofold priesthood, an external priesthood and a spiritual priesthood.[25] Luther wanted to deny a mediatorial, sacrificial power on the part of some Christians (those externally anointed priests) over against all others (the spiritual priesthood). This argument was still set in the context of the positions enunciated in 1520 concerning the sacrifice of the mass and a sacramental system controlled not by the assembly of believers but by an elite group within it whose access to God was conceived differently from all others who constituted the assembly.

The difficulty was not that Luther made such a denial but rather his efforts to state the positive content of the roles of priest and pastor. He could say that because Christ is the only true priest and we are all united with him as brothers and sisters through our baptism, "all Christians have the authority, the command, and the obligation to preach, to come before God, to pray for one another, and to offer themselves as a sacrifice to God."[26] The point seems to be that no one can stand between the individual Christian and God by claiming to offer the only efficacious access to God. If Luther were then to make the contrasting point, that to speak publicly rather than privately is the role of the pastoral office, the distinction would be clear. Indeed he did make such a distinction, but he also spoke of the roles in ways that seem to combine them: "the first office, that of the ministry of the word, therefore, is common to all Christians."[27]

Luther undoubtedly wanted to prevent any group from claiming special favor *coram Deo*, for that would be a denial of Christ's saving death and resurrection opening the kingdom of heaven to all believers without regard for status. If ordination resulted in the creation of such a priestly class it was contrary to the gospel:

> This is the true priesthood. As we have heard it embraces these three things: to offer spiritual sacrifices, to pray for the congregation, and to preach. He who can do this is a priest. They are all obliged to preach the Word, to pray for the congregation, and to sacrifice themselves before God. Let those fools go their way who call the spiritual estate "priests," who, after all, exercise no office other than being tonsured and anointed. If shaving the head and anointing made one a priest, I could even oil and anoint the hoofs of an ass and make him a priest too.[28]

That there was to be a distinction, however, was somehow rooted in a contrast between the individual, priestly responsibility to pray and preach in terms of personal witness and the public pastoral responsibility to speak to and for the whole assembly. In other words the existence of an office distinguished from the priesthood was manifest throughout Luther's argument.

The polemical edge of this sermon was directed toward those who held to the existence of a class of priests who said private masses and were divorced from any public responsibility to and for the assembly of believers. If this situation were corrected, Luther explained how circumstances would be different:

> Thus those who are now called priests would all be laymen like the others, and only a few officiants would be elected by the congregation to do the preaching. Thus there is only an external difference because of the office to which one is called by the congregation. Before God, however, there is no distinction, and only a few are selected from the whole group to administer the office in the stead of the congregation. They all have this office, but nobody has any more authority than the other person has. Therefore nobody should come forward of his own accord and preach in the congregation. No, one person must be chosen

from the whole group and appointed. If desired he may be deposed.[29]

Earlier in this sermon Luther wanted to deny any twofold priesthood, one external and the other spiritual. Yet he here wanted to maintain an external distinction in terms of office. What was the nature of this apparent contradiction?

When Luther explained that the content of the universal priesthood granted to every believer without distinction was to pray and preach, etc., he meant that each person was, as a little Christ, mediator of the gospel to any brother or sister. When the assembly gathered as a worshipping community the public role of such gospel proclamation was to be limited to one "chosen from the whole group and appointed." Luther stated it again later in the sermon when he said that "some can be selected from the congregation who are officeholders and servants and are appointed to preach in the congregation and to administer the sacraments. But we are all priests before God if we are Christians."[30]

Luther went on to argue that he would like to see the words priest and Christian used synonymously. In other words it appears that the key to making sense of the overlapping definitions and apparent contradictions might be rooted in the issue of identification. The individual Christian was identified in baptism as one who had access to the promises of God in Christ, both to speak and hear them. The ordained person, on the other hand, had an identity only in relation to a specific community, but consequently also to the whole church insofar as that specific community was the local embodiment of it.

To be sure, the priesthood of individual Christians could not exist apart from the community, apart from the story mutually told as an objective external word of God over against one's personal subjectivity. But the community's priestly identity extended beyond its visible assembly for worship. Contact with the priestly proclamation of the gospel was not restricted to those moments when the community was assembled. Did ordination imply a restriction of any kind to what could only happen in the midst of the assembly?

The issue of what ordination signified was pursued at length in the one extended treatise which Luther devoted specifically to ministry, the 1523 work "Concerning the Ministry."[31] Here in the midst of a polemic against the Roman concept of *ordo* Luther recovered a scriptural sense of the *sacra ordinatio*:

> Ordination indeed was first instituted on the authority of Scripture, and according to the example and decrees of the Apostle, in order to provide the people with ministers of the Word. The public ministry of the Word, I hold, by which the mysteries of God are made known, ought to be established by holy ordination as the highest and greatest of the functions of the church, on which the whole power of the Church depends, since the church is nothing without the Word and everything in it exists by virtue of the Word alone.[32]

No one received the competence to do the work of the pastoral office in ordination if it took place *sine verbo*, which, of course, was Luther's opinion of consecration to the priesthood in his day.[33] The target of Luther's polemical critique was a sacrificial priesthood (*Opfer-priestertum*), not an ordination that properly set a person in the office of preaching in relation to a specific community.

The situation of compromise in Bohemia, sending priests to Rome for ordination only to have them return and deny what they had vowed concerning communion under both species, was unique. One might expect Luther to have told the church there to abandon ordination completely, especially to reject those ordained in Rome under false pretenses. Yet he did not do so. In spite of harsh sounding language which appeared to condemn ordination as such, the issue for Luther was misuse of both the intent and substance of the act of ordaining:

> But he who came into the ministry through these masks, let him carry on, assume the office and administer it in a pure and worthy manner. Rejecting the office of sacrificing the mass, let him teach the Word of God and govern the church. This he can do while inwardly condemning and hating the anointing and the whole form of ordination by which he came into the office. For it is not necessary to leave the place of ministry though you may have reached it by wrong and impious methods, as long as the mind has mended its ways and the method has been condemned.[34]

The masks of which Luther spoke were those elements of the rite of ordination that obscured its proper purpose, which was to make one a minister not to consecrate one a priest. One was born a priest through baptism, but one was made a pastor: "Christ has been made the first priest of the New Testament without shaving, without anointing, and so without any of their 'character' or all the masquerade of episcopal ordination. He made all his apostles and his disciples priests, but through no such masks. So this mask of ordination is unnecessary. And if you have it, it is not enough in order to be a priest."[35]

Again the point was clear: ordination could not make a person a priest. Ordination was therefore irrelevant *to that concern*. Only baptism made one a priest. To conclude from this, however, that Luther believed ordination to be an unnecessary rite is to ignore the point of the argument. One cannot state too strongly that the polemic was directed toward a false understanding of priesthood and baptism. All Christians are united in their access to God through the one priest Jesus Christ because in being united with him through baptism all Christians are priests.

No one can ever claim to control that access on behalf of others because it is a public, communal reality. Neither can any individual Christian claim possession of the word apart from the community that bears it. The famous phrase *priesthood of all believers* refers always to a communal reality before it is understandable as an affirmation of the individual's priesthood. Even the latter is necessarily rooted in one's meeting God in Christ through the external word so that the communal aspect is never absent. As St. John put it, no one has ever seen God; revelation is always mediated. For Christians it is mediated by the community that is the body of Christ in the world.

Luther's advice to the Bohemian church was that it recognize the ecclesial foundation for priesthood and ministry. The positive content of the office of ministry in distinction from the common priesthood was to be understood in light of the fact that ordination was a liturgical act of the whole church, embodied in the life of a specific congregation:

> ...let those who come together cast their ballots and elect one or as many as are needed of those who are capable. By prayer and the laying on of hands let them commend and certify these to the whole assembly, and recognize and honor them as lawful bishops and ministers of the Word, believing beyond the shadow of a doubt that this has been done and accomplished by God. For in this way the common agreement of the faithful, those who believe and confess the gospel, is

realized and expressed.[36]

The efficacy of the act was assured in the trust that God heard the prayer of the church.[37] One must remember that Luther was advising the church in Bohemia to abandon the practice of sending candidates to Rome to be ordained as priests only to have them return and deny what they had vowed with regard to the controversy about administering both bread and wine in the eucharist. This was for Luther the false maintenance of an episcopal consecration that was divorced from the reality of the ecclesiastical emergency in which the Bohemian church found itself. He could also argue that episcopal consecration was appropriate, indeed the norm, if done in accord with the Word.

As Luther observed in a sermon on May 23, 1524, the problem with Roman consecration was that it did not live up to the biblical example and take the communal reality of priesthood and office properly into account. The biblical precedent made it clear that the way to make a pastor (*mos formandi prebyteros*) was before the church (*coram ecclesia*).[38] A proper ordination was not the same as the anointing in consecration. The former made one a pastor by giving to a qualified person the "authority to preach the word and administer the sacraments."[39] The latter confused the office of ministry with the priesthood given in baptism.[40] This was the basis of Luther's denial of any bestowal of character in ordination, in the sense of a quality of being like that established for the Christian in baptism. Luther stated that only priesthood, the character of baptism, was perpetual.[41]

Some ten years later in "The Private Mass and the Consecration of Priests (1533)," Luther was still making the point that the problem with papal ordination was the incorrect use of anointing and a focus on secondary ritual elements. Lieberg interpreted correctly that this was not a rejection of *ordinatio canonica* by Luther but rather an appeal to recover earlier forms and understanding.[42] One passage is worth quoting at length because it helps to clarify the source of confusion from Luther's perspective. He noted that there was patristic precedent for anointing in papal consecration, but the precedent was only superficial. Luther explained:

Luther's Liturgical Definition of Ordination 57

> I want to excuse the dear, holy fathers, and they should be excused, that they, too, consecrated or ordained with chrism and called those who had been consecrated clerics or priests. For they did not in this way consecrate private clerics nor anyone for private masses; rather, when they called someone to the true Christian office of the ministry or care of souls, they wanted to adorn and portray such a calling for the community with such pomp to distinguish them [i.e., the priests] from others who had not been called, in order that everyone might be sure and know who was supposed to exercise this office and who had the mandate to baptize, preach, etc. For basically consecration should not and cannot be anything other (if it is carried out rightly) than a call or a conferring of the office of the ministry or the office of preaching. The apostles without chrism merely laid their hands on the heads and prayed over those whom they called to the office or sent out, as happened to St. Paul and Barnabas, Acts 19 [13:3] and as St. Paul instructs Timothy not to be hasty in laying hands upon someone [I Timothy 5:22].[43]

A fair reading of this passage makes it self-evident that Luther's concern was to establish scriptural precedent for ordination in order to insure that it was both done and interpreted in accord with the gospel. It was highly suspect to suggest, as did Rietschel, that in this passage Luther believed that "ordination is not some sort of ecclesiastical act of consecration but is rather the call and conferring of the office of preaching."[44] One cannot set call and ordination in opposition to each other and claim justification in Luther's works.[45]

When Luther said that "the apostles without chrism, merely laid their hands on the heads and prayed over those whom they had called to the office or sent out," the point was precisely that a liturgical act of the community took place, albeit without chrism.[46] What Rietschel and others who have followed his interpretation have not demonstrated is what positive content a call to ministry has when divorced from the liturgical action by which the community makes that call on behalf of the whole church. One can make a distinction between call and ordination only if the word call is understood as a purely juridical agreement between pastor and congregation.

The ecclesiological issue here is analogous to one in baptism. When a person is baptized by a specific pastor in a specific congregation the baptism is not into that parish alone but into the church, the whole Christian church. Even apart from the argument of its not being a sacrament, ordination in a specific congregation done by a specific pastor is not ordination into that calling parish alone but ordination into an office of the whole Christian church. This distinction clarifies the relationship of installations, which can be repeated as acts celebrating the juridical promise between pastor and specific congregation, to ordination, which is an unrepeatable act done in the name of the whole church.

When Luther said, "we shall see to it that we get pastors and preachers on the basis of baptism and God's word, without their chrism, ordained and confirmed by our election and call"[47] he was not implying that it occurred without the broader process which included the pivotal liturgical act of prayer and laying on of hands. Again, Luther's intended distinction between consecration (anointing with chrism) and ordination (prayer and laying on of hands) merits reviewing at length:

> Therefore, consecration or chrism is vastly different from ordination or a call to the public Christian office of preaching and the parish ministry, even though they have maintained that they have not called as pastor or preacher someone who was not consecrated but have only taken some of them from the consecrated company. Now this action and custom of theirs, according to which they consecrate clerics without a parish and yet do not ordain a pastor without consecration, do not constitute an article of faith for us so that it would have to be thus. We simply want to show at this point that their consecration does not lead to the ordination of a pastor or to a Christian office among the community of Christians but alone to the creation of a private cleric.[48]

There is no question that Luther's concern here was the gathered Christian community and appropriate leadership within it. The last sentence above indicated that his argument with contemporary practice was that ordination occurred divorced from the assembly which constituted the body of Christ the church. The root of the issue was therefore ecclesiological, and specifically liturgical with regard to the process of ordaining.

This leads to the question of how Luther understood the proper relationship of call and ordination. Were the two concepts synonymous as some have argued? It has already been indicated that this was not the case in light of Luther's arguments about priestly consecration versus proper ministry. Yet a call from a specific congregation and ordination

Luther's Liturgical Definition of Ordination 59

by the whole church were considered to be part of one ecclesial reality.

The simplest way to put the matter is this: Luther believed that in the church's action of choosing, training, examining, electing, and praying for individuals the process of call and ordination took place. To ask for differentiated moments of equivalency, that is, what part of the process constituted call and what part ordination, is to ask a question not unlike that sometimes put to the eucharistic celebration: at what specific point does consecration occur?

For those who need such a before and after analysis, it is fair to suggest that the church's historical and theological wisdom is that the liturgical act of ordaining a person sets them apart in a way that the rest of the call process without that community action does not. In this case, call is the broader, more inclusive term for the process. Ordination is then the action by which, in worship, the community realizes or enacts the call in a way that commends the one ordained to the whole church as a pastor of and for the whole church. An installation is the locally specific act of celebrating the relationship between a pastor and congregation.

The prior issue begging exploration here is whether the framework within which a moment of consecration question can be asked is helpful or even legitimate. Perhaps it should be said that the issue is not what the minimum must be in order for the process to be valid. For to put the question that way is to trap oneself in a juridical framework for answering it. Ordination is primarily a theological, not a juridical issue, even though the structures of human community demand attention to juridical concerns.

The upshot of an investigation of the 1533 treatise is that Luther did not employ the concept *ordinirn* as synonymous with call in a way that contrasted it with a liturgical act of consecration through prayer and laying on of hands (as Rietschel argued).[49] Instead Luther wanted to maintain the traditional canonical act of ordaining as a liturgical act, but purified of abuses.

The substance of this liturgical action was expressed in the concepts *commendare* and *confirmare*. Luther had made this point in the earlier treatise "Concerning the Ministry (1523)": "Proceed in the name of the Lord to elect one or more whom you desire, and who appear to be worthy and able. Then let those who are leaders among you lay hands upon them, and certify and commend them to the people and the church or community."⁵⁰ The liturgical action of laying on of hands with prayer in the midst of the assembled community served both to identify publicly the person chosen and confirm the choice. It was the point at which the office and the person called were recognized as having been definitely brought together.⁵¹ Thus Luther could say that after this liturgical action had occurred those chosen were to be "recognized and honored as lawful bishops and ministers of the Word."⁵²

In other words the whole vocational process came to a definitive conclusion in the liturgical act of ordination with prayer and laying on of hands. A universal recognition of that fact should result because the act was, done in accord with the gospel, *coram ecclesia*. One can see, therefore, that Luther wanted to affirm what he believed to be of apostolic origin (prayer and laying on of hands) and repudiate only those aspects of the vocational process and ordination in the Roman tradition of consecration which had blurred this essential focus.

During the period under discussion thus far, 1520–1533, there is little evidence that Luther acted on the theological positions he was articulating and actually began ordaining people in rejection of episcopal consecration in the Catholic church. On the one hand this was due to the fact that, at least prior to the 1530 presentation of the *Augsburg Confession* and its subsequent rejection, Luther entertained hopes for genuine reform being embraced by the whole church, including Catholic bishops who would continue ordaining. One can only assume that when ordinations occurred during these years they followed the traditional medieval rites of consecration for the minor and major orders. Churches adopting the Reformation cause would therefore be served by pastors who had been ordained as priests but considered themselves part of the evangelical movement.⁵³ There is some evidence that by the time of the first major visitation in Saxony (1528) the situation of a shortage of pastors was becoming so acute that some may have been accepted as preachers because of the circumstances without much training or ordination.⁵⁴ But if that indeed occurred it was viewed by most as an unfortunate compromise brought about by emergency needs.

The Development of Evangelical Ordination

As the Reformation began to take hold in various cities and territories after 1520, the question of where pastors would come from was not raised immediately because there was no clear break with Catholic traditions surrounding the ordination of persons into ministry. As long as priests previously consecrated by bishops were available, the matter was not an issue.

The situation began to change as bishops refused to embrace the Reformation cause and the supply of ordained individuals decreased. What is the evidence for the ways in which such changes resulted in specific steps leading to the establishment of an evangelical process for calling and ordaining people to the office of ministry? A chronological approach will be followed in evaluating the information available.

An early pertinent text is a sermon by Luther on May 23, 1524. Commenting on Acts 13:3 Luther stated:

> This was the custom of making a presbyter, etc., they do not call him rather the Holy Spirit calls him, but they confirm this call. Our bishops imitate this, but badly. Yet priests ought to be similarly established so that they might be prayed for in the presence of the church, and so that the preaching of the Word of God might be entrusted to them.[55]

At this point it is clear that Luther was alluding to a rite. He wanted something other than what presently was taking place badly in imitation of biblical practice. In other words, he desired a way of making pastors that took seriously the evangelical concerns he had expressed in the preceding four years.

A few months later, on October 16, 1524, Luther commented in detail on consecration and priesthood at the end of a sermon on John 4:47ff. He made the point that whoever heard the word of God and received it was an heir of Christ and possessed everything through faith. He then continued: "The bishops anoint nobody except those who want to deny the gospel. We ought in time, therefore, to ordain preachers, for which reason I wish you to be certain, because each Christian is a brother of Christ if he keeps His Word."[56] What he intended with the words "to ordain preachers" was made clear in contrast to papal consecration:

> We will preach and anoint in ways other than those bishops. But we, who already have ministries, will recommend into our ministry. To ordain is not to consecrate. If, therefore, we know a pious man, we take him out and by virtue of the Word that we possess we give him the authority to proclaim the Word and to administer the sacraments. This is what it means to ordain.[57]

Less than a year later Luther performed what is believed to be the first evangelical ordination of record when he made Georg Rörer a deacon on May 14, 1525. There is no record concerning the rite except that it took place in the city church of Wittenberg, before the gathered community, with prayer and laying on of hands.[58] But this was the only such liturgical act of evangelical ordination in the 1520's of record.[59] The simple explanation for this is that prior to 1530 the possibility still existed for bishops to call and ordain evangelical preachers. After 1530 that possibility rapidly disappeared.

On December 16, 1530, Luther wrote to the priest Peter Hackenberg, who wanted to embrace the Reformation cause: "Everywhere there is a great lack of faithful pastors, so that it is almost the case where we will be forced to ordain by our own rite or to establish ministers without shearing, without anointing, without a mitre, without hand laying, without a ring, without a thurible, and finally without these bishops."[60] This indicated that although ordinations were not yet occurring to replace the contemporary practice of consecration there was growing pressure to move toward such a reform, and that Luther was preparing to do so.

At this point one must address briefly the distinction between ordination and installation, for the latter was taking place as those already consecrated were assigned to Reformation parishes. It was not a universal custom in Germany for pastors who were consecrated as priests to be installed with a liturgical celebration in the parish to which they had been assigned.[61] Occasionally this did occur and when it did it involved prayer and laying on of hands. In city parishes the other pastors of the town were the ones to lay on hands. In the country this was done by the pastors of neighboring communities. But there was no set form or rite by which pastors were recognized as having the responsibility to serve a specific parish. For those consecrated by bishops the lines of accountability and authority were clear, at least theoretically, and assignment was simply episcopal prerogative or patronal privilege. Members of parishes knew that the church's canon law provided for the proper process (again, at least in theory) leading to ordination and appointment.

The case was different as the Reformation took hold and candidates began to emerge who had not come through the Catholic church's episcopal system, and who had not been confirmed by any evangelical action. Such called but unconsecrated, unordained pastors faced a crisis of conscience concerning the legitimacy of their office. The situation of Johann Sutel in Göttingen discussed below is a case in point. Also, parishes were not always accepting of those who had not been properly ordained in terms of the processes to which they were accustomed (whether corrupt or not). The period of transition resulted in a variety of makeshift measures and anomalous situations as leaders and people struggled to discern what specific changes in the structure of Christian life were being brought about by the Reformation.

As soon as the bishop of a given diocese refused to recognize or confirm evangelically-minded priests, the need arose for new measures to be developed that would test pastoral candidates, confirm them as fit for leadership, and introduce them into the community for which they were chosen. In other words, structures to circumvent and replace the abandoned episcopal system began to develop. The initial need was for a recognized authority that could carry out the process with some sort of legal power. And there was yet no universally accepted way for that to occur. Thus, for example, in 1525 the "*gemeine Landesordnung des Herzogstums Preussen*" ordered that chosen persons be tested by the bishops of Samlund and Riesenburg and sent back to their community, while to the bishop of Heisberg, who was not evangelically-minded, that right of examination was not given.[62]

Other examples abound, including the work of Bugenhagen as he developed new church orders late in the 1520's. These concerns will be discussed in subsequent chapters dealing specifically with the emergence of the evangelical church orders. At this point, it is necessary only to recognize that local installations did not answer for evangelical churches the theological and ecclesiological problem of how to ordain into the office of ministry.

That a problem existed was attested by the example of Johann Sutel's question to Luther in 1531. Sutel had been called as preacher at St. Nicholas church in Göttingen, but without any public, liturgical act of ordination. He wanted to know whether he could celebrate the eucharist without presbyteral consecration. Luther answered in a letter dated

March 1, 1531, in which he couched his reply in a somewhat cryptic comment about the seriousness of the congregation at Göttingen for the gospel:

> Wherefore about that which you seek, whether you ought to administer the supper of the Lord if not tonsured or anointed. I am able to answer nothing. For if there is nothing serious there, I wish that you abstain, as up to this point; if indeed there is something serious, then you will receive the power and authority to administer the meal, publicly before the altar from the other pastors with prayer and laying on of hands.[63]

The issue is what Luther was referring to when he advised Sutel to abstain.[64] The point seems to have been this: it is not proper to celebrate the eucharist (so abstain from that) without having been ordained with prayer and laying on of hands—in spite of the fact that Sutel had been legitimately called. In other words Luther intended here to advise Sutel that he should not preside at the eucharist without having been properly ordained to that responsibility. In the developing sense of what the situation in Germany might require, the point therefore was that Luther advocated a liturgical resolution for an unsettling ecclesiological consequence of the Reformation movement: having no episcopally consecrated priests to preside.

The 1533 work "On the Private Mass and Consecration of Priests" was discussed above with regard to the fact that Luther's argument there did not preclude his inclusion of the liturgical act of prayer and laying on of hands as essential to the process of calling to the office of ministry. Thus when he said, "we shall see to it that we get pastors and preachers on the basis of baptism and God's word without their chrism, ordained and confirmed by our election and call,"[65] this election and call was not seen as divorced from the liturgical act of prayer and laying on of hands.

Of concern here is the discussion that followed in which Luther made a case for Roman Catholic acceptance of evangelical ordination on the basis of a comparison with canon law's acceptance of ordinations done by heretics. The question is whether his language indicated that evangelical ordinations were already occurring in 1533. Luther argued the point as follows:

> Even the pope himself has ordered in his spiritual statutes (though they were taken from the ancient fathers), that one should regard the consecration or ordination performed by heretics as a true consecration and not reconsecrate those who had been consecrated by heretics. Now we Lutherans are not heretics;

this the papists themselves must admit. For that reason they should regard our consecrating and ordaining as valid.[66]

There can be no doubt that Luther had the liturgical act of consecration in mind since he was arguing on the basis of canon law and the sacramental character of the act of ordaining which it presupposed. Thus when he said, "for that reason they should regard our consecrating and ordaining as valid,"[67] he did not mean the process of election and call in some vague form divorced from the liturgical action on which the comparative analysis was being based.

Luther anticipated the possible objection that heretics whose ordinations were recognized were legitimate bishops and therefore in apostolic succession. He countered that on the basis of the New Testament and St. Jerome "bishops and pastors are the same thing."[68] When discussing an additional historical example drawn from St. Augustine Luther touched on the question at issue here:

> And the same little pastor or bishop, St. Augustine, consecrated and ordained many pastors or bishops in his little parish...who were sought and called by other cities, as we ordain and send them out of our parish at Wittenberg to other cities which want them and do not have any pastors among them. For ordaining should consist of, and be understood as, calling to and entrusting with the office of ministry... .[69]

The words that Luther used here, "wie wir aus Pfarrhen zu Wittenberg ...mügen,"[70] indicate that ordinations had probably not yet begun in Wittenberg in 1533. Luther was only making the case for the legitimacy of such action. On the other hand, one cannot rule out the possibility that there were some instances of people being ordained in Wittenberg for calls in other communities before 1533 or that ordinations in local communities had begun to occur.

The real point at issue was the distinction being made between ordinations taking place in Wittenberg for other parishes over against having calls being accepted and pastors somehow introduced or installed in the local congregations that called them. The former represented the development of an ecclesiastical structure to replace the episcopal hierarchy and its attendant patterns for regulating ordained ministry. The latter had already begun to occur in the mid–1520's because ordination as a liturgical act of the whole church was not an issue for those already consecrated according to the still accepted episcopal structures of the church. Karant-Nunn explained that "there is evidence to suggest that after the Catholic bishops' sway over the parish clergy had come to an end, *Amtmänner* and *Schösser* had appointed, dismissed, and inducted pastors. In some places there may have been no one else to do it. The practice became entrenched and was difficult to eradicate."[71]

The evidence of a May 9, 1535 sermon by Luther corroborates the conclusion that prior to 1535 ordinations were not occurring in Wittenberg:

> For the first time we think to ordain with a public assembly. You have now German baptism, eucharist, preaching and catechism and whatever is Christian. Although the preaching office and call also ought to be put in the German language.[72]

The words "for the first time" indicated exactly that: an evangelical rite for ordination had not yet replaced the episcopal process.

A major turning point for the Reformation churches occurred in 1535. Without an ecclesiastical structure for approving candidates there was no way to prevent false teachers or ill-trained pastors from creating turmoil in parishes. So Elector John Frederick issued a decree in 1535 centralizing ordinations in Wittenberg. No extant copy of the decree itself exists but we know its content on the basis of instructions of the Elector to the visitors of Meissen and Vogtland, dated May 12, 1535, Torgau.[73] They were to inform the superintendents that henceforth everyone who desired an office in the electorate should be examined by the superintendent and then sent, with a letter of attestation, to the faculty at Wittenberg to whom the Elector had given the mandate "to ordain and thus to give the power and authority of the office of priest and deacon." This establishment of a regulated way of ordering the church was clearly viewed as parallel to and a replacement for episcopal consecration.[74]

Luther discussed issues relevant to the electoral decree in his October 20, 1535 sermon.[75] He recognized that the shortage of pastors had become acute and that new ways had to be established for filling the office of ministry:

> Pastors may die, but the office of the ministry remains. It alone is the gift of God to the Church, so that the Gospel, baptism, the keys, the sacrament, and the preaching office remain. One pastor after another dies, but the office remains. Because of this we can send replacements if we desire.[76]

That Luther had in mind the Elector's decree about ordination as a liturgical act was made clear in the comments that followed on the papist ways in which the rite focused on externals (anointing, tonsure, vesting, etc.), in contrast to the evangelical way in which it ought to have been understood.[77] Ordination is the placing of a person in office; it is done publicly with the gathered community present; it is entrusting the office to someone through prayer and laying on of hands.

What was new for Luther as a result of the action taken by the Elector was that ordinations would now officially occur in Wittenberg for other communities.[78] Rörer's ordination in 1525 had been in the city church at Wittenberg for service in that community. This decree represented something else. In a Latin version of part of this sermon there was an even stronger emphasis on ecclesiastical regulation of the process of call and ordination. The Elector carried out the examination process through the authority granted to the theological faculty at Wittenberg. The ordination functioned as an episcopal confirmation of call (vocation) before and for the whole church. It both gave persons the office and sent them out.[79] A translation of the Latin version reads as follows:

> You know that the ordination of the church with its rite is necessary. But because the Pope does not promote the course of the gospel, but hinders it, we will be vigilant and pray. Our Elector has necessarily ordered that we should choose and ordain educated men and pious ministers of the Word of God and see that none among us who are ignorant stand up and teach. Therefore he has desired and decreed that from all the dioceses of Franken, Meissen, etc., candidates are to be sent to us to be examined, confirmed, and then sent back. You ought to be witnesses of this public rite, and beseech God most fervently to give us us pious and sincere preachers of his word.[80]

The first unassailable evidence for this taking place is a record of the examination of Hieronymus Hirscheider, a school teacher at Reichenbach in Vogtland, who was tested by the Rector of Wittenberg University on August 14, 1535.[81] Hirscheider passed the examination. Melanchthon noted that the rite of ordination was still a necessary part of the process: "the bishops do not allow our men to teach, and it is still necessary that this rite be retained on account of order in the church."[82] Evidently this area in Vogtland adhered to the necessity of a replacement for episcopal consecration, which is why Hirscheider sought certification from the Wittenberg faculty as a legitimate evangelical preacher. It is apparent, therefore, that response to the electoral mandate was quick, and that probably from May 1535 on ordinations were occurring in Wittenberg.

Drews rhetorically raised the question whether prior to Luther's October 20 sermon the ordinations that took place were done by members of the faculty without the participation of the congregation.[83] He answered negatively, noting that the process was not purely the preserve of the University. But Luther as ordinator did make the liturgical, congregational action an integral part of the process. When Bugenhagen returned to Wittenberg late in August of 1535 after a long absence in Pomerania he was made aware of the newly developing custom based on the electoral edict. The theological faculty also gave him, as city pastor and general superintendent, the office of ordinator in Wittenberg.

Four days after the October 20 sermon Luther wrote to Friedrich Myconius in Gotha, most likely concerning the ordination that had just occurred the preceding Sunday:

> We send back to you your Johann, who was called and elected by you. He has been examined by us and ordained and confirmed publicly before our congregation, with prayer and praise of God in accord with the mandate of the Elector. Dr. Pomeranus [Bugenhagen] was not present willingly since he still believes that ordination should be done in the local church by the presbyters. That will eventually happen once this new thing and order has established deeper roots and has become more customary.[84]

The letter outlined well how the process of calling and ordaining would be done in accord with the electoral mandate. It also raised the question of Bugenhagen's understanding of that mandate and whether he and Luther agreed on the significance and place of the liturgical act of ordaining within the process.

That there was a question is supported by the report of the papal legate Pietro Paulo Vergerio concerning a conversation he had with Luther and Bugenhagen.[85] Vergerio was in Wittenberg from November 7–12, 1535. The conversation occurred on November 7. In it he reported that with regard to the newly established custom of ordaining in Wittenberg Luther observed, "we are forced to do this" (*nos cogimur ita facere*). Luther meant that since bishops would not ordain or examine candidates the reformers were forced to deal with the circumstances and thus give authority to one among them to function as ordinator in place of the bishop. That the one among them meant Bugenhagen was clear from Vergerio's comment: "He is the one who lays on hands and ordains for this whole sect. He told me himself that he was given this authority by Brother Martin and the other members of the Academy."[86]

Bugenhagen believed that a liturgical act like prayer and laying on of hands had to take place with and before a congregation. There is some question about how he interpreted this liturgical act, that is, whether it was an ordination in the traditional sense or an installation and confirmation of the call that somehow circumvented the question of ordination.[87] The confusion had more to do with the issue of whether there needed to be an evangelical replacement for episcopal ordination (especially centralized in Wittenberg) than with a liturgical action being an essential part of the whole process of calling/ordaining. The fact that Bugenhagen quickly adopted Luther's rite after 1535 for his Church Orders indicates that he, like Luther, was more concerned about the negative implications of papal consecration than about the positive content of a proper ordination. And at least initially the act of installing may have been considered an act of ordaining, especially when one remembers that the central content of ordination for Luther, prayer and laying on of hands, could occur in both.

He also believed that it was the proper responsibility of the pastor of a congregation and not the members of the theological faculty to preside at this liturgical act. Thus for Bugenhagen every ordination ought to occur in the community by which the person had been called. On this point he and Luther were apparently in some disagreement since Luther fully supported the move to centralized ordinations. Luther's closing comments in the letter to Myconius demonstrate, however, that he was sympathetic to Bugenhagen's position. Subsequent developments never allowed the implications of that sympathy to be realized.

The hesitation indicated in Luther's use of *cogimur* as reported by Vergerio had nothing to do with the legitimacy of ordinations taking place in Wittenberg, but rather referred to the fact that Luther and the others did not want for themselves what they considered properly to be an episcopal authority and responsibility—to ordain. The rest of the report made that plain.[88] Luther argued that the role of the bishop in the early church was to act as a "supervisor or visitor" who "watches over and supervises his people in regard to teaching and life."[89] But since that role had been abandoned by contemporary bishops, there was only one recourse:

> ...we would like to have seen the true episcopal office and practice of visitation re-established because of the pressing need. However, since none of us felt a

call or definite command to do this...no one has dared to undertake it...we have respectfully appealed to the illustrious and noble prince and lord, John, Duke of Saxony...[to]...call and ordain to this office several competent persons.[90]

Again in evidence was Luther's reluctance to have anyone assume the episcopal responsibility to ordain. Faced with the necessity both the Elector and the faculty at Wittenberg acted to supply congregations with properly trained, called, and ordained evangelical pastors.[91]

When the general council of the church for which Luther had hoped was initially called by Pope Paul III in June, 1536 to meet in Mantua the following May (even though it did not convene until 1545), the Elector asked Luther to prepare a statement of those things on which the reformers were willing to compromise for the sake of peace and unity and those things which were not negotiable. The *Smalcald Articles* were the result.[92] Of value are the comments Luther made in Article X of Part III, on "Ordination and Vocation":

> If the bishops were true bishops and were concerned about the church and the Gospel, they might be permitted (for the sake of love and unity, but not of necessity) to ordain and confirm us and our preachers, provided this could be done without pretense, humbug, and unchristian ostentation. However, they neither are nor wish to be true bishops. They are temporal lords and princes who are unwilling to preach or teach or baptize or administer Communion or discharge any office or work in the church. More than that, they expel, persecute, and condemn those who have been called to do these things. Yet the church must not be deprived of ministers on their account. Accordingly, as we are taught by the examples of the ancient churches and Fathers, we shall and ought ourselves ordain suitable persons to this office. The papists have no right to forbid or prevent us, not even according to their own laws, for their laws state that those who are ordained by heretics shall also be regarded as ordained and remain so. St. Jerome, too, wrote concerning the church in Alexandria that it was originally governed without bishops by priests and preachers in common.[93]

This summary statement of Luther's position, specifically requested to state the limits of compromise, provides an unambiguous confirmation of the line of argument followed in his works thus far. The criticism of episcopal consecration was the "pretense, humbug, and unchristian ostentation" the rite contained. That there ought to be a rite was never questioned. What was at issue was whether it would be a truly reformed rite that eliminated the "humbug." If the bishops had been willing to engage in such reform there would have been no need to take the steps Luther defended in the second paragraph above (a defense already discussed).

Given all this, it is somewhat surprising that the official Wittenberg ordination register had its first entry dated July 29, 1537. Rietschel interpreted this to mean that because of Bugenhagen's belief that ordinations should be done locally few candidates were actually ordained in Wittenberg from 1535-37.[94] Only after Bugenhagen left for Denmark in 1537 and Luther took his place as primary ordinator did the frequency increase. Lieberg considered this to be a reasonable explanation, although emphasizing that ordinations for other communities were in fact occurring in Wittenberg from 1535 on.[95]

NOTES

1 See, for example, Heinz Schütte, *Amt, Ordination und Sukzession* (Düsseldorf: Patmos Verlag, 1974); Robert H. Fischer, "Another Look at Luther's Doctrine of the Ministry," *Lutheran Quarterly* 18 (1966): 260-271; Lowell C. Green, "Change in Luther's Doctrine of the Ministry," *Lutheran Quarterly* 18 (1966): 173-183; Brian A. Gerrish, "Priesthood and Ministry in the Theology of Luther," *Church History* 34 (1965): 404-422.

2 See, for example, Richard Walter Schoenleber, "The Sovereign Word: The Office of Ministry and Ordination in the Theology of Martin Luther" (Ph.D. Dissertation, University of Iowa, 1983).

3 See the brief survey of secondary literature in the Introduction.

4 See, for example, Frieder Schulz, "Evangelische Ordination," *Jahrbuch für Liturgik und Hymnologie* 17 (1972): 1-54; Hellmut Lieberg, *Amt und Ordination bei Luther und Melanchthon* (Göttingen: Vandenhoeck and Ruprecht, 1962), [cited hereafter as "Lieberg"].

5 Luther himself succumbed to the problem. The tract "That a Christian Assembly or Congregation Has the Right and Power to Judge All Teaching and To Call, Appoint, and Dismiss Teachers, Established and Proven by Scripture (1523)," WA 11, 408-416 (LW 39, 304-314), is often used to support the argument that Luther held a radically congregational view of ministry. Yet as Susan C. Karant-Nunn, *Luther's Pastors: The Reformation in the Ernestine Countryside*, (Philadelphia: Transactions of the American Philosophical Society, Vol. 69, Part 8, 1979) has observed: "A measure of the extent to which Luther was caught up in theory and separated from reality is his tract on the right of each Christian community to call, examine, seat, and unseat its own spiritual teachers. Later, better aware of local conditions, he completely disowned this democratic notion" (21).

6 Vilmos Vajta, *Luther on Worship* (Philadelphia: Muhlenberg Press, 1958), x. Originally published as *Die Theologie des Gottesdienst bei Luther* (Stockholm, 1952).

7 See, for example, Frank C. Senn, "Martin Luther's Revision of the Eucharistic Canon in the *Formula Missae* of 1523," *Concordia Theological Monthly* 44 (1973): 101-118.

8 Frieder Schulz, "Luthers Liturgische Reformen," *Archiv für Liturgieswissenschaft*, Heft 3 (1983): 249-275.

9 Ibid., 263-264.

10 Paul Drews, "Das Ordinationsformular," WA 38, 401-433; Ulrich Leopold, LW 53, 122-126.

11 Bryan Spinks, "Luther's Other Major Liturgical Reforms: 2, The Ordination of Ministers of the Word," *Liturgical Review* IX, 1 (1979): 20-21.

12 As an example, how can one claim that Luther lacked familiarity with the rite when he could be as specific as this: "For these were the words the consecrating bishop spoke when he placed the chalice into your anointed hand and said: 'Receive the authority to consecrate and sacrifice for the living and the dead' (...wie die wort des Weybisschoffs lauten, da er dir den Kelch jnn die gesalbeten hand gab, und sprach: Accipe potestatem consecrandi et sacrificandi pro vivis et mortuis)"; WA 38, 199, 17-19 (LW 38, 152)?

13 Peter Manns, *Martin Luther* (N.Y.: Crossroad, 1983), 27-28. Bonemilch was the "*Weihebischof*" for the Archbishop of Mainz.

14 WA 6, 404-469 (LW 44, 115-217), "To the Christian Nobility of the German Nation Concerning the Reform of the Christian Estate, 1520"; WA 6, 497-573 (LW 36, 3-126), "The Babylonian Captivity of the Church, 1520"; WA 7, 1-38 (LW 31, 327-377), "The Freedom of a Christian."

15 WA 6, 407, 13-15, 19-23 (LW 44, 127): "Dan alle Christen sein warhafftig geystlichs stands, unnd ist unter yhn kein unterscheyd, denn des ampts halben allein...Das aber der Bapst odder Bischoff salbet, blatten macht, ordiniert, weyhet, anders dan leyen kleydet, mag einen gleysner und olgotzen machen, macht aber nymmer mehr ein Christen odder geystlichen menschen." Cf. WA 6, 408, 11-13 (LW 44, 129): "For whoever comes out of the water of baptism can boast that he is already a consecrated priest, bishop, and pope... (Dan was ausz der tauff krochen ist, das mag sich rumen, das es schon priester, Bischoff und Bapst geweyhet sey...)."

16 WA 38, 227, 20-23 (LW 38, 185): "Aber, das ist aller erst der rechten grewel einer widder die liebe und selige Tauffe, das sie sich rhumen, wie sie mit irem Cresem und Weyhe Pfaffen machen inn der heiligen Kirchen, das ist einen weit, weit höhern und heiligen stand, denn die Tauffe gibt."

17 WA 6, 564, 16f. (LW 36, 113); Luther made it clear that he did not condemn the rite but rather wanted to recover its original sense as "a certain rite by which the church chooses its preachers (ritus quidam eligendi Concionatoris in Ecclesia)"; Cf. WA 6 566, 30ff. (LW 36, 116): Ordination is "a certain rite whereby one is called to the ministry of the church (ritus quendam vocandi alicuius in ministerium Ecclesiasticum)."

18 WA 6, 561, 26–33 (LW 36, 108–109): "Quare permitto, ordinem esse quendam ritum Ecclesiasticum, quales multi alii quoque per Ecclesiasticos patres sunt introducti, ut consecratio vasorum, domorum, vestium, aquae, salis, candelarum, herbarum, vini et similium, in quibus omnibus nemo ponit sacramentum esse, nec ulla in eis est promissio: ita ungere manus viri, radi verticem et id genus alia fieri non est sacramentum dari, cum nihil eis promittatur, sed tantum ad officia quaedam, ceu vasa et instrumenta, parentur."

19 WA Br 1, 595, 31–33: "All other things are equal if you take away the ceremonies and human statutes. We wonder where Holy Order found the name of sacrament. Are these things not amazing to you? (Cetera omnia sunt equalia, si ceremonias et humana statuta demas. Et satis miramur, unde ordo nomen sacramenti invenerit. Mira hec tibi nonne?)."

20 Compare the fate of penance in this regard; its "sacramental" nature was finally rooted in baptism. It is worth recalling as well that in the *Apology to the Augsburg Confession*, Article XIII, 7–13 (T. Tappert, *The Book of Concord* (Philadelphia: Fortress Press, 1959), 212), Melanchthon (and Luther?) was willing to accept the office as a sacrament.

21 WA 7, 633, 12–15 (LW 39, 157): "Also macht die weyhe keynen pfaffen, sie macht aber pfaffen knechte"; Cf. WA 7, 633, 16–18 (LW 39, 157): "All of us in the whole mass of people are priests without the consecration of the bishop. But through consecration we become the stewards, servants, and administrators... (Wyr alle mit dem gantzenen hauffen seyn priester, on des Bischoffs weyhen, aber durch das weyhen werden wir der andernn priester knecht, diener und amptleut...)." Lieberg, (172–173), correctly criticized the positions of both G. Rietschel and G. Hök for overlooking the fact that Luther here saw ordination as indeed *making* one a servant in the office. Thus consecration set one in office. Hök argued that for Luther the consecration had no significance for the call into office. The difficulty with such a view is that it separates "call" from "ordination" as if the former were some independent, discrete act. What is its content? The issue raised is how the relationship between Church (in the sense of both a specific congregation and the broader Christian community) and pastor is realized, made public, formalized, recognized. If nothing is ever said or done publicly to make known the relationship between a community and its leader, how is the "call" ever known? And even more importantly, how is the Church's prayer, which is Christ's prayer, to be understood in connection with this relationship?

22 WA 12, 179–180 (LW 40, 21): "But let us go on and show from the priestly offices (as they call them) that all Christians are priests in equal degree. For such passages as, 'You are a royal priesthood' (I Pet.2 [:9]) and, 'Thou has made them a kingdom and

priests' (Rev. 5 [:10]), I have sufficiently treated in other books." See, for example, WA 6, 407ff. (LW 44, 127ff.); WA 8, 247ff. (LW 39, 229); WA 7, 56, 35ff. (LW 31, 354).

23 WA 12, 309, 1-10 (LW 30, 55); Cf. WA 12, 189, 17-27 and 40-41 (LW 40, 34); 190, 1-26 (40, 34-35).

24 WA 6, 408, 11ff. (LW 44, 129).

25 WA 12, 307, 10-12 (LW 30, 53): "We ask further whether St. Peter is differentiating between spiritual and secular, as today one calls the priests the clergy and the other Christians the laity (Weytter fragen wyr, ob er eyn unterscheyd macht unter geystlichen und welltlichen, wie man ytzt die pfaffen 'geystlich' heysst, die andern Christen 'welltlich')." Cf. WA 12, 180, 24-28 (LW 40, 22): "But some imagine a twofold priesthood, one spiritual and common to all, the other external and limited, and say that Peter here speaks of the spiritual one. But what is the function of this limited and external office? Is it not to declare the wonderful deeds of God? But this Peter enjoins on the spiritual and universal priesthood (Dicant igitur illi, qui duplex fingunt sacerdocium, unum spirituale et commune, aliud speciale et externum, et Petrum hic de spirituali faciunt loquentem, quod sit officium sui specialis et externi sacerdocii? An non est virtutes dei annunciare? At hoc Petrus hic mandat spirituali et communi illi sacerdocio)."

26 WA 12, 308, 4-7 (LW 30, 54): "Drumb weye er priester ist, und wyr seyne bruder sind, so habens alle Christen macht und befehl, und mussens thun, das sie predigen und fur Got treten, eyner fur den andern bitte, und sich selbs Gotte opffere. Und trotz das ymand anhebe das wort Gottis zu predigen oder zusagen, er sey denn eyn priester."

27 WA 12, 180, 17-18 (LW 40, 21): "Primum igitur officium, nempe verbi ministerium, esse omnibus Christians commune." Cf. 180, 1-6 (LW 40, 21): "Mostly the functions of a priest are these: to teach, to preach and proclaim the word of God, to baptize, to consecrate or administer the Eucharist, to bind and loose sins, to pray for others, to sacrifice, and to judge of all doctrine and spirits. Certainly these are splendid and royal duties. But the first and foremost of all on which everything else depends, is the teaching of the Word of God (Sunt autem sacerdotalia officia ferme haec: docere, praedicare annunciareque verbum dei, baptisare, consecrare seu Eucharistiam ministrare, ligare et solvere peccata, orare pro aliis, sacrificare et iudicare de omnium doctrinis et spiritibus. Magnificia plane et regalia sunt haec. Primum vero et summum omnium, in quo omnia pendent alia, est docere verbum dei)."

28 WA 12, 309, 24-31 (LW 30, 55): "Das ist nu das rechte priesterthumb, wilchs ynn den dreyen stucken stehet, wie wyr gehort haben: Das man geystlich opffere, und fur die gemeyn bete, und predige. Wer das thun kan, der ist priester, die sind alle schuldig, das sie das wort predigen, fur die gemeyn beten und sich fur Gott opffern. So lass nu yhene narren faren, die den geystlichen stand "priester" nennen, wilche doch keyn ander ampt furen, denn das sie platten tragen und geschmyrt sind. Wenn das bescheren und

schmyeren eyn priester macht, so kund ich eym esel auch wol die pfotten schmyeren und salben, das er auch eyn priester were."

29 WA 12, 309, 1-10 (LW 30, 55): "Also, das die, so ytzt priester heyssen, alle leyhen weren, wie die andern, und nur ettliche Amptleutt von der gemeyn erwelt wurden zu predigen. Also ist nur eyn unterscheyd euserlich des ampts halben, datzu eyner von der gemeyne beruffen wirtt. Aber fur Gott ist keyn unterscheyd, und werden nur darumb ettliche aufs dem hauffen erfurtzogen, das sie an statt der gemeyne das ampt furen und treyben, wilchs sie alle haben, nicht das eyner mehr gewalt habe denn der ander. Darumb soll keyner von yhm selb auff tretten und ynn die gemeyn predigen, sondern man muss eynen aufs dem hauffen furtzihen und auff setzen, den man muge wider absetzen, wenn man wollt." Cf. WA 12, 193-195 (LW 40, 40-42).

30 WA 12, 317, 4-7 (LW 30, 63): "Es konnen ettliche aufs der gemeyne herfur gezogen werden, die da amptleut und diener sind, und datzu gesetzt, das sie ynn der gemeyn predigen und die sacrament aussteylen. Aber alle sind wyr priester fur Gott, so wyr Christen sind."

31 WA 12, 160-196 (LW 40, 3-44).

32 WA 12, 172,35; 173, 1-7 (LW 40, 11): "Nam cum ista ordinatio autoritate scripturarum, deinde exemplo et decretis Apostolorum in hoc sit instituta, ut ministros verbi in populo institueret: Ministerium publicum inquam verbi, quo dispensantur mysteria dei, per sacram ordinationem institui debet, ceu res, quae omnium in Ecclesia et summa et maxima est, in qua tota vis Ecclesiastici status consistit, cum sine verbo nihil constet in Ecclesia et per solum verbum omnia constent."

33 WA 12, 174, 23-29 (LW 40, 13-14): "Such are the things which ought justly to move not only you in Bohemia but all pious hearts everywhere to tolerate anything rather than to be sullied by these sacrilegious ordinations. And they who have already been ordained should grieve that they thus have been misled through masks of falsehood. For if these ever rightly celebrated the mass or fulfilled the ministry of the church, it certainly was not by virtue of a sacred ordination, which is mere falsehood and derision of God, but by virtue of the faith and spirit of the church which has had to tolerate these masks in place of a true ministry (Haec itaque sunt, quae non solum vos Boemos, sed plane omnia pia corda merito debent movere, ut quidvis aliud patiantur, quam istis sacrilegis ordinibus fedari. Atque ii, qui hactenus ordinati sunt, doleant sese sic fuisse per mendacii larvas illusos. Nam si unquam consecrarunt aut officium ministri Ecclesiastici expleverunt, id certe non virtute sacri ordinis sui, qui est merum mendacium et irrisio dei, fecerunt, sed virtute fidei et spiritus Ecclesiae, quae eos in loco ministerii huius toleravit et admittere coacta fuit)"; Cf. WA 15, 720, 20f.: "It is not an order for it is without the word, and no one ought to be called ordained by virtue of this ordination (Non est aliquid ordo, quia sine verbo fit, neque aliquis debet vocari ordinatus ex virtute huius ordinationis)."

34 WA 12, 174, 33-38 (LW 40, 14): "Qui has autem per has larvas ad locum

ministerii venit, age, ministerium apprehendat et deinceps pure ac digne administret, sacrificandi officium deserat, docens verbum dei ac regens Ecclesiam, caeterum uncturam et totam ordinationem, qua intravit, ex animo damnet ac detestetur. Neque enim necesse est locum quoque ministerii relinquere, licet impiis ac perversis modis ascenderis, dum animus ipse corrigatur et modus ipse damnetur."

35 WA 12, 179, 25-29 (LW 40, 20): "Sic etiam pulchre sequitur: Christus factus est sacerdotes primus novi testamenti sine rasura, sine unctura, denique sine Charactere illo et sine omni illa Episcopalis ordinationis larva, fecitque Apostolos omnesque discipulos suos per nullam talem larvam sacerdotes. Quare non est necessaria illa ordinationis larva, neque si assit, sufficit, ut fias sacerdos." Cf. WA 12, 178, 26-28 (LW 40, 19): "Sacerdos enim novo praesertim testamento non fit, sed nascitur, non ordinatur, sed creatur. Nascitur vero non carnis, sed spiritus nativitate, nempe ex aqua et spiritu in lavacro regenerationis (For a priest, especially in the New Testament, was not made but was born. He was created, not ordained. He was born not indeed of the flesh, but through a birth of the Spirit, by water and the Spirit in the washing of regeneration)." Cf. also 12, 178, 21-22 (LW 40, 19): "Stet itaque primum tibi rupes illa inconcussa, in novo testamento sacerdotem externe unctum nullum esse nec esse posse (First, regard as an unmovable rock that the New Testament knows of no priest who is or can be anointed externally)."

36 WA 12, 191, 21-25 (LW 40, 37): "...aut oportere conventu facto communibus suffragiis ex suo gremio eligere unum vel quotquot opus fuerit idoneos, et orationibus ac manuum impositionibus universitati commendare et confirmare, atque eos tum pro legitimis Episcopis et ministris verbi agnoscere et colere, indubitata fide credendo, a deo gestum et factum esse, quod hac ratione gesserit et foecerit consensus communis fidelium, Euangelion agnoscentium ac profitentium."

37 WA 12, 191, 32-37 (LW 40, 37): "If then the agreement of these three or two in the name of the Lord makes all things possible, and Christ endorses as his own the things they do, how much more may we not believe that it has happened or can happen with his approval and guidance when we come together in his name, pray together, and elect bishops and ministers of the Word from among ourselves. Even before such election we have been born and called into such a ministry through baptism (Si igitur trium aut duorum consensus in nomine domini omnia potest, et Christus agnoscit sese esse autorem eius facti, quod tales faciunt, quanto magis illo probante et operante fieri et factum esse credendum est, si in nomine eius congregemur, oremus et eligamus Episcopos et ministros verbi ex nobis ipsis, qui iam sine electione eiusmodi per baptismum nati et vocati sumus ad eiusmodi ministerium)." Cf. WA 12, 194, 21-26 (LW 40, 41) where a few pages later Luther was willing to recognize that this might not be what the Bohemian church desired: "But if you are altogether too weak to dare attempt this free and apostolic way of establishing a ministry, I suppose we must endure your weakness and permit you to go on accepting those ordained by papal bishops, such as your Gallus. Use these instead of the papal bishops, to call and elect and ordain such as they think capable and you will endure, according to the foregoing and to the teaching of Paul (Quod si omnino infirmiores estis, quam ut hunc liberum et Apostolicum ritum instituendi

sacerdotii audeatis tentare, age feremus infirmitatem vestram et permittamus, ut iam ordinatos ab Episcopis papisticis accipiatis, scilicet Gallum illum vestrum et sui similes, et utamini illis vice Episcoporum papalium, ut illi vocent et eligant atque confirment, quos viderint idoneos et vobis tolerabiles esse, iuxta praescripta et doctrinam Pauli)."

38 WA 17/I, 511, 3-7: "This was the custom of making a presbyter, etc., they do not call him rather the Holy Spirit calls him, but they confirm this call. Our bishops imitate this, though badly. Yet priests ought to be similarly established so that they might be prayed for in the presence of the church, and so that the preaching of the Word of God might be entrusted to them (Hic fuit mos formandi presbyteros etc. non vocant eum, sed spiritus sanctus, sed confirmant vocationem hanc. Hoc imitantur nostri Episcopi, sed male, sed iterum institui debent sacerdotes, ut coram ecclesia pro eis oretur eisque commendaretur verbum dei praedicandum)." An editorial note in the Weimar edition by G. Buchwald (17/I, 511, note 1), states that the words "sed iterum institui debent sacredotes" raise the question whether evangelical ordinations were occurring in Wittenberg at that time. See below, pp. 61-63, for a discussion of this issue.

39 As Luther stated in a sermon later in the same year, October 16, 1524, (WA 15, 721, 3-5): "Therefore if we know a pious man, we take him out and by virtue of the word that we possess we give him the authority to proclaim the word and to administer the sacraments. This is what it means to ordain (Si ergo scimus pium hominem, extrahimus eum et damus in virtute verbi quod habemus, auctoritatem praedicandi verbum et dandi sacramenta. Hoc est ordinare)."

40 WA 15, 721, 9-12: "That person is a priest who is a brother in Christ, and has been anointed with the Holy Spirit as was Christ: whenever one comes out of baptism he is a priest. Whoever, therefore, wishes to make a priest in order to become a minister of the word blasphemes God because he was already a priest before such an attempt (Ille sacerdos est qui frater Christi est et qui unctus est spiritu sancto ut Christus: quando ex baptismo prodit, est sacerdos. Qui ergo vult facere sacerdotem, ut fiat minister verbi, blasphemat deum, quia iam ante est)."

41 WA 15, 721, 15f.: "The priesthood is perpetual which we receive from Christ (Perpetuum est sacerdotium, quod a Christo accepimus)."

42 Lieberg, 174ff.

43 WA 38, 228, 19-33 (LW 38, 186): "Die lieben heiligen Veter wil ich entschüldigen, und man sol sie auch entchüldigen, wo sie auch mit Cresem geweyhet odder geordinirt und jre geweyheten die Pfaffen odder Priester genennet haben, Denn sie haben da mit keine Winckel Pfaffen noch jemand zur Winckel messen geweyhet, Sondern wenn sie jemand zum rechten Christlichen Pfarrampt odder seelsorgen haben beruffen, haben sie solchen beruff fuer die gemeine mit solchem geprenge wollen zieren und malen zum unterscheid der andern, die nicht beruffen sind, auff das jederman gewis wurde und wüste, welche person solch ampt füren solte und befelh hette zu Teuffen, Predigen, u. Denn es sol und kan im grunde die weyhe nichts anders sein (sol es recht zu gehen) denn

ein beruff odder befelh des Pfarrampts odder Predigampts. Die Apostel haben on Cresem allein die hende auffs heubt gelegt und gebettet uber die, so sie zum ampt berieffen odder sandten, wie Actuum am neunzeheden Capitel Sanct Paulus und Barnabas geschach und Sanct Paulus seinen Timotheon leret, Er solle nicht bald einem die hende auff legen." Note that the final sentence of the LW translation has "merely" for "allein" (...the apostles without chrism merely laid their hands...). This seems to be a somewhat prejudicial rendering which does not do justice to the contrast Luther was making here. The point was not to denigrate the liturgical act of ordaining with prayer and laying on of hands, as "merely" can imply. Cf. WA 41, 457, 19; and 38, 238, 7f.: "ordinirn sol heissen und sein beruffen und befelhen das Pfarrampt"; the Latin translation of this line made by Jonas was "Verum sacramentum ordinis, vera ordinatio est vocatio ad pastoralem curam" (cited by Drews, WA 38, 401).

44 Georg Rietschel, *Luther und die Ordination* (Wittenberg: R. Herrose, 1889), 50; "...nicht etwa in irgend einen kirchlichen Weiheakt, sondern in den Beruf und Befehl des Predigtampts selbst die Ordination." Lieberg, (174), noted that Rietschel himself had to modify the stark way in which he drew the contrast at this point. Rietschel explained, "All dieses zusammengefasst ist nach Luther die ordinatio oder der rechte evangelische ordo" (52). The "all" refers to examination, election, confirmation with laying on of hands before the community, and prayer. In other words, Lieberg argued, there is a significant difference in saying on the one hand that ordination is *not* a liturgical act of consecration *but rather* the election and call, while on the other hand saying that it is election, call, *and* the liturgical action of the community which *together* constitute for Luther the content of ordination. Lieberg rightly criticized Rietschel for focusing so narrowly on this treatise in making the former claim.

45 Perhaps even more challenging for those who emphasize "call" exclusively as the insight of Luther concerning ministry and church structure (important insight though it was) is the following passage where Luther commented on the role of Apollos in Acts 18:24ff.; WA 12, 192, 2-7 (LW 40, 37-38): "This man was afterward even made an apostle without the formality of ordination, and not only functioned in the ministry of the Word but also proved himself useful in many ways to those who had already come to faith. In the same way any Christian should feel obligated to act, if he saw the need and was competent to fill it, *even without a call from the community* [emphasis added]. How much more then should he do so if he is asked and called by the brethren who are his equals, or by the whole community? (Et hic vir postea factus est etiam Apostolus nulla alia accedente ordinatione, non solum fungens ministerio verbi, sed et multum utilis iis, qui iam crediderant. Ita quilibet Christianus facere tenetur, si viderit opus esse verbo et idoneus sit, etiam si non vocet eum universitas, quanto magis, si rogetur voceturque a fratribus aequalibus seu tota universitate)."

46 Quoting the careful wording of the German text, Lieberg (175) argued: "A proper consecration in Rome is, 'nicht mehr eine Weyhe zum beruff odder Pfarrampt *blieben*' (as was the case originally according to apostolic example), 'sondern eine Winckel Weyhe *worden*', (namely, in the historical process of distortion and perversion), 'zu ordinirn Winckel Pfaffen zur Winckel messe' [Lieberg cited in a note here WA 38, 229,

Luther's Liturgical Definition of Ordination 79

4ff.; cf. 230, 32f., 34f.; 234, 30ff.]. And this perversion of correct consecration in Rome corresponds with the necessity of its reformation: 'Und wo die Bepstissche Weyhe recht wolt thun solt sie nichts anders thun denn solche geborne Pfaffen beruffen zu Pfarrampt' [Lieberg cited in a note here WA 38, 230, 21ff; cf. 54, 428, 3f.: Ordo non est sacramentum. Sed ministerium und vocatio ministrorum Ecclesiae; 437, 1f.: ...ein gebot, Befelh und Beruff zum Ampt der Christlichen Kirchen]."

47 WA 38, 236, 30–32 (LW 38, 195): "... wir wollen sehen, wie wir Pfarrhern und Prediger kriegen aus der Tauffe und Gottes wort, on jren Cresem, durch unser erwelen und beruffen geordinirt und bestetigt."

48 WA 38, 220, 34; 221, 1-9 (LW 38, 177): "Und ist also die Weyhe odder Cresem gar weit gescheiden vom ordinirn odder beruff zu dem gemeinen Christlichen ampt des predigens und Pfarrampts, wie wol sie das gehalten haben, das sie keinen ungeweyhten zum Pfarher odder Prediger beruffen, sondern allein aus dem geweyheten hauffen etliche haben genomen. Nu, solch jr thun und brauch, das sie on Pfarre, Pfaffen weyhen und doch on die weyhe keinen Pfarrher ordinirn, macht uns keinen Artikel des glaubes, das drumb also sein muesse, Wir haben itzt daran gnug, das jre weyhe keinen Pfarher noch Christlich ampt unter die gemeine der Christen ordinirt, sondern allein einen Winckel Pfaffen."

49 Lieberg believed the point was unambiguous. In support (see note 68, 178), he cited Vilmos Vajta's conclusion that Luther's criticism of Roman consecration was that it "was not a call to the preaching office, but a consecration to a particular status, which did not exist in the church of Christ" (217; page references are to the German edition), viz., to a sacrificial priesthood (218). Vajta also suggested that for Luther ordination was the "call to the preaching office with prayer and laying on of hands" (218). Against the position of Drews, Vajta emphasized that "it cannot be maintained that Luther...wanted to abandon ordination with prayer and laying on of hands as a liturgical act before the community. Ordination was not thought of by Luther as a mere juridical act" (218, note 80). Thus, Lieberg argued, Vajta had implicitly taken up a position against Rietschel who attempted to play off *vocatio* against *ordinatio* in Luther's writing. When Vajta, on the contrary, said that ordination was for Luther the "public call to the office" (216) he meant that the call took place publicly in the liturgical act of ordaining with prayer and laying on of hands. Thus Lieberg wondered why Vajta did not bring more clearly to expression his opposition to Rietschel's long standing position.

50 WA 12, 193, 37–39; (LW 40, 40): "...procedatis in nomine domini et eligite quem et quos volueritis, qui digni et idonei visi fuerint, tum impositis super eos manibus illorum, qui potiores inter vos fuerint, confirmetis et commendetis eos populo et Ecclesiae seu universitati... ."

51 Compare the comments in the sermon on Acts 13:3 cited below (note 55). Lieberg observed (180, note 73), that Rietschel had commented on the fact that *confirmare* and *commendare* were not synonymous (Rietschel, 61). The latter was introduction to the community, the former an act of the whole community in validating the call.

52 WA 12, 191, 24f. (LW 40, 37): "...and recognize and honor them as lawful bishops and ministers of the Word (atque eos tum pro legitimis Episcopis et ministris verbi agnoscere et colere)"; Cf. 12, 194, 1f. (LW 40, 40): "In this way let them become your bishops, ministers, or pastors (sintque hoc ipso vestri Episcopi, ministri seu pastores)."

53 See Karant-Nunn, pp. 8–13, for a helpful analysis in which she argued that the first generation of Lutheran pastors were probably almost all formerly consecrated clerics.

54 See Lieberg, 183; Karant-Nunn, 13-20.

55 WA 17/I, 511, 3–7 (see above, note 38, for the Latin text). The editorial comment in the Weimar edition stated that the words "sed iterum institui debent sacerdotes" raise the question whether evangelical ordinations were already occurring, but also cautioned that the subjunctive forms of "pray" and "entrust" indicated that it was something yet to be realized. There is some evidence that a year earlier in 1523 Luther had installed Bugenhagen as pastor in Wittenberg by standing in the chancel and declaring him "confirmierte und bestätigte" in the office because he was worthy of it (Hering, *Doktor Pomeranus* (1888), 21; cited by P. Drews, *Die Ordination*, Prüfung und Lehrverpflichtung der Ordinanden in Wittenberg 1535 (Giessen: Otto Kindt, 1904), 1). But Bugenhagen had already been ordained as a Catholic priest, so this is not evidence for the establishment of any precedent with regard to evangelical ordinations. It was, however, a clear indication of the importance for Luther of having pastors called by a local congregation and committed to it.

56 WA 15, 720, 13–15: "Episcopi neimen ungunt nisi qui velint abnegare Euangelium. Debemus tamen cum tempore praedicatores ordinare, quare velim vos certos esse, quod quisque Christianus sit Christi frater, si verbum eius habet."

57 WA 15, 721, 1–5: "Nos praedicabimus et ungemus aliter quam illi Episcopi. Sed nos qui iam habemus ministeria, commendabimus in nostrum ministerium. Ordinare non est consecrare. Si ergo scimus pium hominem, extrahimus eum et damus in virtute verbi quod habemus, auctoritatem praedicandi verbum et dandi sacramenta. Hoc est ordinare." Lieberg (182), argued that there is no doubt that Luther was using the word "ordinare" to include both the selection of persons (*extrahimus*) and the transmission of authority to preach and administer the sacraments via a public liturgical act of ordaining. Paul Drews (WA 38, 402) was more cautious in his assessment of whether the appointment (*bestellen*) aspect of the call had to occur through a liturgical act, although he made it clear that such an idea was not excluded in the way Luther expressed himself here.

58 WA 16, 226, 6, note: "Dominica Cantate quae erat 14. Maii quo ordinatus sum in diaconum Ecclesiae Wittenbergensis praesente tota ecclesia Wittenbergensi imponentibus mihi manum Luthero, Pomerano, Phi[lippo] Consu[le], Iud[ice], Anno.25." WA 17/I, 243, note: an editorial comment here observes that written above the title of the Sermon of May 14, 1525, "Dominica Cantate Luth. Ioh.16" are the words "quae erat 14.Maij ordinatus."

Luther's Liturgical Definition of Ordination 81

59 The only exception is the argument of Enders (Enders, *Briefwechsel*, 7, 137; cf. 132, note 1) that Wencel Kilmann was ordained in 1529 (although Enders' manuscripts have the date 1539). Drews (WA 38, 406), points out that the date is neither 1529 nor 1539, but 1536 as shown by Kawerau, *Theologische Studien und Kritiken*, 1899, 137.

60 WA BR 5, 700, 12-15: "Magna ubique penuria fidelium pastorum, ita ut prope sit, quo cogemur proprio ritu ordinare seu instituere ministros, sine rasura, sine uncura, sine infula, sine chirothecis, sine baculo et sine thuribulo, sine denique istis episcopis." In his editorial comments, (WA 34/II, 574), Georg Buchwald stated that this passage along with comments by Luther in a May 21, 1531 sermon indicated clearly that ordinations were occurring in Wittenberg in 1531: "Finally, of importance as evidence for the fact that at that time, May 1531, ordinations were taking place in Wittenberg, are Bd. 34/I, 437, 16/17, and Luther's remarks on Dec. 16, 1530 (Enders 8, 332 [=BR 5, 700, 12f.])." The comments from the May 21 sermon (WA 34/I, 437, 16-17) are as follows: "Likewise whenever we ordain an official, because it is done in obedience to the church, to whom it has been entrusted... (Item quando ordinamus parochum, quia es ghet ynn dem gehorsam ecclesiae, cui commissum...)." Cf. WA 34/I, 432, 5ff.: "Just as today the papists sit in a legitimate office, they themselves baptize, give the sacrament, ordain priests, consecrate marriages, so we [do also] (Sicut hodie Papistae sitzen ynn dem rechten ampt, ipsi baptisant, dant Sacramentum, ordinant sacerdotes, consecrant coniuges ut nos)." Lieberg (178, note 67) agreed with Drews (WA 38, 404-405) that Buchwald was in error in seeing this as evidence that ordinations were practiced in Wittenberg at this point for other communities.

61 See Drews, WA 38, 405-407, from which the following summary is drawn.

62 Sehling, IV, 38.

63 WA BR 6, 44, 15-20: "Quare de hoc quod petis, an coenam Domini non rasus neque unctus debeas tractare, nihil respondere possum. Nam si nihil serium ibi fuerit, vellem te, ut hactenus, abstineres; si vero serium fuerit, tum publice coram altari a reliquis ministris cum oratione et impositione manuum testimonium accipies et autoritatem coenae tractandae."

64 Enders' interpretation (Enders 8, 368, note 5) that "abstain" referred to "tonsure and anointing" was refuted by O. Clemen in his editorial notes in the Weimar edition of the letter (WA BR 6, 44, note 9). He argued that the sense of the whole passage should be taken as follows: "This thing that the people complain about when they are supposed to pay the pastor a bit more in wages, signifies that they do not seriously seek the gospel. That is why (because I suspect the people do not take it seriously), I cannot definitely answer your question as to whether you should administer the Lord's Supper without presbyteral ordination. The answer must be given in conformity with whether the people are serious or not. If not, I desire that you abstain from administering the sacrament as you have up to now, but if they are serious...[then do as the letter recommends]." Clemen goes on to explain that the contrast is not "tum publice..." with "tonsura et unctione", but with "tum accipies autoritatem... ." As supporting evidence he cites BR

5, 659 15f., (an October 26, 1530 letter of Luther to Nicholas Hausmann): "lest in any way he try to hold the eucharist secretly, since he is not a minister called to this task (Ne vllo modo tentet Eucharistiam clam porrigere, cum non sit vocatus minister ad hoc opus)," and BR 6, 338, 2ff.: "I have given advice to the man, whenever a preacher has been called, and concern is present about the sacrament, he himself meanwhile should abstain, and should allow the host to administer according to his own custom, he himself being content with teaching (Ego homini consilium dedi, quandoquidem praedicator esset vocatus, et periculum adesset propter sacramenti ministerium, ipse interim abstineret, et parochum sineret more suo ministrare, ipse docendo contentus)." Clemen saw additional support for his interpretation in Drews' refutation of Enders (WA 38, 408), but disagreed with Drews' conclusion that the intent of the passage was to show that Luther thought a special evangelical rite of ordination was a concession to human weakness. Lieberg (184, note 95) concluded that Clemen was correct and believed that for Luther prayer with laying on of hands was required before one administer the sacrament.

65 WA 38, 236, 30-32 (LW 38, 195): "...wir wollen sehen, wie wir Pfarrhern und Prediger kriegen aus der Tauffe und Gottes wort, on jren Cresem, durch unser erwelen und beruffen geordinirt und bestetigt." See Lieberg's argument, 176-178.

66 WA 38, 237, 4-9 (LW 38, 196): "Hat doch der Bapst selbs jnn seinen geistlichen rechten geboten (wie wol aus den alten Vetern genomen), Man solle der Ketzer weyhe odder Ordinirn fuer rechte Weyhe halten und nicht widderumb Weyhen, die so von Ketzern geweyhet waren. Nu sind wir Lutherisschen nicht Ketzer, das muessen die Papisten selbs bekennen, Darumb sollen sie unser Weyhen und Ordinirn lassen recht sein... ."

67 WA 38, 237, 4ff. (LW 38, 196): "Darumb sollen sie unser Weyhen und Ordinirn lassen recht sein"; Cf. WA 50, 248, 16ff., and 53, 257, 1ff.

68 WA 38, 237, 19-23 (LW 38, 196): "If they claim that the heretics who consecrated in this way were bishops and that is why the pope and fathers have allowed their consecration to be valid, this is true. They were bishops, not princes or lords; but as St. Jerome and St. Paul prove, bishop and pastor were one and the same thing (Und ob sie für geben, die Ketzer so geweyhet haben, sind Bisschove gewest, darumb hat der Bapst und die Veter jr Weyhen lassen gelten, Das ist war: Sie sind Bisschove gewest aber nicht Fursten noch herrn, sondern, wie Sanct Hieronymus aus Sanct Paul beweiset, ist Bisschoff und Pfarrher ein ding gewest)." The editorial note in LW gives the reference to Jerome as: 'The presbyter is the same as the bishop...the bishops should have known that they were greater according to custom rather than according to the truth of the Lord's ordinance.' [*Jerome, Commentary on the Epistle to Titus* (*Commentariorum in epistolam ad Titum*, Titus 1:7 ; *MPL* 26, 562]. Cf. WA 12, 387, 14-15 (LW 30, 133): "...the words 'bishop' and 'priest' had one and the same meaning."

69 WA 38, 238, 1-8 (LW 38, 197): "Und der selbe kleine Pfarrher odder Bisschoff Sanct Augustinus hat viel Pfarrher odder Bisschove jnn seiner kleinen Pfarrhen geweyhet und geordinirt..., die von andern Stedten begert und beruffen wurden, Wie wir aus unser

Pfarhen zu Wittenberg andern Stedten, so es begern und bey sich keine haben, ordinirn und senden muegen. Denn Ordinirn sol heissen und sein beruffen und befelhen das Pfarrampt... ." Lieberg (177) had no doubt that Luther was referring to the liturgical act of ordaining in this passage. Drews, (WA 38, 405), following the reasoning of Rietschel, believed that this was not the case. Cf. WA 38, 252, 23-26. (LW 38, 211): "[Christ has begun]...to assure and make available to the church once again the call or true consecration and ordination to the office of the ministry, as it possessed it from the beginning, but which the great bishops arrogated to themselves alone and took away from the small bishops or pastors (...den beruff odder rechte Weyhe und ordinirn zum Pfarrampt widderumb der Kirchen zu sprechen und ein reumen, wie sie von anfang gehabt hat, welche die grossen Bisschove zu sich allein gerissen, der kleinen Bisschoven odder Pfarrhern genomen haben...)."

70 As Lieberg, (177), pointed out in his analysis of Rietschel's position.

71 Karant-Nunn, 65.

72 WA 41, 240, 33-35; 241, 1: "Nos gedenken 1 mal mit eim offentlichen gepreng ordinare. Habetis nunc deutsche taufe, Sacramentum, praedicationem et Catechismum et quicquid Christiani. Quanquam predig ampt und beruff auch halten, tamen etiam in die deutsch sprach bringen." Lieberg (178) stated that it remained a possibility so to interpret this passage that Luther was thinking here about ordinations done in German and that ordinations in Latin were in fact already a matter of practice. But he himself conceded that it was difficult to sustain such an interpretation in light of subsequent evidence in the sermon.

73 The text was reprinted by Paul Drews, *Die Ordination*, Appendix, 33. The Elector explained that he was making this innovation "in order hereafter to provide that the shortage and lack of preachers and deacons who bring the Word of God and administer the sacraments may with time fall away, since those who in accordance with the old custom had themselves ordained to the priesthood by bishops are dying out... ." Drews believed that it was highly likely that the Elector issued similar instructions to visitors in his other territories. A line from Luther's October 20, 1535 sermon (see below) supports that: "in franken sachsen meisschen durigen" (Drews, ibid., Appendix IV, 36).

74 See the witness provided by the ordination of Hieronymus Hirscheider, *Corpus Reformatorum* II, 901-902; discussed by Drews, ibid., 10-11.

75 Lieberg (186), believed the sermon was "without question an ordination address." Drews, in the earlier *Die Ordination* (3), had also accepted that as the case, but in his introduction to the Weimar edition of Luther's rite (WA 38, 409) stated that it was not an ordination address but rather a sermon delivered on a Sunday when an ordination was going to occur. What the point of this distinction was for Drews is not clear.

76 WA 41, 457, 1-5: "Ehe sterbe, wer da wolle, bleibt ministerium, quod solius dei, donec Ecclesia est, hic manet Euangelium, baptismus, claves, Sacramentum, predigampt.

1 pfarrher stirbt nach dem andern, ampt bleibt. Si hoc, mogen wir andere an die stad setzen."

77 WA 41, 457, 7-10, 15-16: "The papists whenever they ordained gave a chalice, keys and other official signs of the office, shaved their heads, clothed them with a chasuble and anointed them with chrism. We do none of this, for they think priests are made through these things. We desire to give the office, but to set a person in this office, which is prior, we only receive a person who will be a laborer (Papistae, quando ordinaverunt, dederunt calicem, claves u. zu warzeichen officii und kopff beschoren und kasel angezogen und finger mit kresem. Nos non, quia ipsi putant per hoc fieri sacerdotes. ...Wir willig officium damus, sed setzen 1 ein in hoc officium, quod prius est, tantum accipimus personam, quae sol operarius sein)."

78 WA 41, 457, 33-35: "Das ist zur vorrhede, cum simus ordinaturi aliquem in aliam Eccclesiam. Prius non fecimus, ne Papistae, et in conspectu vestro, ut sitis testes." Lieberg, (187), tried to render intelligible the sense of this difficult passage, based on Rörer's broken up notes, as follows: "Up to now we ourselves have not ordained for other communities, because we still waited to see whether or not the Roman bishops would confirm our pastors. But since that has become hopeless, we do it now, and indeed *coram ecclesia*, which brings with it the office of witness." Drews, *Die Ordination*, (35) rendered both the text and the translation differently: "Das ist zur vorrhede, cum simus ordinaturi aliquem in aliam Ecclesiam. Prius non fecimus ne Papistae et in conscientia vero ut sitis testes," which was then translated, "we have such an ordination, in which one ordains someone for another community, but by doing that we are not again papists and encumbered in conscience" (4-5). G. Buchwald, "Wann hat Luther die erste Ordination vollzogen?," *Theologische Studien und Kritiken*, (1896), 151ff., had argued on the basis of this sentence that this date represented the first evangelical ordinations in Wittenberg. Drews pointed out that the passage made sense even if Luther had already done a few ordinations. Furthermore, other evidence indicated that ordinations had taken place in Wittenberg prior to October 20, 1535.

79 On the "sending" aspect, cf. TR 5, 111, 24f.: "...to which we call and send you through God's authority, just as God has sent us (zu welchen wir dich durch Gottes gewaldt ruffen und senden, gleichwie ons Gott gesandt hat)." On the "giving" aspect, compare the words of the electoral edict already cited above: "...to give the power and authority of the office of priest and deacon (Macht und Gewalt ihres Priester- und Diakoneamts zu geben)."

80 WA 41, 762, 18-21; 763, 1-5: "Scitis ordinationem ecclesiae cum suis ritibus necessariam esse. Sed quia papa non promovet, sed impedit cursum euangelii, nobis vigilandum et orandum est. Noster elector necessario ordinavit, ut eligantur et ordinentur hic docti viri et pii ministri verbi dei, et ne quis ignorantibus nobis surgat et doceat. Ideo vult et decrevit, ut ex omnibus dicesibus Francken, Meissen, etc. ad nos mittantur et examinentur et confirmentur et, quo mittendi sunt, mittantur. Illius publici ritus vos debetis esse testes, deum ardentissime orare, ut ipse det nobis pios et sinceros praedicatores sui verbi... ."

Luther's Liturgical Definition of Ordination 85

81 *CR* II, No.1299, 901-902. The text is also printed by Drews, *Die Ordination*, (Appendix 3, 34-35). The Rector at that time was the Jurist Sebaldus Münsterer. Melanchthon was also present. The exam took place in Jena because the faculty had fled there to escape the plague in Wittenberg in July of 1535. Hirscheider did not have a definite call at the time of the examination.

82 *CR* II, No.1299, 902: "Quod autem petivit a nobis, ut vocant, ordinari, si quidem episcopi nostros non admittunt ad docendum, et tamen necesse est propter ordinem in Ecclesia hunc ritum retineri."

83 Drews, *Die Ordination*, (11). The following summary is drawn from Drews, 11-13.

84 WA BR 7, 302, 3-10: "Remittimus vestrum Ioannem per vos vocatum et electum, per nos quoque examinatum et publice coram nostra Ecclesia inter orationes et laudes Dei in vestrum comministrum ordinatum et confirmatum ad mandatum Principis nostri, licet D. Pomeranus non satis facilis ad hoc fuerit, ut qui adhuc sentit, quemlibet in Ecclesia sua ordinandum per suos presbytros. Quod fiet tandem, ubi ista res nova et ordinatio radices altius egerit et mos firmior factus fuerit." Drews, *Die Ordination*, (5), observed that *ordinatio* in the last sentence referred to the order of the Elector (*Ordnung*) and not to "ordination."

85 For the text of the report see Walter Friedensburg, ed., *Nuntiaturberichte aus Deutschland. Erste Abteilung 1533-1559, Erster Band, Nuntiaturen des Vergerio 1533-1536* (Gotha, 1892; reprint Frankfurt: Minerva G.M.B.H., 1968), 544.

86 As quoted by Drews, *Die Ordination*, (12). Drews also noted that this fit with the way in which Melanchthon concluded examinations of candidates with the remark: "Admittet vos dominus pastor."

87 See Lieberg's summary, 188-189, note 119.

88 Against Drews, WA 38, 408, and Rietschel, *Luther und Die Ordination* (68f.), Lieberg, (190, note 125), commènted: "With the remark, 'nos cogimur ita facere,' an inner indifference to ordination itself is not expressed but rather exactly the opposite: the conviction about the necessity of ordination, which was taken up by pastors instead of bishops only in an emergency. If one did not maintain that ordination was necessary for appointment to office it would not be necessary to examine how one then was supposed to be 'forced' to the actual doing of ordination. Indeed, one could simply discount it."

89 WA 26, 196 (LW 40, 270).

90 WA 26, 197, 15-19, 22ff. (LW 40, 271).

91 Drews, *Die Ordination*, (6-9), argued that it might not have been simply a response

to an emergency situation but rather part of a larger, well-conceived plan on the part of the Elector. Karant-Nunn's analysis supports the latter; see especially 60-74.

92 For the text of the articles and an introduction see, Theodore Tappert, ed. *The Book of Concord* (Philadelphia: Fortress Press, 1959), 287-318. The letter from the Elector to Luther is dated December 11, 1536.

93 Ibid., 314.

94 Rietschel, *Luther und die Ordination*, 71ff.

95 Lieberg, 190-191. Drews, WA 38, 409, believed that Rietschel's claim that the evidence in the Register showed that Luther did not complete his rite for ordination before 1537 could not be substantiated. Drews also argued that the reason for so few ordinations in 1535-36 lay simply in the nature of the situation in Wittenberg (and elsewhere) at the time (e.g., the plague). He did not believe that it had anything to do with an "unfavorable disposition" toward the idea of Wittenberg ordinations by Bugenhagen. How, Drews rightly asked, could Bugenhagen have refused to ordain anyone approved and sent to him by the Wittenberg University faculty? Cf. *CR* 3, 235-236; which contains a letter Spalatin wrote early in 1537 to Melanchthon: "aufs höchest vonnöthen sey, wie die Ordination zu bestellen sey. Denn alle verständige Christen wissen, dass niemand ohne Vocation öffentlich lehren soll, derhalben an solcher Vocation merklich und viel gelegen." Lieberg, (191), noted that this implied that at the start of 1537 the correct manner of ordaining was not yet settled. Rietschel, *Luther und die Ordination* (74), saw this as additional evidence for dating Luther's rite in the first half of 1537. Drews clearly demonstrated, however, that the oldest manuscript witness was from 1535. Thus, Lieberg believed, what accounted for Spalatin's comment was probably the infrequent use of the rite due to Bugenhagen's reluctance (or according to Drews, due to the situation in Wittenberg at the time).

CHAPTER 3

A DECADE OF TRANSITION: RITES FROM 1525-1535

The well-known fact that Luther ordained Georg Rörer a deacon in the city church at Wittenberg in 1525 does not answer the question whether it was the first evangelical ordination, as Rörer himself had claimed. It was not an act of episcopal ordination since Luther was not a bishop. It was into the diaconate, not the presbyterate. Insofar as it substituted for episcopal ordination into one of the major orders it could be considered the first. It involved the laying on of hands and prayer in the midst of the gathered community, thus fulfilling historical, theological and liturgical criteria for ordering ministry that Luther had been advocating in his writing.

Yet this was an anomaly in the Reformation currents of the 1520's. Only when the episcopal structure of the medieval Catholic church, including its rites for ordaining, could no longer function did the characteristics of substitute evangelical structures emerge. That was a gradual process as already noted. In the case of a rite for ordaining pastors the critical combination of factors that established a new, evangelical standard did not come together until the years 1535-39.

Elector John Frederick was responsible for the legal facets of an evangelical process for calling and ordaining, the superintendents and Wittenberg faculty for the educational, and Luther and Johannes Bugenhagen for the liturgical. Together these facets of that process and other factors produced an ecclesiastical revolution. That Luther was personally responsible for the versions of the rite that bear his name and established the model for subsequent liturgical efforts is beyond doubt.[1] Open to question is the nature of Bugenhagen's influence on Luther in the development of the structure and content of that rite.

Although Luther's rite had the most influence on subsequent liturgical developments, it is true here as in the evangelical reforms of the mass that he was not the first to make the attempt. The 1526 Homberg Church Order (named after the city of Homberg in Hesse), although an aborted effort, contained the first evangelical rite for ordination.

Together with the rites of Bugenhagen's first Church Orders, it provided the first step in movement from the medieval rites to Luther's influential 1535/39 rite.

The *Kirchenordnungen* give direct access to the issues that were in the forefront of reformers' minds as they tackled the problems inherent in changing ecclesiastical structures. The Orders are context specific because they discuss immediate concerns pertinent to their area while providing practical descriptions of solutions to problems, or methods to be used in addressing them. As the Orders develop through the years one can trace the changing sense of identity in the Protestant churches and assess the theological (and political) currents prevailing in the areas from which they come.

The 1526 Homberg Church Order (Hesse)

The origin of the Reformation of the church in Hesse can be traced directly to Melanchthon's influence on Hesse's prince, Philip, whose place in history ranks next to that of Luther and Melanchthon in terms of his influence on the success of the reform movement in Germany.[2] It can be argued, of course, that Philip's concerns and motives were more political than theological, but his commitment to the cause of church reform cannot be questioned. Although Melanchthon's 1524 *Epitomae* convinced Philip of the need for evangelical reform, he was reluctant to act. The 1526 Diet of Speyer provided the political freedom he and other princes needed. In October, 1526, under the urging of Franz Lambert of Avignon, Philip convened a synod in the city of Homberg. It met from October 21–23 and was the formal beginning of the Reformation in Hesse.[3]

On the last day of the Homberg synod the only official action of the meeting was taken: that a few men should "set in order based on God's Word, ...what should be reformed in all of the church in Hesse."[4] On the basis of this action Lambert produced the first known effort in establishing a new, evangelical Church Order, the *Reformatio*.[5] It was probably completed in December 1526 and was sent by Philip to Luther for his appraisal. On January 7, 1527 Luther responded advising Philip against printing the Order or introducing it in the territory. The basic reason for this negative judgment was simply that Luther thought the action to be premature. The people were not yet ready for it.[6] Because of Luther's assessment Philip abandoned the *Reformatio* and it never gained any official status or influence.

This Homberg Order is helpful, nevertheless, exactly because it was the first attempt to formalize what shape church life should take in the movement from Catholic tradition to evangelical reform. More important for our purpose, it contained a description of a rite for ordaining ministers: *De ordinatione ministrorum ecclesiae per orationem et manuum impositionem*.[7] The fact that it was never actually used does not detract from its importance as a witness to the kinds of changes being considered at this early stage (four years before the presentation of the *Augsburg Confession*).

In the Homberg Order the congregation had the right to elect and install its pastor because the congregation had the task of judging the voice of the shepherd: "Let any church choose or depose its own bishop, because it is the church's task to judge the voice of pastors."[8] But the Order noted that the congregations needed to be instructed in the task of discerning the shepherd's voice. Until that occurred the prince, in consultation with the Visitors, had the responsibility and authority to call a pastor to a congregation.[9]

The decree of the prince provided the legitimation that normally would have come from within the ecclesiastical hierarchy. Thus the move in Hesse to have the prince function as an emergency bishop (albeit in consultation with the Visitors) predated Luther's support of the same in Saxony nine years later. Again, that power was temporary, as made clear by the statement that when properly educated to the task congregations were to assume this responsibility.

Ordination was discussed under the general title "The ordination of bishops, electors of the synods, visitors, and all other ministers." On the one hand this indicated a leveling of hierarchical distinction since all those listed were to be ordained in the same way, through prayer and laying on of hands.[10] Yet the descriptions also made it clear that these were different offices with differing requirements, and the fact that the confirmation of the election and call was accomplished through an ordination performed by others already in the pastoral office maintained some sense of clergy/laity distinction.

Sunday was designated as the occasion for the election of the pastor (bishop).[11] The ordination was to occur as part of the community's worship: "The church will be gathered together and all will pray, along with those elected."[12] As would be the case in Luther's rite, the specific comment about the community's prayer for the ordinands communicated the point that congregational intercession was an integral part of the process. The description of the rite was minimal. After the congregation's prayer the ordinator laid on hands along with two other ordained people. One of two formulas was said: "Receive the Holy Spirit...(John 20:22)" or "Receive the keys of the kingdom of heaven... (Matthew 16:19)." This was done for each candidate, one at a time.[13] While this individual formula was being said for each candidate an expanded prayer formula was also spoken.

Niebergall interpreted the latter as the formula for ordaining deacons, but there is no clear justification in the text for such a restriction. The description and prayer state:

> While the bishop, or the visitors, or the thirteen electors, or the assistants of the bishop [deacons] are being ordained, one of those laying on hands should say, "Receive the Holy Spirit." And while hands are being placed on the others one of them should say: "May the Lord fill you with his Spirit, may the Lord teach your heart, and strengthen it with faith, so that you might worthily fulfill the ministry to which you have been elected. Response: Amen."[14]

It is not clear whether the ordinands or the whole congregation said the response. Whether the *aliis* meant deacons other than those noted so that the longer prayer formula applied only to them, as Niebergall seemed to interpret, cannot be stated with precision. A later section describing the office of deacon did not mention a specific formula.[15]

Following the act of laying on hands with both the imperative formula and prayer the ordinator said a Collect:

> Ordinator: The Lord be with you.
> Response: And with your spirit.
> Ordinator: Let us pray: God, who teaches your people to be ruled by your Spirit and Word, we ask that you pour out the gift of your Spirit upon these your

servants, over whom we invoke your holy name, and in whose name we lay hands upon them. Grant that they may worthily and with holiness, to the glory of your name, fulfill the ministry in your church to which they have been elected, through our Lord Jesus Christ, your Son, who lives and reign with you, etc.[16]

That the Collect functioned as a prayer for the ordinands (an ordination prayer) was reinforced by the directive that "if there is only one who is ordained the prayer should be in the singular."[17]

On the basis of the structure and content of this brief rite one can conclude that the ordination was to the ministry of the word in the interest of *utilitas ecclesiae*. Leading a holy and upright life was central to election to office: "No bishop or deacon may be admitted or confirmed unless they will teach the word purely and live the life worthy of ministers of Christ and of the church."[18] The recurring references in the Order to bishop and deacon, no use of the word presbyter or priest, reveal the concern to abandon almost all the minor and major orders and their accompanying distinctions of status. Yet the emphasis on morality, ability to teach, etc., also made it clear that pastoral leaders were to be exemplary in the conduct of their lives.

Although no specific readings were noted for inclusion within the rite, repeated reference in the Order to I Timothy 3 and Titus 1 indicates that these were probably incorporated in the broader liturgy within which the ordination took place.[19] Both of these readings were associated with ordination in the Roman tradition. The December section of the Würzburg lectionary listed the pericope I Timothy 3:8-13 for the ordination of a deacon, and for a priest, Titus 1:1-9.[20] The Homberg Order did not state specifically that its ordination liturgy was a eucharist, and it made no references to communion or the participation of the newly ordained in it.

The dramatic restriction of the act of ordaining to the focused moment of laying on hands with prayer stood in stark contrast to the embellished medieval rite. It also pointed to an unequivocal abandonment of the *traditio instrumentorum* which had become a focus of the Roman rite. The rite had no anointing, no giving of paten, chalice or vestments, no pledge of obedience to anyone, no extended exhortation. The imperative formulas made it clear that the power to forgive sins was still considered a central responsibility of the ordained, but divorced from the larger context of the Roman rite these formulas created less sense of hierarchical distinction. The power may still have been considered personal, but it was also more clearly ecclesial.

The tension between ordination being an act of the universal church and/or the local congregation was evident in the Homberg Order's concern to guarantee congregational participation on the one hand, and provide for an act to communicate universal recognition on the other:

> When the churches have been instructed through the Word and can choose their own bishop, it will be sufficient for them that the election be confirmed by two Visitors if three cannot be there. If the Visitors themselves cannot come together personally to lay hands on those elected, they should write a letter to show that they confirm the bishop elected. Three neighboring bishops should then be called for the ordination of the elected bishop.[21]

The role of those already ordained stood in relationship with the role of the congregation in the process of calling and ordaining. In other words both a theological and juridical or political dimension were present. This was due to the dismembering of what had been an ecclesiastical whole, where the ordained hierarchy had fulfilled both the theological and jurisdictional roles. Now the territorial prince and the Visitors approved by him carried out the juridical role, while the congregation and other pastors regained their theological place as the agents for calling and ordaining.

The emergence of a variety of brief Church Orders designed to speak to specific needs in the regulation of ecclesiastical life characterized the decade following the Homberg Synod.[22] As in Saxony the means for establishing what those needs were was to provide for a visitation of the territory. Already in August of 1525 Philip appointed Adam Krafft Visitor.[23] His task and that of his fellow Visitors initially was to visit and make an inventory of the cloisters of Hesse prior to the decision to dissolve them in 1527. But that task soon expanded to include assessing the state of congregations and pastors, schools, and administrative offices. The Visitors reported directly to the prince. In subsequent developments the jurisdictional power appropriated by the prince from the episcopal structures of the Catholic church was delegated to the superintendents (who were often the Visitors). The office of superintendent eventually absorbed the duties of the office of Visitor. The implications of these later developments for the emerging ordination rites in Hesse are discussed in the next chapter.

The 1529 Hamburg Church Order

Johannes Bugenhagen (1485-1558) was one of the chief leaders of the Reformation, especially in northern Germany and parts of Scandinavia. Although born and raised in Pomerania, he went to Wittenberg in 1521 and became a close associate and life-long friend of Luther.[24] He served as pastor in Wittenberg and was an official member of the University faculty there from 1533 until his death. A prominent leader, he made his influence felt by organizing the reform movement in several key cities, authoring or co-authoring church orders for each: Braunschweig (1528), Hamburg (1529), Lübeck (1531), Pomerania (1535), Denmark (1537), Schleswig-Holstein (1542), Braunschweig-Wolfenbüttel (1543), and Hildesheim (1544). All but the 1528 Braunschweig order contained ordination and/or installation rites.

Bugenhagen's early Church Orders for Hamburg (1529), Lübeck (1531) and Pomerania (1535) came before Luther's 1535/39 rite. It is worth noting, therefore, that Bugenhagen's influence was perhaps as important as Luther's at this early stage. He had a perspective different from Luther's on the question of what constituted ordination. In the later Church Orders which he wrote or influenced he adopted Luther's rite, but at this early stage (1528-35) he was struggling, perhaps more so than Luther, to produce a liturgical expression of Reformation concerns about ordered ministry in the church.

On April 23, 1525, three weeks before Luther's ordination of Rörer, Bugenhagen commented on the fact that the liturgical act of laying on of hands was not necessary for a person to be ordained:

> Titus and Timothy did this [lay on hands] not because it was something before God but because it was a sign, after a gathering of the community had been called, that the person had been chosen and was known to have been chosen. I would have been able to do this also, but because the various enthusiasts do so, I am unwilling. Whoever is chosen by the church and accepted is ordained.[25]

Clearly Luther did not share this reservation and Bugenhagen himself backed away from it later.

It was, as stated explicitly, only a reaction by Bugenhagen based on his not wanting to be identified with the *Schwärmerei* who were apparently using laying on of hands for some identifying purpose, and probably had nothing to do with any kind of theological or historical objection to the act itself. This reaction to the enthusiasts might account for the absence of a liturgical act for confirming persons in their call in the 1528 Church Order for Braunschweig.[26] In his later church orders he did include a rite of laying on of hands and prayer, although he may have considered this (initially) to be an act of installing rather than ordaining.[27] The confusion is understandable at this point because episcopal ordinations were still occurring in the 1520's and there was no reason to develop a liturgical alternative for a need that did not yet exist.

The first of Bugenhagen's efforts was the 1529 Hamburg Church Order. The Hamburg Order contained an act of installation in its Article 12, *Van der Annehminge solcher denere des wordes in der Kercken*, which resembled closely the rite for ordination developed by Luther six years later.[28] After the candidates had been called and properly examined they were to receive the spiritual order (*den geistlichen Orden*). They were subsequently called *ordinati ad ministerium spiritus non literae*, ordained to preaching the gospel of Christ (*verordnete zu predigen das Evangelium Christi*).

The rite took place in the context of regular Sunday morning worship after the epistle reading. Thus Bugenhagen retained the traditional medieval placement of the rite. The ordination began with an announcement to the community:

> Dear friends in Christ, you know that we have prayed that God for Christ's sake would send us a good superintendent, pastor or chaplain, or preacher. Those who have been entrusted have done their duty and chosen, N., whom they have, with as much judgment and understanding as humanly possible, judged to be honest, just, capable and not envious. He is blameless to himself and to those around him. He has the strength to teach the Word of God the Lord to the consciences, to stop the mouths of those who would contradict, as Saint Paul teaches in Timothy and Titus, and Christ teaches in the faithful and wise servant (Matthew 24: 45ff.). Pray therefore that God, through Jesus Christ, would give him grace to carry out his office and lead us to salvation. Remember the example that Christ has given us in Luke 6: On the morning on which he wished to teach and choose his twelve disciples for the office of preaching, he had prayed to God on the previous night alone on the mountain. If God commands this matter according to our prayers, then it cannot fail, even if we were possibly to choose a Judas. But this, N., shall be presented before this altar with song, prayer and the laying on of hands so that he may be commended to the grace of God and so that this congregation may know that this person has been commended by us to such an office. I admonish all of you—councilmen, deacons, citizens, and common folk, young and old—to pray while the children's choir sings the Alleluia.[29]

An examination was clearly assumed to have occurred in the vocational process, of which the liturgical act of ordaining was, therefore, only a part. The scriptural foundations cited, Timothy and Titus, became a standard source for readings in evangelical rites subsequently. The verses usually chosen (for example, I Timothy 3:1-7) specified the kind of life an ordained person should lead. Both Bugenhagen and Luther emphasized repeatedly that the moral conduct of pastors needed to be above reproach. The reference to Matthew 24 reinforced Bugenhagen's contention that servanthood was the key to understanding the role of pastor. It was an anti-clerical, anti-hierarchical, congregationally oriented theme that Bugenhagen shared with Luther which found expression in the mention of this text.

The admonition to prayer which followed the scriptural references was not a casual aside as the subsequent explanation of the significance of Luke 6 demonstrated. To link the act of ordaining with Christ's prayer and choosing the twelve disciples would appear to establish a *de iure divino* argument for its importance. It is at least clear that for Bugenhagen the prayers of the community were central to ordaining. The candidate who was prayed for, "even if a Judas," could not negate the power of that ecclesial action. This was the beginning of a Reformation focus on the community's prayer, theologically rooted in pneumatology, which was to appear universally in the evangelical rites that followed.

The three focal points of the rite according to this introduction were song, prayer, and laying on of hands. The song and prayer were communal since the gathered congregation was involved in them. Yet, in spite of Bugenhagen's congregational emphasis, there is a distinguishing of the role of those already ordained ("commended by us") in the vocational process. At least two facets of that distinction are the role of training and examining, and within the ordination rite itself the act of laying on hands. Prior to the latter the choir was to sing *Veni Sancte Spiritus*. The hymn invoked the Spirit through whom the prayers of the community for the grace of God to empower the candidate for pastoral ministry were realized. The hymn was part of Durandus' rite and thus represented a point of contact with the content of the medieval ritual tradition for ordination.[30]

During the singing the ordained clergy present were to gather at the altar with the ordinand and all were to kneel until the hymn concluded. The clergy then rose (the ordinand remained kneeling), all laid their hands on the candidate's head, and one among the clergy (not necessarily the superintendent) said the following prayer:

> Let us pray: Almighty, eternal Father, you have taught us through our master Jesus Christ that the harvest is great but the workers are few, therefore pray the Lord of the harvest, that he may send into his harvest laborers who will be good workers. That is, preachers who by your grace admonish with hearty prayer to improve. We ask you in your boundless mercy that you would look with favor upon this, your servant, our elected preacher, that he may be diligent with your word, preaching Jesus Christ for our salvation, instructing our consciences, comforting us, and punishing, warning and admonishing us with forbearance and teaching; that he may preach the pure, holy gospel without deadly human doctrine; that he may abide with us and bring from among all of us the fruits of salvation, through the same, our Lord Jesus Christ. Amen.[31]

The reference to Matthew 9 on the laborers in the harvest appeared for the first time here but it became a recurring theme in Reformation rites. The emphasis on laborers gave voice to the concern of the reformers that pastors should indeed work in ministries of word and sacrament in the congregations that had called them. Bugenhagen, like Luther and others, criticized absentee pastors who lived on benefices without ever serving in the churches which supported them.

The prayer as a whole emphasized the leading and teaching role of the pastor. The visitations had made it clear how ignorant of scripture and doctrine both clergy and laity were. Furthermore, pastors were needed who could protect the congregation from false teachers and, of course, articulate the Reformation cause in light of Catholic intransigence.

Praying during the laying on of hands was not restricted to a presidential prayer. At the close of the latter the community was instructed to sing, "Now pray we to the Holy Spirit." The congregation's prayer at this point was a reinforcement of Bugenhagen's belief that ordination was a congregational act. In spite of his maintaining the traditional practice of having only those already ordained lay on hands, Bugenhagen's use of the congregational prayer indicated a clear shift of focus from the medieval rite.

At the conclusion of the hymn, the clergy around the ordinand knelt again and placed these things in the care of God through Jesus Christ (*und befehlen Gott durch Jesum Christum diese Sache*); they then departed (*gehen ehrlich aus der Kirche*).[32] The normal order of worship continued with the Gospel reading and sermon. An outline of this Hamburg rite reveals the simplicity of its focus:

> Presentation of the Candidate
> Address to the Community
> *Veni Sancte Spiritus* (Choir)
> Laying on of Hands
> Presidential prayer
> Congregational Song ("Now pray we")
> Silent Prayer
> Gospel
> Sermon (and remainder of the Sunday liturgy)

Rietschel argued that this was a matter of installing not ordaining.[33] The point is significant in light of the 1535 Church Order for Pomerania.[34] There an act of episcopal confirmation of call was separated from the liturgical act of installing in the community. Bugenhagen ordered the vocational process in 1535 in this way: 1) examination; 2) presentation to the bishop, by the congregation or patron; 3) confirmation of the candidate and exhortation by the bishop concerning the responsibilities of office; and 4) those episcopally confirmed were accepted in the community: a) with laying on of hands by the other ordained pastors present along with a specific member of the congregation, whenever the ordination took place in the city, or b) with laying on of hands by the two nearest pastors if it occurred in a village church. The rite was to come after the epistle reading within a regular Sunday liturgy.[35] The ordination was done according to the Hamburg rite described above, taken from the 1531 Church Order for Lübeck where it had also been adopted:

> Then on a Sunday the same pastor shall be accepted and given into the care of the church before the altar (if it is in the city), after the epistle with the laying on of hands by the other presiders and someone from the congregation, from the eldest, using the ceremonies from the Lübeck order.[36]

Rietschel interpreted Bugenhagen's separation of the episcopal act of confirming from the installation in the congregation as the starting point for understanding the formation of evangelically established ordinations.[37] But the separation was clearly a concession to prevailing tradition in Pomerania (and to Bugenhagen's desire to work with the bishop there). Bugenhagen in fact wanted to reconcile the right of the bishop to do the ordaining with what he considered the congregation's right to participate in it. The Pomeranian church order made it plain that the episcopal act was not essential: "Now the ones who already assume this position in good order, who are examined and installed, do not need a confirmation but are to be considered confirmed."[38]

Only when these actions, the episcopal confirming (or a substitute) and the prayer with laying on of hands before the community were combined into one ecclesiastical–liturgical action was the development of a new, evangelical way of ordaining complete. Commenting on Kliefoth's point that Bugenhagen's inclusion of a member of the congregation (not ordained) in the laying on of hands was in conflict with Luther's reform of ordination, Rietschel argued that the conflict disappeared when one recognized the Pomeranian action as an installation and not an ordination: "When the whole action of the congregation in this church order is seen clearly as an act of installation and obviously not an ordination, since the word ordination or *ordinatus* does not appear anywhere in it, then one can understand it as an exceptional moment in comparison with Bugenhagen's earlier church orders."[39] The creation of an action equivalent to the episcopal confirmation (ordination), distinct from the installation in the congregation (investiture) first happened, according to Rietschel, in Wittenberg with Luther's centralizing of ordination.[40]

Luther's 1535/39 Rite

Various manuscripts of Luther's ordination rite exist, the earliest dated at 1535, but it was not published in Wittenberg until 1539. Few scholars have contested the conclusions on manuscript dating drawn by Drews in the Weimar edition.[41] For our purpose it is sufficient to summarize the origins of the major manuscripts. The oldest is that of the Hamburg city library (designated "H" by Drews). It was prefaced by part of an ordination address which was closely related to the 1535 ordination sermon by Luther, especially in its conclusion.[42] That close connection is what helped Drews to date the rite to 1535. Parallel to the Hamburg version except for a few details was that uncovered by Rietschel in the Jena University library (designated "J" by Drews).[43] Drews proved it to be the second oldest version next to that of Hamburg although it cannot be dated precisely.

Another witness stems from the year 1538. It was used by Melanchthon to ordain two preachers for Culmbach (designated "C" by Drews).[44] This version was closely related to another discovered in the

A Decade of Transition

city archives of Freiberg (Saxony) from 1538 (designated "F" by Drews).[45] Two other early handwritten versions were discovered by Rietschel in the Wittenberg pastoral archives from the year 1539 (designated "R" by Drews).[46] Lieberg observed that it was impossible to ascertain which of these versions represented the purest expression of Luther's intent. Perhaps the Hamburg rite has some claim to that distinction as the oldest. Yet given the ongoing development of liturgical expression it is difficult even to frame the question in that way. Almost from the start the rite went through changes, recognizable in additions and emendations made by Luther, or by Bugenhagen with Luther's approval.[47]

All of the versions noted were in German, the rubrics in Latin. A Latin version was also produced by Luther for foreign students not familiar with German who came to Wittenberg to study and be ordained.[48] It was a free rendition rather that a literal translation of the German version. It did have one noteworthy expansion of the ordination prayer at the laying on of hands which referred to the act of ordaining as a *confirmatio vocationis* (discussed below). A final witness is the entry in Luther's *Table Talks* describing the ordination of Benedict Schumann in 1537.[49] It is included as additional evidence for the shaping of the rite between the years 1535–1539.

As preparation for discussing the rite in detail a structural outline and comparative synopsis of the texts follows to serve as a guide and framework for subsequent analysis. It should be noted that all of the rites assume that an examination of candidates had taken place prior to the rite being celebrated.[50] Because the focus here is on the rite itself the issue of how candidates were chosen and examined will not be discussed.

The 1539 version of the rite, the one first published officially in Wittenberg, will serve as the standard for analysis. It is the fullest of the editions. Structurally it contains all the elements of the other versions, although differing in content at certain points. The translations following are those of the American edition, *Luther's Works*, supplemented where necessary.

A Structural Comparison: The Manuscript Versions of Luther's German Ordination Rite[51]

H and J: 1535/36	S: 1537	C and F: 1538	R: 1539
1. Prayer for candidates and for the whole ministry.		1. Prayer for candidates and for the whole ministry.	1. Prayer for candidates and for the whole ministry.
2. Choir: Veni sancte spiritus.		2. Choir: Veni sancte spiritus.	2. Choir: Veni sancte spiritus.
3. Versicle: Send your spirit [or Create in me... Response: And renew a right spirit...]		3. Versicle: Create in me... Response: And renew a right spirit...	3. Versicle: Create in me... Response: And renew a right spirit...
Collect: [Deus qui corda]		Collect: [Deus qui corda]	Collect: [Deus qui corda]
4. Address by Ordinator [I Tim.4:4–5]			
5. Readings: a. I Tim.3:1–7 b. Acts 20:28–31	1. Readings: a. Acts 13 (3) b. Acts 20 c. I Tim.3:1–7 d. Titus 1 (6–9	4. Readings: a. I Tim.3:1–7 b. Acts 20:28–31	4. Readings: a. I Tim.3:17 b. Acts 20:28–31
	2. Address by Ordinator	5. Address by Ordinator (longer form)	5. Address by Ordinator (shorter form)
		6. Promise of the Ordinand	6. Promise of the Ordinand
6. Laying on of hands with the Lord's Prayer	3. Laying on of hands with the Lord's Prayer	7. Laying on of hands with the Lord's Prayer	7. Laying on of hands with the Lord's Prayer
7. Ord. Prayer	4. Prayer	8. Ord. Prayer	8. Ord. Prayer

A Decade of Transition

8. Reading: I Pet.5		9. Reading: I Pet.5	9. Reading: I Pet.5
	5. Blessing and congratulations to ordinands		10. Blessing (with the sign of the cross) of ordinands
	6. Song: "Now Let Us Pray to the Holy Spirit"	10. Song: "Now Let Us Pray to the Holy Spirit"	11. Song: "Now Let Us Pray to the Holy Spirit"
			12. Singing of the Lord's Prayer by the Ordinator
9. Communion	7. Communion	11. Communion	13. Communion

Textual Comparison Of The Rite According To The Major Manuscripts

H (Hamburg Codex) 1535	F (Freyberg Codex) 1538	R (Wittenberg) 1539
	Form by which those called to the ministry of the word and of the church will be ordained at Wittenberg.	The Ordination of Ministers of the Word
1. First. It is recommended, therefore, for the prayers in the church, that the congregation in public shall pray for them and for the whole ministry, that God would deign to send many faithful laborers into his harvest, for the sanctification of his own name, for the building up of the kingdom of heaven and	1. The candidates shall be examined either on the same or on the preceding day. If they are worthy, the congregation after due admonition by the preacher shall pray for them and for the whole ministry, namely, that God would deign to send laborers into his harvest and preserve them faithful and constant in sound doctrine against the gates	1. The candidates shall be examined on either the same or on the preceding day. If they are worthy, the congregtion after due admonition by the preacher shall pray for them and for the whole ministry, namely, that God would deign to send laborers into his harvest and preserve them faithful and constant in sound doctrine against the gates

for the salvation of all peoples, and preserve them pure and constant in sound doctrine against the gates of hell, and against the powers of this world, because the ministry of the church is most important and necessary for all churches and is given and preserved by God alone.	of hell.	of hell, etc.
2. After the prayer all kneel before the altar and the choir sings: "Veni sancte spiritus."	2. Then the ordinator and the minister or presbyters of the church shall place the ordinand in the center before the ordinator and all shall kneel before the altar. And the choir shall sing: "Veni sancte spiritus."	2. Second. The Ordinator and minister or presbyters of the church shall place the ordinand in the center before the ordinator and all shall kneel before the altar. And the choir shall sing, "Veni sancte spiritus."
3. Versicle: "Send your Spirit," etc., [J has the versicle: "Create in me a clean heart, O God," with Response: "And renew a right spirit within me."]	3. Versicle: "Create in me a clean heart, O God." Resp.: "And renew a right spirit within me."	3. Versicle: "Create in me a clean heart, O God." Resp.: "And renew a right spirit within me."
Collect: [Proper for Pentecost], "Lord God, dear Father, who (on this day) through your Holy Spirit did enlighten and teach the hearts of your faithful people: Grant to us that we may have right understanding through the same Spirit and at all times rejoice in his comfort and power; through the same your Son Jesus Christ our Lord. Amen.	The customary Collect of the Holy Spirit shall be read [Deus qui corda].	The customary Collect of the Holy Spirit shall be said [Deus qui corda].

A Decade of Transition

4. Afterwards the ordinator ascends the high step, and turning to the ordinands shall say: St.Paul says, "Every creature of God is good," etc., "for it is sanctified," [I Tim.4:4-5]. You are not only good creatures, sanctified by the Word and the sacrament of baptism, but in a second sanctification you have also been called to the holy and divine ministry, so that many others may be sanctified and reconciled to the Lord through your word and work. This goes to show how devoutly and worthily you ought to hold your holy office so that you may be sound in faith, pure in word, irreprehensible in conduct, and that you may be found good stewards in word and deed of the mysteries of God and useful ministers of Christ in the day of the Lord, as St.Paul teaches in I Timothy:	4. After this the ordinator shall ascend the step of the predella and facing the ordinands shall recite with a clear voice I Timothy 3. Thus writes St.Paul in the First Epistle to Timothy in the third chapter [1-7]:	4. Third. After this the Ordinator shall ascend the step of the predella and facing the ordinands shall recite with a clear voice I Tim. 3. Thus writes St.Paul in the First Epistle to Timothy in the third chapter [1-7]:
"This is a true saying," etc., up to the end of the section, "snare of the devil," etc., Acts 20: "Take heed to yourselves," etc. [Thus the two readings are I Tim.3:1-7 and Acts 20:28-31]	"This is a true saying, whoever desires the office of bishop," etc., up to the end of the section, namely, "the snare of the devil," or the whole chapter. To these is added Acts 20: "Take heed to yourselves," etc., up to	"This is a true saying. If a man desire the office of bishop he desireth a good work. A bishop then must be blameless, the husband of one wife, vigilant, sober, of good behavior, given to hospitality, apt to

the end of the section "with tears."	teach...[R continues with the full German text of I Tim.3:1–7 and Acts 20:28–31].
5. Then the Ordinator addresses the ordinands in these or similar words (or if he is willing, this can be omitted because they have been admonished enough from what has been said before, lest it become a tradition, increased henceforth ad infinitum): First, you hear that the Holy Ghost called and ordained you bishops in his flock or church. Therefore, you must believe for certain that you were called by God, because the church sent you here and secular authority has called and desired you. For what the church and secular authorities do in these matters, God does through them, so that you may not be considered intruders. Second, you hear here how in personal conduct you should live and what is to be done by you in the church: namely, that you should tend and mind it, for you are not called to watch over geese and pigs, but the flock of Christ, which he purchased with his own blood; to feed them with the pure word of God, and to be on guard lest wolves and sects	5. Fourth. The Ordinator addresses the ordinands in these or similar words: herein you hear that we bishops–i.e., presbyters and pastors–are called not to watch over geese or cows, but over the congregation God purchased with his own blood that we should feed them with the pure Word of God and also be on guard lest wolves and sects burst in among the poor sheep. This is why he calls it a good work. Also in our personal conduct we should live decently and honorably and rule our house, wife, children, and servants in a Christian way.

burst in among the poor sheep. That is why he calls the office of bishop a good work and praises it. If you are now ready and willing to accept and faithfully to exercise such an office, then on the command of the church and by means of our office we ordain and certify you, as St.Paul commanded Titus and Timothy, that we install priests in the cities and entrust the Word to those who are qualified to instruct others.

6. Response: We will.	6. Are you now ready to do this? Answer: Yes.
7. Then while the whole presbytery impose their hands on the heads of the ordinands, the Ordinator says the Lord's Prayer over them, and if he desires or time permits he may add this prayer, which explains more fully the three parts of the Lord's Prayer:	7. Fifth. Then while the whole presbytery impose their hands on the heads of the ordinands, the ordinator says the Lord's Prayer in a clear voice. Let us pray. Our Father, etc. And if he desires or time permits, he may add this prayer which explains more fully the three parts of the Lord's Prayer:
8. [text of F prayer parallels R]	8. Merciful God, heavenly Father, you have said to us through the mouth of your dear Son our Lord

Jesus Christ: "The harvest truly is plenteous, but the laborers are few. Pray therefore the Lord of the harvest, that he will send forth laborers into his harvest" [Matthew 9:37–38]. Upon this your divine command, we pray heartily that you would grant your Holy Spirit richly to these your servants, to us, and to all those who are called to serve your Word, so that the company of those who publish the good tidings may be great, and that we may stand faithful and firm against the devil, the world, and the flesh, to the end that your name may be hallowed, your kingdom grow, and your will be done. Be also pleased at length to check and stop the detestable abomination of the pope, Mohammed, and other sects which blaspheme your name, hinder your kingdom, and oppose your will. Graciously hear this our prayer, since you have so commanded, taught, and promised, even as we believe and trust through your dear Son, Jesus Christ our Lord who lives and reigns with you and the Holy Ghost, world without end. Amen.

7. The passage from I Peter 5 should be read: "Tend the flock of God."	9. The passage from I Peter should be read: "Tend the flock of God," etc., up to "you will obtain the unfading crown of glory." Then they depart, each to his own place. Moreover, first those ordained shall commune with our congregation.	9. Sixth. The ordinator shall address the ordinands with these words of St. Peter 5 [:1–4]: Feed the flock...[text of the passage is included in German].
8. The ordinands will first commune with the congregation. Afterwards they will be sent out to pursue their vocation.		
		10. Seventh. The ordinator shall bless them with the sign of the cross and use these or other words: The Lord bless you that you may bring forth much fruit. After this each one shall return to his own place.
	10. If it is desired this is sung: "Now Let Us Pray to the Holy Ghost." Then the mass proceeds.	11. If it is desired the congregation may sing "Now Let Us Pray to the Holy Ghost."
		12. This ended the presbyter chants: Our Father, etc.
		13. And first the ordinands shall commune with the congregation, then likewise the

ordinator if he so desires.

The Latin Version

"Latin form of ordination, which is used whenever pilgrims approaching to seek ordination do not understand the German language"

[The Latin version does not include any of the rubrics. It is a translation only of those portions of the rite done in German; i.e., the scripture readings and the prayer texts.]

The Apostle Paul, describing what kind of people ought to be bishops, spoke thus in the third chapter of I Timothy [I Tim. 3:1-10]: "The saying is sure: if anyone aspires to the office of bishop, he desires a good work. Now a bishop must be above reproach, the husband of one wife, temperate, sensible, dignified, hospitable, an apt teacher, not quarrelsome, not violent but gentle, not a lover of money. He must manage his own household well, keeping his children submissive and respectful in every way (for if a man does not know how to manage his own household, how can he care for God's church). He must not be a recent convert, or he may be puffed up with conceit and fall into the condemnation of the devil. Moreover he must be well thought of by outsiders, or he may fall into reproach and the snare of the devil. Deacons likewise must be serious, not double-tongued, not addicted to much wine, not greedy for gain, they must hold the mystery of faith with a clear conscience. And let them also be tested first; then if they prove themselves blameless let them minister."

In another place Paul gave a reminder to the elders at Ephesus using these words [Acts 20: 28-31]: "Take heed to yourselves and to all the flock, in which the Holy Spirit has made you bishops, to feed the church of the Lord which he obtained with his own blood. I know that after my departure fierce wolves will come in among you, not sparing the flock; and from among your own selves will arise men speaking perverse things, to draw away the disciples after them. Therefore be alert, remembering that for three years I did not cease night or day to admonish every one with tears."

You have heard the serious reminder of the Apostle that we bishops are called not to watch over a flock of geese or over pigs, but over the church which God purchased with his own blood, that we should feed it with the pure word of God and also be on guard, watching carefully and being wary lest any wolves and sects burst in among the poor sheep. This is why Paul calls it a good work.

Also, in our personal conduct we should live decently and honestly and rule our house, wife, children and servants in a modest and pious way.

Promise now in public, with a clear voice, that you will do these things to the best of your ability.
Answer: I promise.
Laying on of hands.
Let us pray: Our Father...Amen.

Most merciful God, eternal Father, you have said to us through the mouth of your chosen Son, our Lord Jesus Christ: "The harvest truly is plenteous, but the laborers are few. Pray therefore the Lord of the harvest, that he will send forth laborers into his harvest" [Mt. 9:37]. Upon this your divine command, we pray heartily that you would grant your Holy Spirit richly to these seeking confirmation of their call from this church, to us, and to all those who are called to serve your Word, so that the company of those who publish the good tidings may be great, faithful and constant, strengthened by your labor and protection against the devil, the world, and the flesh, so that although we are unworthy and weak, your name may be hallowed, your kingdom grow, and these things be pleasing to you and of benefit to many. Be also pleased at length to check and stop the detestable abomination of the pope, Mohammed, and other sects which blaspheme your holy name, try to destroy your kingdom, and oppose your will. Graciously hear this our prayer, since you have so commanded, taught, and promised, even as we believe and trust through your chosen Son, our Lord Jesus Christ, who lives and reigns with you and the Holy Spirit, world without end. Amen.

Now therefore we depart with the words of the Apostle Peter [I Pet. 5:2-4]: "Tend the flock of Christ that is your charge, not by constraint but willingly, not for shameful gain, not as domineering over those in your charge but by being examples to the flock. And when the chief shepherd is manifested you will obtain the unfading crown of glory."

The Lord bless you, that you may bear much fruit.

The Rite in Detail

In the different manuscript editions of the rite one finds some with titles and some without. The 1539 Wittenberg version stated simply: "The Ordination of Ministers of the Word." The 1538 Freyberg Codex was more explicit: "Form By Which Those Called To The Ministry Of The Word And Of The Church Will Be Ordained At Wittenberg." The Latin version had a clear statement of its specific purpose over against the standard German forms. In each case the heading was purely descriptive of function and provides no particular historical or theological information of import beyond that identification.

Ordination was not a self-contained liturgy but rather a rite occurring within the context of a regular worship service, usually though not exclusively on Sunday.[52] It took place after the sermon, which concluded with a brief exhortation concerning the ordination about to occur and asking for silent prayer by all for the ordinands. When the ordination was completed the service continued as usual.

The rite was laid out rubrically, that is, it explained what was to be

A Decade of Transition 109

done at each point, frequently but not always providing the content of the action called for by the rubric. The following analysis uses the arabic numeral references for each section as assigned in the preceding structural outline for the Wittenberg 1539 version ("R"). The letter designations assigned by Drews as noted in the outlines above refer to the manuscripts.

Section 1. Exhortation to Prayer

The sermon functioned as the transition point for the ordination rite within the eucharistic liturgy. "After due admonition by the preacher," the congregation was instructed to pray for the ordinand and the whole ministry. What they were to pray for was noted explicitly and formed the content of the preacher's admonition: "that God would deign to send laborers into his harvest and preserve them faithful and constant in sound doctrine against the gates of hell etc." This exhortation may have occurred as an integral part of the sermon itself but more likely functioned as an appended conclusion to provide a transition to the rite. Very few instructions were given about the physical aspects of executing the rite, but one can assume that the ordinands and others involved in the action directly were taking their places immediately after this period of silent prayer. Because the preacher of the day was not necessarily the ordinator this opening rubric still represented a transitional moment in preparation for the rite.

In the medieval consecration of presbyters the transition from the normal course of the liturgy into the rite for ordination occurred after the tract and the epistle reading. Whether there was any theological significance in the specific placement of the rite within the eucharistic liturgy is questionable. One can make a case for symbolic connections such as, for example, ordaining a deacon between the epistle and gospel reading so that the one ordained might perform the function of the office for the first time within that liturgy. In the case of episcopal and presbyteral ordination such a focused liturgical definition of role was not present, although a person ordained as presbyter prior to the eucharistic rite might then preside over the meal for the first time. Of course if more than one person were being ordained that symbolic connection of immediately exercising a function of the office into which one was ordained would be muted (but not lost, since one from among the group could be understood to be functioning representatively for the rest; or as the medieval Roman rite indicated, all the newly ordained could concelebrate). It seems unwise to make more of the placement of the rite than practical considerations demand. At this point the evangelical placement was relatively in keeping with the medieval structure discussed in Chapter One.

Both R and F ended the exhortation to prayer at the point of admonition about sound doctrine against the gates of hell. R had an "etc." indicating that more could or should be said. The Hamburg Codex of 1535 provided an example of the content of that etc.: "...because the ministry of the church is most important and necessary for all churches and is given and preserved by God alone." The comment was theologically consistent with what Luther had said at many other points.[53]

It provided an example because it was clear from the versions themselves that Luther felt some freedom in adapting the content of the rite. Emphasizing the divine origin of the church's ministry of the word was something Luther did at every point in his career, no matter who his theological opponents happened to be. The fact that it was said here in the context of an ordination might indicate a more narrow interpretation: that God instituted not only the "ministry in general" of the priesthood of all believers but also the specific ministry of the ordained. Since the two are not mutually exclusive, both notions can be said to be intended.

Such a dual focus was implicit in the use of the biblical text about sending laborers into the harvest. All Christians were such laborers insofar as the missionary task was to proclaim the gospel in a hostile world ("preserve them faithful and constant in sound doctrine against the gates of hell"). This included the ordained. The congregation was to "pray for them and for the whole ministry." If Luther had said "pray for them and for all other pastors" a different case might be made, although even then one could not on the basis of the whole rite make any claim for the ordained being the only ones who were ministers of the gospel in the world.

The overlapping definitions of the priesthood of all believers and the

A Decade of Transition

ordained pastoral ministry were discussed in detail earlier. Nevertheless with reference to the ordinands themselves the text indicated that they were not yet in the particular, public office prior to the ordination, even though the call of God to them to be such laborers was evident in their vocation prior to this. Thus the congregation prayed "in order that God would deign to send laborers." In other words the ordinands were not yet officially sent into the harvest but rather the sending was about to occur in the ordination itself. That is why the prayer was petitioning the Lord with respect to this beginning of the act of ordaining.[54]

The exhortation, given by the preacher of the day (not necessarily the ordinator), established the context and purpose for the church's ministry. As the expanded version of H put it: "for the sanctification of his own name, for the building up of the kingdom of heaven and for the salvation of all people." In that vocation both lay and ordained had roles because together they constituted the church as a visible community in the world. One must conclude that the gathered community was not simply a witness for an act that could in fact occur without them. They were to participate through their prayer specifically for the ordinand as well as the whole ministry of the church. The assembly's prayer both initiated the act of ordaining and embraced the whole of the rite.[55]

Section 2. *Veni Sancte Spiritus*

After the silent prayer of the whole congregation those who were to participate took their place with the ordinand "in the center before the ordinator." This probably meant at the front of the nave but not in the chancel since a later rubric indicated that the ordinator ascended the predella, presumably from the position he had at this point. Along with the ordinator and ordinand were "the ministers or presbyters of the church." This meant those pastors from the city or neighboring areas who were present. All were instructed to kneel before the altar as the choir sang.

The participation in a particular way of those who were already ordained was significant. Nothing in the prayer indicated that others holding the office should join in the act of ordaining in a manner different from what the rest of the participating congregation was doing.

Luther made no mention of any other non-ordained person being involved. The medieval Catholic liturgical tradition included the participation of all other priests present in the ordination of a new priest. Why did Luther advocate this action here if, as some have argued, he wanted to do something completely new having nothing in common with preceding traditions? Did this action, retained from earlier rites of ordaining, embody liturgically some specific Reformation doctrine concerning ministry in the church? One should entertain the possibility that Luther retained a sense of setting individuals in office by means of their being confirmed in it by those whom the church had already called and ordained. Because of Bugenhagen's inclusion of a non-ordained person in the laying on of hands, the more restricted role maintained by Luther makes such an interpretation reasonable.

In light of the exhortation that preceded it and the congregation's prayer for "the whole ministry," such an action would tend visibly to provide an identifying focus for the congregation's prayer, namely those who were gathered before the altar: the ordained pastors of the church and one about to enter their company. Insofar as those pastors also represented congregations that had called them, their presence together embraced the symbolic presence of more than those who were ordained. Yet it is worth pondering why Luther did not have a lay representative of the congregation also involved as, for example, Bugenhagen did in his 1535 rite for Pomerania.[56]

The concern here is not to demand doctrinal judgments about the significance of a college of presbyters or apostolic succession and its importance but rather to discover what the rite as described communicated apart from theological presuppositions about what one thinks it ought to say. In other words, seeing and hearing this rite in its context what would be understood by this action occurring at this point? It indicated that those who already held the pastoral office had a special function to fulfill, otherwise the action would not have been restricted to them. It is not yet clear from the rite itself what the function was.

While the ordination group was kneeling the choir sang *Veni Sancte Spiritus*. The whole of the rite was permeated by prayer for and reference to the Holy Spirit. Here the text of the *Veni Sancte Spiritus* asked that the Spirit come; on whom and for what purpose? Again, with the ordinator, ordinand, and other pastors kneeling before the altar, the logical conclusion to be drawn was that they were the focus of the petition. All who served in this office were in need of the Spirit anew, and especially the ordinand who was only about to undertake the responsibilities of the office. This is not to say that the text cannot be interpreted more broadly. The question is simply this: What was its function in this rite at this point? Why this particular chant?

In the late medieval presbyteral rite *Veni Sancte Spiritus* was sung if the ordination took place on the Ember Saturday of the octave of Pentecost. Durandus indicated that the second alleluia verse of Pentecost, *Alleluia. Veni sancte spiritus, reple tuorum corda fidelium et tui amoris in eis ignem accende*, was used with its sequence. Other than that when an ordination took place the normal procedure was for *Veni Creator Spiritus* to be used. In Durandus' rite the singing preceded and accompanied the anointing of the hands. If there were many ordinands so that the anointing went on for a longer time Durandus noted that the sequence for Pentecost should also be sung, the *Veni sancte spiritus et emitte coelitus*.[57]

Luther's choice was a departure from the Roman rite insofar as *Veni Creator Spiritus* was the hymn traditionally associated with ordination. But it is not clear whether he had the alleluia verse or the Pentecost sequence in mind here since he did not list the full text but only the first three words which both pieces have in common. Luther had written a series of hymns in 1524 based on all these texts, which serves to confuse the matter further. His *Kom heyligen geyst herre Gott* was based on the *Veni sancte spiritus, reple*. His *Nu bitten wyr den heyligen geyst* was based on a popular German *Leise* intoned at the conclusion of the choir's singing of the Latin sequence *Veni sancte spiritus et emitte* on Pentecost. He also produced a version of the *Veni Creator Spiritus*, his *Kom Gott schepfer heyliger geyst*. Because Luther closed the rite with the *Nu bitten wyr*, it is reasonable to assume that he intended the *Veni sancte spiritus, reple* at this point.[58]

In Luther's service the hymn functioned as an introduction for the main body of the rite to follow. It is a bit surprising that Luther was willing to retain the singing of the *Veni Sancte Spiritus* because of its connection with the part of the medieval rite he most vehemently rejected—the anointing. Yet the choice was consonant with Luther's knowledge of this hymn being used on Pentecost Sunday, apart from ordination services, and its appropriate petition for the gift of the Spirit. It is well known that Luther was a lover of hymnody and of traditional Latin texts. The retention of this hymn betrays once again Luther's conservatism and his conviction that in a proper context liturgical texts and actions which had heretofore been problematic could be beneficial and "rightly" interpreted.[59]

Section 3. Versicle and Collect

The appointed versicle was linked to the Collect, *Deus qui hodierna die corda fidelium*, which was the proper Collect for Pentecost. It was often appended to the hymn "Now Let Us Pray to the Holy Spirit" in later Lutheran hymnals.[60] Along with the *Veni Sancte Spiritus*, also drawn from the liturgical propers for the festival of Pentecost, the collect and its accompanying versicle served to alert the ordinand and community of the pivotal role of invocation of the Spirit in the ordination rite, as well as make connections with the celebration of Pentecost.

Section 4. Scripture Readings

Two readings were included in all versions of the rite, I Timothy 3:1–7 and Acts 20:28–31. The 1535 Hamburg text prefaced these two readings with two verses from I Timothy 4 (4–5) and an extended comment on them. This extended comment was significant because it articulated a theological comparison between the sanctification of baptism and a "second sanctification" in the call to ordained ministry. The two readings common to all the versions will be discussed first.

Luther interpreted ordained ministry on the basis of scripture as one might expect. Rarely did he make a theological case for a doctrine or practice of the church not based on some scriptural precedent. Thus the choice of readings as well as scriptural allusions elsewhere in the rite give clues for discerning what Luther understood the act of ordaining to do.

I Timothy 3:1–7 began, "if someone desires the office of bishop he desires a good work." This was linked with the earlier exhortation. There the intent was to pray for workers to be sent (by virtue of the act of ordaining and the whole of the call process) into the harvest. At this point the text was directed to those who "desired" the office but were not yet in it, even though they already had a call. Before they were recognized as office holders they were to be made aware of the responsibilities it entailed.

The subject of the passage was the moral life of the one who desired the office. It provided a brief summary of the kind of persons pastors were to be and the kind of life they were to lead. Since the text detailed the duties of a bishop one was reminded of Luther's contention that there was no distinction between a bishop and a presbyter with regard to the primary task of being a minister of the word. It is important to note that Durandus' pontifical specified I Timothy 3:1-7 as the reading for a bishop's consecration.[61] The choice of this text also betrayed a primary concern of the reformers to improve the pitiful condition of pastoral leadership which existed in Luther's day. Pastors were often ignorant, blatantly immoral, corrupt, lazy, and generally incompetent.[62]

In his lectures on I Timothy in 1528 Luther had emphasized the shepherding role of the pastor, who was to be a forthright and even combative guardian of the gospel:

> Because the ministry is so important...he must absolutely be strong, firm, and good who says: "I see that the erring brethren do not understand the sound Word. They are my brothers. I shall run into that fire. I shall oppose those errors and iniquities of Satan." .....For bishop means "watchman," "visitor," that is, one who goes to visit, who visits to see people. He looks around to see what is being taught and how people live. He watches with open eyes that no false doctrine breaks in....[63]

Luther made clear the ecclesial context within which these comments were to be interpreted by his earlier argument in the same section about the "many fickle, big-talking false teachers who kept rushing about in all directions, saying that they were driven by the Spirit, by wisdom and by their talent."[64] Only those properly called and ordained by the church had the power to perform the tasks outlined. This was the case because proper calling and ordaining were the church's act, and therefore Christ's act: "If a bishop thinks about his calling, he sees that he is a bishop by the rite, the oracle, and the command of God, and secondly, that he has in his hand the possession and the property of Christ. What is that? It is the Gospel and the sacraments."[65] The passage from I Timothy also made it clear that Luther was concerned to provide educated and morally upright pastors for evangelical congregations. The focus was ethical, not sacerdotal.

Acts 20:28-31 was obviously chosen in the context of Luther's battles with adversaries on the right and left (Roman Catholics and Anabaptists). The opening verse reminded the pastor to keep watch and be a faithful shepherd over those entrusted to his care. The point of the text, however, was to make one wary of the "savage wolves" within the church who distorted the truth. For Luther the text spoke directly to the conflicts of the Reformation. He knew firsthand through the visitations that evangelical pastors needed to be equipped to withstand what he considered to be the onslaught of heretical teaching. The text thus functioned as an admonition concerning the serious responsibility of standing up for the gospel in the midst of a church plagued with false teaching.

Luther preached a sermon on this passage at the ordination of Nikolaus von Amsdorf in 1542 as bishop of Naumburg.[66] In it he discussed the burden and responsibility which the office brought with it. Recognizing this in light of our weakness, said Luther, made it a wonder that anyone would be willing to bear the office. In a brief polemical comment he also pointed out the dangers inherent in the office, especially being corrupted by its power. Yet, as the biblical text made clear, one could undertake the task because it was done according to God's word and command. In other words, the Acts passage provided a scriptural warrant for the role of leadership (guarding, tending the flock) in the church.

Considering Luther's knowledge of scripture it was significant that he chose this focus for readings within the ordination rite. On the one hand the choices reinforced his position that ordination was not an issue of status; it was not entry into a special priesthood. On the other hand the texts did stress the special responsibility which ordained leaders of the church had to assure that the gospel was proclaimed. "Right teaching"

A Decade of Transition

remained a constant concern of the reformers.

Section 5. Address

An address or exhortation to the ordinands followed the readings in R and F. The form and content were not fixed. The introductory comments indicated that the ordinator was to speak to the ordinands "in these or similar words." The shorter form in R provided a brief reinforcement of the readings. The fact that freedom existed here suggests that extemporaneous elaboration could occur. This is supported by the inclusion of additional material in F. Its content indicated that the situation of evangelical pastors was precarious. They were open to the charge of being illegitimate pastors since they were not ordained in the normal episcopal process. Both they and the churches they served needed the assurance that F included: "the church sent you here and secular authority has called and desired you. For what the church and secular authorities do in these matters, God does through them, so that you may not be considered intruders." The appeal to secular authority was more than a casual reference. Without the support of the princes evangelical pastors would have had no way to challenge the Roman Catholic hierarchy.

The conclusion of the address in F also included an affirmation of the right of those performing the ordination to do so. Enough ambivalence about the propriety of evangelical ordination existed to warrant constant reference to the legitimacy of the action. This was but another indication of the difficulty of this transition period as the episcopal structures of the medieval church were abandoned.

Lieberg argued that the point here was that ordinations occurring in Wittenberg were acts of the universal church and not simply acts of investiture in a specific, local call. The mere fact that within the same rite many ordinands, each with a different call, were ordained made this clear. The longer address in F was especially keen on this point when it said "thus on the command of the church (*aus bevelh der kirchen*) we ordain and confirm you on the basis of our office (*durch unser ampt*)."[67] Lieberg rightly emphasized the significance of these phrases. The act of ordaining was rooted in the "command of the church." This referred not to the call of the local congregation but to the decree of the Elector. For Luther, the Elector functioned as an emergency bishop and thus it was as an instrument of the universal church that he ordered the ordination.[68]

Luther traced the specific responsibility of the church to ordain, now done through the Elector because of the lack of evangelical bishops, to the command of Paul to Timothy and Titus to establish priests in cities and order the Word. And the ordinator was the one who realized the mandate in specific terms. As Lieberg remarked:

> The command of the Apostle binds the church to do the same thing today, namely—now just as then—*through the pastoral office*. That is why Luther emphasizes that the ordaining and confirming occur "through our office." St. Paul gave Titus and Timothy the mandate to establish priests because as office bearers themselves they were in the position to judge a person's suitability. ...The office indeed has the function of ordaining "on the command of the church." The ordinator embodies, so to speak, the church itself in the act of ordination, he ordains not only as an office bearer himself but also as an organ of the whole church.[69]

Although Lieberg supported his argument with texts beyond these few lines in one manuscript tradition of Luther's rite, one should be cautious about reading too much into the phrases "command of the church" and "through our office." The fact that they did not occur in H and R indicated that Luther did not consider the making of the point within the rite essential. But Lieberg was right to argue that the theological and ecclesiological framework within which Luther operated demands that we recognize the critical significance of the liturgical act of ordaining being an act of the whole church. Who commanded that it be done as well as who actually did it were not immaterial points. The public liturgical act assured the universal recognizability of the ordination.

Section 6. Promise

Of the three major manuscript families, only R had a question directed to the ordinands at the conclusion of the address. F included a response (*volumus*), but it was not prefaced by a question. Nevertheless, one can assume that the ordinator would make the transition from the

A Decade of Transition

address to the ordinand's response by asking a question. In R the promise was a simple yes. In later developments more extended oaths were used, as will be discussed below. The assent here was to the responsibilties of the office as just described by the readings and address: "to guide Christian flocks with none other than the pure word of God, to prevent incursion by wolves and heretical factions, to live honorably, and to raise and keep members of their families in the Christian faith."[70] Unlike the medieval presbyteral rite, Luther's version had no promise of obedience to those doing the ordaining nor to any person in a hierarchy.

Section 7. Laying on of Hands with Prayer

As a liturgical gesture laying on hands has a rich and varied history in Christian tradition.[71] It has been used in a variety of contexts for divergent purposes: to confirm, to bless, to heal, to empower, to commission, to transfer authority. Its history alone should be enough to tell us that as a liturgical action laying on hands will not submit to any single interpretation. One must pay strict attention to traditions, cultural context, and the specific rite within which the gesture occurs in order to discern its significance.

From the beginning of his theological reflection on ministry Luther understood the biblical precedent for prayer and laying on hands to be the foundation for confirmimg people in the office of ordained pastor.[72] There can be no doubt that he considered it to be a liturgical action of importance and substance. Did Luther consider it to be necessary for ordination?

Those who have distinguished "call" and the liturgical act of ordaining, as if to say that the two are mutually exclusive, or at least that the former can exist without the latter, would clearly answer no. Yet this is in some sense to ask an irrelevant question. Fundamentally, nothing is necessary for the Christian but God's grace—not baptism, not confirmation, nor eucharist, nor ordination, nor anything else. But such a theoretically affirmable theological assertion is vacuous if "necessary" presupposes a view of instrumentality that is foreign to the Incarnation's message of the inevitable embodiment of God's grace. For Luther necessity did not mean compulsion. God's own self-communication in

Jesus revealed that the good news is a materially mediated reality for Christianity. For Luther, prayer with laying on of hands defined the (biblical) content of ordination.

Luther made a clear and strong case for the significance of laying on hands with prayer in a 1544 sermon.[73] The *Hauspostille* collection in which it occurs makes it suspect as a witness, but it may serve to corroborate views that can be demonstrated from other of Luther's uncontested works. A revealing passage in this sermon runs as follows:

> The Christian should know that a bishop, pastor, chaplain or whatever one calls him no longer belongs to the servants of the church just because he has an irreproachable way of life, a good understanding of Christian teaching, and can communicate the same to others. Where such a person is, there he may no longer remain unless he is called by the authority, so that the preaching office and other service of the church is entrusted to him publicly. It is not to be doubted that with such prayer and laying on of hands the Holy Spirit not only surely comes, but does not depart without bearing fruit, for it accomplishes that for which it is sent according to the promise of Christ: where two or three are gathered in my name, whatever they ask of the Father will be given to them. That is why Christians should ordain their pastors, for it follows the example of the apostle and the early church.[74]

Thus, according to apostolic and early church precedent, an ordination for Luther occurred correctly through laying on hands with prayer and not, as he was still stressing, through secondary ritual elements which obscured that focus (such as anointing, tonsure, handing over of vessels, etc.).[75]

One of the most provocative passages for sorting out Luther's thinking on liturgical prayer and blessing is his commentary on Isaac's blessing of Jacob in the Genesis lectures of 1535–45. The opening comments on Genesis 27:5–10 make evident that Luther had a liturgical perspective: "Here belongs a description of the rites which the fathers used both when bestowing and when receiving a blessing."[76] Furthermore, it is obvious that Luther was thinking in terms of the story's application to the Christian assembly so that his reflections have direct connections with how one is to understand what happens in Christian worship.

He was discussing the sacrifices of Jacob and Isaac necessary in the

A Decade of Transition

procedures established for giving and receiving the blessing of primogeniture when he observed: "First it was necessary to prepare some food for the father. This was not done without a sacrifice. Both offered a sacrifice to God, and thus the beginning was made with a sacrifice, just as in our public assemblies we commence with a prayer of thanksgiving, and just as we pray when we lay hands on those who are being ordained for functioning in the church."[77] Luther was always clear about his understanding of divine initiative having priority over all human response. So here he explained that it was the Holy Spirit that blessed through Isaac. But it was exactly because of that understanding that Luther had such profound respect for what occurred when God spoke or acted through people by the power of the Holy Spirit. Thus with regard to the unrepeatability of Isaac's blessing, Luther argued that "when God has rendered a verdict, He does not change or retract it, as men are wont to do...the gift and call of God are irrevocable [Romans 11:29]."[78]

The significance of the commentary here is the insight it gives into how Luther understood the connection between liturgical prayers and gestures and the work of the Spirit. Specifically, it helps to clarify what is meant when one says that they pronounce a blessing. As might be expected from Luther, the foundation for faith in divine action on our behalf was baptism.[79] This line of thought might lead one to conclude that in the end Luther would apply the implications of his assessment of prayer and blessing only to the sacraments of baptism and eucharist. But Luther's vision of the church's life ranged more broadly, even though one cannot deny the centrality of baptism and eucharist for everything else Luther said about Christian worship.

The broader vision incorporated the act of ordaining when Luther commented on Genesis 28:17. The physical signs by which God communicates are the means by which God speaks. Our task is to discover the voice/spirit of God in them, including the laying on of hands in ordination.[80] It is in one sense remarkable that Luther linked ordination with baptism and eucharist in the argument that follows:

> For the flesh fixes its eyes only on the water, on the bread, on the wine, and on the ground where Jacob slept; but the spirit must see the water, the hand, the

> Word of God, and God in the water. The flesh sees so keenly that it judges that the water is water and excludes God, as the Sacramentarians and the Anabaptists do. Therefore one must learn contrary to the view of the flesh that it is not a simple word and only an empty sound, but that it is the Word of the Creator of heaven and earth. Thus the imposition of hands is not a tradition of men, but God makes and ordains ministers.[81]

Yet this is entirely consistent with everything explored thus far in Luther's analysis of ministry, call and ordination.

In light of the context in Genesis, which was specifically about Isaac's imposition of hands in blessing Jacob, it also makes sense that ordination emerge as an example. On the other hand, the words *sic impositio manuum non est traditio humana: sed Deus facit et ordinat ministros*, appear to contradict explicitly the passage quoted earlier from the *Babylonian Captivity* which stated that laying on hands was introduced by the church fathers like many other secondary ritual elements of Christian life.[82] One should recall that the earlier comment was made in the context of a misunderstood (according to Luther) concept of priesthood. In an evangelical context where the office of ministry was held properly in view as an office, Luther's early negative response was vitiated.

Yet it should also be recalled that as early as 1528 Luther spoke positively about the gift received in the act of laying on hands because of its precedent in the early church. Commenting on I Timothy 4:14 ("Do not neglect the gift you have, which was given you by prophetic utterance when the leaders laid their hands upon you"), Luther argued that "...he [Paul] is treating a rite just as earlier: he [Timothy] has this gift from the laying on of hands. At that time the Holy Spirit was being given visibly, when they imposed hands, as the early church did in Acts. Imposition of hands was not anything other than receiving and assigning an office which was being entrusted."[83]

If one assumes that this Genesis passage was from Luther,[84] the implication for understanding ordination is that Luther thought of it in the same *context* as the sacraments (which is not to suggest that he thought of it as a sacrament). The external element, the gesture of laying on hands, was assigned a role like that played by water in baptism and bread and wine in the eucharist. The rite had scriptural foundation.

But again one must exercise caution in pushing the sacramental point too far in light of the broader reflection on this issue already noted in the sweep of Luther's theological thinking from 1520 to 1545. In other words Lieberg was right to observe that "one is probably saying too much at this point to argue that Luther here wanted to teach a divine establishment and ordering of a special rite of the *impositio manuum*. It is more probable that the concept *impositio manuum* is a synecdoche for the whole process of ordination through which God acts in an external-material way and calls a person into office."[85]

Just as Luther did not separate the process leading up to the liturgical act of ordaining from that act, neither did he separate the ordination from the tasks of ministry into which it subsequently led a person. Always his focus was on the means by which God communicated the gospel to humanity: "But whenever I minister, that is, baptize or absolve, I must be certain that my work is not mine, but God's who works through me. Baptism is a work of God; for it is not mine, although I lend my hands and my mouth as instruments. Thus when I absolve you or call you to the ministry and lay my hands on you, you should not doubt that as Peter says, it is God's strength."[86] Thus laying on hands was inextricably bound to prayer and the Word of God. Only when laying on hands (just as water, bread and wine) was used in the context of the Word could it be more than a human ceremony, that is, be the medium of divine action. The Word of God was for Luther the self-evident foundation for ordination as for any other genuinely liturgical act.[87]

Having said all this what did this gesture signify? It signified the approval of others already in the office who were laying on hands and thereby entrusting that office to the one upon whom hands were laid.[88] It attested publicly that the person on whom hands were laid had been properly called and examined. It confirmed the legitimate fulfillment of the whole call process before the gathered church.[89] In this same vein Luther wrote concerning the episcopal consecration at Naumburg (in 1542, discussed in the next chapter): "Laying on of hands, the blessing, confirms and signifies in the same way that a notary and witness confirm a secular matter, as when a pastor in blessing the bride and bridegroom confirms or witnesses their marriage."[90] Along with this function of public attestation Luther mentioned the notion of blessing (*Segenen*).[91]

Laying on hands had this function, of course, as a consequence of its link with prayer.[92]

Laying on hands with prayer functioned as a blessing which imparted a spiritual gift:

> ...it is not to be doubted that with such prayer and laying on of hands the Holy Spirit not only surely comes, but does not depart without bearing fruit, for it accomplishes that for which it is sent according to the promise of Christ: where two or three are gathered in my name, whatever they ask of the Father will be given to them. That is why Christians should ordain their pastors, for it follows the example of the Apostle and the early church.[93]

Luther had said the same thing much earlier in the 1523 treatise "Concerning the Ministry" when discussing the way to call and ordain a pastor. One can trust that God will act through our human words and gestures: "When you have prayed, have no doubt that he to whom you have prayed is faithful and will give what you ask, opening to him who knocks and granting to him who seeks."[94] One can conclude, therefore, that Luther understood the liturgical gesture of laying on hands with prayer in the midst of the assembly's worship to bless, that is, bestow the gift of the Spirit for the work of pastoral ministry in the church.[95]

To say this creates the need to raise a caution: the Spirit was not a possession in Luther's understanding, not a quantity to be passed out to people. Peter Fink's explanation is applicable here:

> There is no hint in the *lex orandi* that the Spirit is given to the ordained in order that they in turn may pass it on to others. That is an unfortunate image drawn once the church is funneled into priest and bishop, and once the personal presence of God becomes imaged as an entity to be doled out in different amounts. In that image set, one can only give what one has received. If the *lex orandi* is given a proper hearing, it becomes clear that the reason why the ordained person goes forth to invoke God's Spirit upon others is the very reason the Spirit was invoked upon him. It belongs to the structure of the church's prayer to invoke God's Spirit whenever a transformation is sought or when a mission is seen which can only be fulfilled by God's help.[96]

Luther's theology of the Spirit, his understanding of blessing, and the sacramental significance of laying on hands as a biblical and apostolic act, indicate the aptness of Fink's comments on today's Roman rite for

A Decade of Transition

describing the concerns of the Reformation period.

Section 8. The Ordination Prayer

The Lord's Prayer accompanied the laying on of hands, along with an optional elaboration of the three parts of the Lord's Prayer according to some versions of the rite. The elaboration began by quoting Matthew 9:37-38, echoing the introductory comments on the rite (section one above). The prayer was a petition for the gift of the Spirit. It made clear at the outset that a dominical imperative lay behind the petition. It was only on the basis of Jesus' word that the prayer could ask for the Spirit to come to servants of the Word. The gift of the Spirit was needed for the battle that had to be waged against "the devil, the world, and the flesh."

Luther's novel use of the Lord's Prayer to accompany the laying on of hands indicated his desire to root this central action in the words and deeds of Jesus. In a sense the Lord's Prayer functioned here like the words of institution in the eucharist. It connected the present action with a foundational dominical event. To be sure, this use of the Lord's Prayer cannot be interpreted as a specific dominical command to ordain. Yet, rather than being foreign to the earlier Western tradition of an ordination prayer, Luther's use and structure reinforced the idea that it was God acting in and through this rite. That this moment of laying on of hands and prayer was pivotal was also supported by the charge to the newly ordained which followed it (section ten below).

The variations in the texts of the manuscripts show that the ordination prayer was not understood as a fixed formula. Two additional pieces of evidence support this: the ordination prayers Luther used in the 1537 ordination of Benedict Schumann and the 1542 ordination of Nicolas von Amsdorf. These latter two prayers had more in common with one another in terms of style and content than either had with the prayer in the Wittenberg rite. In both cases, for example, Luther specifically mentioned the ordinand by name. Also, in the consecration of von Amsdorf as bishop, the Lord's Prayer was not part of the action of laying on of hands with prayer.

The text of the prayer used in the ordination of Schumann follows:

In addition he [Luther] said: "My dear brother, you have been ordained by God to be a faithful servant of Jesus Christ in N. [Naumburg], to further his holy name by the pure teaching of the gospel, to which we call and send you by the power of God, just as God has sent us. Therefore, watch earnestly, be diligent, pray God that he may preserve you in this high calling, that you may not fall away by reason of false doctrine, heresy, sectarianism, or your own thoughts, but rather begin it in the fear of God, faithful diligence, and constant prayer and rightly accomplish it in Christ." This was the main content of his prayer. Afterward he laid hands upon him and, kneeling, prayed the Lord's prayer aloud. When he had risen to his feet, he lifted up his eyes and hands to heaven and said: "Lord God, heavenly, merciful Father, who hast commanded us to ask and seek and knock, and also promised to hear us when we call upon thee in the name of thy Son: In this promise we put our trust and pray: be thou pleased to send this thy servant of thy Word, Benedict, into thy harvest. Help him, bless his ministry and service, and open the ears of believers to the blessed course of thy Word, to the praise of thy name, the increase of thy kingdom, and the growth of thy church. Amen. Therefore, my dear brother, I wish for you moreover, blessing and success, that you may walk in the fear of God and trust in the Lord!" Then "Now Pray We All the Holy Ghost" was sung.[97]

The prayer communicated some of the same concerns expressed in the 1539 rite, especially that it was God who sent persons into the harvest and sustained them in their ministry of the Word. In the Schumann ordination prayer an explicit invocation of the Spirit did not appear, nor did the specific mention of those against whom the newly ordained pastor would need to stand with pure teaching ("the pope, Mohammed and other sects which blaspheme your name"), as was the case in the prayer used in the major manuscript families. But the consistency of prayer for the Spirit occurring within the rite (for example, with the singing of *Nun bitten wir* in the Schumann rite at the point of laying on of hands) makes Peter Fink's comments again appropriate: "The true power that is associated with ordained ministry is nothing else but the fundamental empowering by God which is named the Holy Spirit. Theology in the West has tended to play this Spirit falsely by employing a "some Spirit for you, more Spirit for you" motif as it tried to distinguish baptism from confirmation, and both from ordination. But the Spirit of God is not a quantity; it is God's personal presence in the church."[98] Luther's rite intentionally embodied what Fink has characterized as a non-quantitative view of the gift of the Spirit (especially in relation to baptism), and the necessity of that gift of the Spirit to fulfill the mission to which one was being called as ordained pastor.

Luther was not consistent in his use of the Lord's Prayer as the prayer of ordination. Nor is it clear whether he considered it an appropriate or necessary introduction or conclusion to an *extempore* ordination prayer. The fact that his freely worded prayers were expansions of the petitions of the Lord's Prayer indicates that a model was at work. The function and tone were intercessory and built on the imagery of ministry being a means by which "thy kingdom" was increased. There is no question that Luther abandoned the content of the medieval rite's central ordination prayers (Roman or Gallican form). But the necessity for Luther of connecting prayer and laying on of hands cannot be denied.

Section 9. The Charge

The newly ordained now had the flock of Christ formally entrusted to them. They were now officially in their office. They were to be sent to the congregation that called them on the basis of the ordination having realized that call, that is, by having made it public and proclaimed it as an act of the universal church. I Peter 5:2-4 was used as the charge: "Tend the flock of God that is your charge, not by constraint but willingly, not for shameful gain but eagerly, not as domineering over those in your charge but being examples to the flock. And when the chief shepherd is manifested you will obtain the unfading crown of glory."[99] Thus the act of ordination was the means by which one was sent out as a servant of the Word. It simultaneously set a person in the office and commissioned them to exercise it. Because Luther's rite was used in centralized ordination services in Wittenberg, often involving a number of candidates, the charge helped to specify the local nature of the church and the importance of having been called to serve in a particular congregation. It helped to express the dimension of installation which was lacking in a setting where the participating community was not the one in which a person would be pastor.

Section 10. Blessing

A concluding blessing, with or without the sign of the cross, did not appear in H and F. Of the major manuscripts only R bore witness to its use. The 1537 ordination of Schumann and the 1542 episcopal ordination of von Amsdorf, however, provide additional support for the view that Luther's normal practice was to include such a blessing. This was not the view of Kolde and Rietschel, both of whom argued that the blessing with the sign of the cross in R was a later addition by Bugenhagen.[100] There is no evidence, other than its absence in H and F, to support this position. And even if it were an addition by Bugenhagen it would not have survived in R if Luther had had anything against its use. Secondary evidence for attributing it to Luther is the fact that the blessing was in Latin, for Luther taught Latin and sought to retain its use in liturgical texts in spite of pressures to produce German versions of evangelical rites.

In terms of its positive content, the blessing constituted part of the larger whole where each element lifted up a facet of the candidate's need for God's presence in order to fulfill the responsibilities of office. In other words, the closing blessing was one final affirmation, along with the hymnody, the collect, and the ordination prayers which invoked the Spirit or implored the gift of God's grace. As a concluding word of assurance the blessing sent out the newly ordained minister to serve the church and the cause of the Gospel with the hope for a fruitful ministry. Luther's free wording of it in the 1537, 1539, and 1542 rites also indicates that he understood it as a personal word of blessing.

Peter Brunner elaborated on the meaning of blessing for Luther by emphasizing that the hands laid on a person in ordination were "hands that bless."[101] He also noted that Luther held to a biblical realism with regard to interpreting the act of blessing.[102] The meaning of the sign of the cross in R (not mentioned in the Schumann or von Amsdorf rites) held no particular significance since it was a common ritual gesture. But neither should one treat its baptismal reference as a minor detail. Blessing and sign of the cross together served formally to signal the conclusion of the central portion of the ordination rite, which focused on the individual(s) being ordained. The attention then turned again to the

A Decade of Transition

community for the singing of a hymn.

Section 11. Hymn: "Now Let Us Pray to the Holy Spirit"

This hymn appeared at different points in the ordination rites under discussion here. In the 1539 rite (R) it was the final congregational song prior to the continuation of the rest of the liturgy within which the ordination had taken place. In the 1542 ordination of von Amsdorf (discussed in the next chapter) it was sung after the reading and brief comment by Naumburg's superintendent as he opened the liturgy.[103] The first stanza of the hymn was "a German *Leise* (i.e., a sacred folk song in the vernacular, ending in Kyrie eleison) that was known since early in the Middle Ages."[104] It was often intoned by the congregation at Pentecost after the choir's singing of the Latin sequence *Veni Sancte Spiritus* (discussed above). Luther added three stanzas and turned it into a chorale. The text is significant:

> Now let us pray to the Holy Ghost
> For the true faith of all things the most,
> That in our last moments he may befriend us
> And as home we go, that he may tend us.
>   Kyrioleis.
>
> Thou noble light, shine as thou hast shone,
> Teach us to know Jesus Christ alone,
> Clinging to our Savior whose blood hath bought us
> Who to our true home hath again brought us.
>   Kyrioleis.
>
> Thou sweet Love, grant us favor, that so
> We feel within of thy love the glow,
> That we from our hearts may love true the others,
> And with peace and joy live as good brothers.
>   Kyrioleis.
>
> Thou comfort best in danger or blame,
> Help us to fear neither death nor shame,
> That we may not falter when all shall fail us
> And the foe with his taunts shall assail us. Kyrioleis.[105]

The first stanza's petition for the true faith was, argued Ulrich Leupold, particularly fitting if it was first printed with Luther's additional stanzas "around Pentecost of the year 1524 (May 15), a time when Luther was greatly disturbed by the activities of Karlstadt, Münzer, and other enthusiasts and had ample reason to pray for preservation in the true faith."[106] Kolde thought that its placement in the rite at this point made no liturgical sense, that is, to pray for the coming of the Spirit for true faith when such was a prerequisite for the rite to have occurred at all.[107] Lieberg noted that such a perspective failed to take into account that the hymn was also used as a gradual verse or as a song after the sermon in the Sunday liturgy.[108] More important, the hymn's petition for the Spirit played a part in the larger whole in which each piece served to reinforce the rite's central imagery.

The intense focus on the Spirit throughout the rite revealed Luther's liturgical and theological sense that when the community called a minister, when the person heeded the call, was educated, examined and approved, when the ritual act of ordination celebrated the *vocatio*, *benedictio*, *missio* of the candidate, and when the newly ordained servant of the Word began the challenging task of ministry in the world, God's Spirit empowered and sustained each part and the whole.

Section 12. Lord's Prayer

It is not clear why the Lord's Prayer was repeated here when it had just been used as the ordination prayer. One can assume, however, that it provided the transition to the communion since Luther's 1526 *Deutsche Messe* stated that "after the sermon shall follow a public paraphrase of the Lord's Prayer and admonition for those who want to partake of the sacrament."[109] The German Mass then proceeded with the Words of Institution. The liturgy used with the ordination rite may have been Luther's German Mass, so that the rubric provided no new information about the liturgical context.

Section 13. Communion

The final rubric stated simply that the liturgy continued with the

A Decade of Transition 131

celebration of communion. Only R noted that the ordinands were to commune first. There is no indication that any of those newly ordained were to preside at the eucharist to follow.

The preceding material represents the first generation of reform in the struggle to reshape the liturgical practices associated with medieval episcopal polity in which bishops controlled the vocational process leading to ordination. An evangelical process in which the role of the bishop and congregation had to be reinterpreted was underway. It resulted in part from the simple fact that no Catholic bishops in Germany embraced the Reformation cause. But the deeper biblical, theological and liturgical perspectives which emerged in these transitional years revealed that more was at stake in how ordinations were done than the issue of episcopal succession.

The liturgical decisions that were made to meet the needs of the reforming churches were formulated first by Bugenhagen and Luther. Yet they were not alone in the way they approached the task. Franz Lambert's work in the 1526 Homberg Church Order indicates that a ritually focused, ceremonially austere evangelical rite was from the beginning a norm among reformers who took up the task of preparing new liturgical material. It is particularly clear in the work of Bugenhagen and Luther that there was to be almost no liturgically expressed distinction among deacon, presbyter or bishop. The role of the community in the rite, the whole of a gathered congregation and not just the ordained clergy present, was considered essential. The song and prayer of the congregation constituted the liturgical act and validated it. The ordination rite was never treated as an independent ritual act but rather occurred within a regular worship gathering, usually a Sunday eucharistic celebration.

Who presided at the ordination was not an issue in the early stages. Once new rites were developed it was always indicated that those already ordained, since they were in fact already leading the worship life of the community, were obviously the ones responsible for the ordaining. But again it was the congregational context which made the question of who the ordinator was less troublesome than it might have been. The evangelical rites were not seeking to abolish distinction between clergy and laity, but they were certainly redefining what the nature of that distinction was. Only when the issue of ordination and investiture (or installation) was addressed in the years after 1535 did the difference between two fundamental models for ordaining begin to emerge.

As has been set out in the preceding analysis, Bugenhagen and Luther differed on this point. Bugenhagen was more congregational than Luther when he argued that ordinations should always occur in the congregation to which the candidate had been called. Luther, on the other hand, maintained that ordinations should be centrally controlled. The congregational context was not lost, of course, since Luther also believed that the ordination should occur within the regular liturgical life of the community, in his case one of the churches in Wittenberg. The question here, however, is what distinguishes these two perspectives liturgically. There are variations in the ritual structure and content, but one would be hard pressed to explain liturgically that something different was happening in one over against the other. Were installations in reality a reordination? No one ever argued such a point, but the ritual content demands that the question be pursued.

If one uses, for example, the analogy of baptism, it is clear that one is not being rebaptized when accepted into a congregation other than the one in which the baptism originally took place because the ritual act of being immersed in water in the name of the Trinity is not repeated (although some other ritual affirmation may occur). Was there a similar ritual focus in the development of evangelical ordination which made it clear that once done, it was not and need not be repeated?

Part of the answer to this question must lie in broadening one's definition of the liturgical action. It is not a matter only of texts. Any distinctions made with regard to who presided, who laid on hands, who sang what prayers or hymns (choir, congregation), and so forth are part of the ritual action. Furthermore, these rites did not exist in an ecclesiastical vacuum. The larger context involving matters such as whether the ordination took place in a city or country parish, what magistrates or patronage privileges were involved, how cities and territories related to one another (including rivalries, jealousies, feuds) also contributed to the way in which the ritual action was experienced and understood, accepted or rejected. Some of these matters began to

A Decade of Transition

resolve themselves within the first generation of reform as consensus gradually emerged concerning evangelical approaches to ordination, and as cities and territories learned and borrowed from one another. But by no means can one speak of unanimity. The emerging consensus was still characterized by freedom and variety. The ecclesiological implications of these issues will be taken up again in Chapter 5.

NOTES

1 See Drews, WA 38, 410–422. No one seriously questions the authority of the manuscript traditions or Luther's authorship of the rite. Paul Vetter, "Das älteste Ordinationsformular der lutherischen Kirche," *Archiv für Reformationsgeschichte* 12 (1915): 64–75, argued for a different dating of the manuscript relationships, but Drews has shown his analysis to be faulty (see Drews, WA 38, 416ff.).

2 See Melanchthon's *Epitomae renovatae ecclesiasticae doctrinae ad illustrissimum principem Hessorum*, 1524; in *Corpus Reformatorum I*, 703ff.

3 The following historical summary is drawn from Hannelore Jahr's "Introduction" in Sehling, VIII, 3–36.

4 W. Schmidt, *Die Homberger Synode und ihre Vorgeschichte* (Festschrift zur Vierhundertjahrfeier der Homberger Synode, 1926), 90, 70; as cited Sehling, VIII, 12.

5 See Sehling, VIII, 43–65 for the text.

6 For the text of Luther's letter see WA Br.4, 1071, 157–158.

7 Sehling, VIII, 58.

8 Homberg Order, ch.23, 123 (Sehling, VIII, 59): "Eligat quaevis ecclesia aut deponat episcopum suum, quod ad eam spectet iudicare de voce pastorum."

9 Homberg Order, ch.23, 124 (Sehling, VIII, 59).

10 Homberg Order, ch.21, 112 (Sehling, VIII, 58): "The ordination of bishops, of electors of the synod, of visitors, and of all ministers should be done by prayer and laying on of hands according to the example of the apostles (Episcoporum, electorum synodi, visitatorum et omnium ministrorum ordinatio apostolorum exemplo per orationem

et manuum impositionem fiat...)." Alfred Niebergall, "Die Anfänge der Ordination in Hessen," in *Reformatio und Confessio*, Festschrift für D. Wilhelm Maurer (Berlin: Lutherisches Verlaghaus, 1965), 141–160, correctly pointed out that the Homberg Order was attempting to abolish hierarchical distinctions: "This is revealed in Ordination. All spiritual offices, not only the congregation's pastor/bishop, ...should be ordained according to the same order in which one prays and lays on hands as in the example of the Apostle" (143; the reference is to the Homberg Order ch. 21, 112).

11 Homberg Order, ch. 15, 62, 63, 71 (Sehling, VIII, 52–54).

12 Homberg Order, ch. 21, 113 (Sehling, VIII, 58): "Congregabitur ecclesia, et omnes simul pro his, qui electi sunt, orabunt... ." Cf. Homberg Order, ch. 22, 127 (Sehling, VIII, 60): "Moreover let the ordination of bishops be before the church through laying on of hands and prayer (Episcoporum autem ordinatio, fiat coram ecclesia per manuum impositionem cum oratione)."

13 Homberg Order, ch. 21, 114 (Sehling, VIII, 58): "...three will place their hands on the first elected, and of these one will say in a loud voice, "Receive the Holy Spirit, those whose sins you forgive etc.," or this, "Receive the keys of the kingdom of heaven, and whatever you bind on earth etc." And let it be done for each, one at a time (...tres manus imponent super primo electo, quorum unus alta voce dicet: Accipe spiritum sanctum, quorum remiseris peccata etc. Vel sic: Accipe claves regni coelorum, quodcunque ligaveris super terram etc. Et sic fiat super singulis)."

14 Homberg Order, ch. 21, 116 (Sehling, VIII, 59): "Dum episcopi, aut visitatores, aut 13 electi, aut adiutores episcoporum ordinantur, unus manus imponentium dicat: Accipite spiritum sanctum etc. Dum vero aliis manus imponuntur, unus eorum dicat: Impleat te Dominus spiritu suo, et erudiat cor tuum, illudque fide roboret, ut digne perficias ministerium, ad quod electus es. Resp. Amen."

15 Homberg Order, ch. 24, 141 (Sehling, VIII, 61): "Let any church choose a helper for its own bishop whom it might confirm with prayer and laying on of hands before the whole church (Eligat quaeveris ecclesia sui episcopi adiutorem, quem cum oratione et manuum impositione coram tota ecclesia confirment...)."

16 Homberg Order, ch. 21, 117 (Sehling, VIII, 59): "In omni manuum impositione tandem dicatur haec oratio ab eo, qui praeest ordinationi, hoc praemittens: Dominus vobiscum. Resp.: Et cum spiritu tuo. Oremus: Deus qui tuo spiritu et verbo praecipis populos tuos regi, supplices te deprecamur, ut his famulis tuis, supra quos invocavimus nomen tuum sanctum, et in ipso nomine tuo manus nostras imposuimus tui spiritus charismate infundas, et da illis, ut digne, sancte, et ad gloriam nominis tui ecclesiae tuae utilitatem impleant ministerium, ad quod electi sunt per Dominum nostrum Jesum

A Decade of Transition

Christum, filium tuum, qui tecum regnat etc."

17 Ibid.

18 Homberg Order, ch. 23, 140 (Sehling, VIII, 60-61): "Nullus episcoporum aut diaconorum eorundem admittatur aut confirmetur, nisi sub conditione, scilicet quandiu sincere, pure sanctum verbum docuerint, et vitam vixerint Christi et ecclesiae ministris dignam."

19 See, for example, Homberg Order, ch. 22, 122; 23, 131, 134; 24, 142, 144 (Sehling VIII, 59-61).

20 G. Morin, "Le plus ancien comes ou lectionnaire de l'Eglise romaine," *Revue Benedictine* 27 (1910): 41-74; see 65.

21 Homberg Order, ch. 23, 125 (Sehling, VIII, 60): "Cum autem ecclesiae verbo doctae fuerint, et eligerint episcopos suos, sat illis erit, ut a duobus visitatoribus, si tres adiri nequeunt, ipsa electio confirmetur, et si ipsi visitatores personaliter convenire nequeunt, ut eisdem manus imponant, rescribant paucis ecclesiae epistolam, qua ostendant se confirmasse episcopum ab eis electum committantque illi, ut vocet tres ex vicinioribus episcopis ad sui episcopi ordinationem. Si ecclesia inutilem et insincerum episcopum elegerit, deponatur a visitatoribus, et alium mittant."

22 For example, the *Stipendiatenordnung* 1529 was concerned with scholarships for educating pastors; the *Kastenordnung* 1530 regulated the distribution of goods; the *Kirchendienerordnung* 1531 established the number and jurisdiction of superintendents; the *Kirchenordnung* 1532 described worship. For the texts of these various Orders see Sehling, VIII, 66-100.

23 Sehling, VIII, 15.

24 The standard biography of Bugenhagen is that by Karl August Traugott Vogt, *Johannes Bugenhagen Pomeranus*. Leben und ausgewählte Schriften (Elberfeld: R. L. Friderichs, 1867).

25 G. Buchwald, *Ungedruckte Predigten Joh. Bugenhagens aus den Jahren 1524 bis 1529* (Leipzig, 1910), 217, 31ff.; cited by Drews, WA 38, 403.

26 When he went to Braunschweig, Bugenhagen assembled all the pastors of the city in the Andreas Church on the evening before the Ascension and evidently "confirmed" them all as evangelical leaders of the church with prayer and laying on of hands. But this act of confirmation or ratification did not occur before the assembled congregation. See

Drews, WA 38, 403. Nevertheless, A. Scholz, "Bugenhagens Kirchenordnungen in ihrem Verhältnis zueinander," *Archiv für Reformationsgeschichte* 10 (1912/13): 1-50, argued that the comments in the 1528 Braunschweig Church Order paralleled passages in the 1529 Hamburg Order, and probably also presupposed a liturgical setting (see especially pages 32-36).

27 Drews, WA 38, 403, discussed Bugenhagen's Church Orders, as did Lieberg (Lieberg, 188, note 119). See the summary of this issue provided by A. Scholz, cited above, especially 32-38.

28 See Sehling, V, 481-503; cf. Richter, I, 128f., for the Hamburg rite. Drews, WA 38, 404, drew attention to the liturgical structure and content of this act. A translation of the rite is provided in Appendix II, below pp. 253-255.

29 Sehling, V, 502.

30 For a discussion of the use of *Veni Sancte Spiritus*, see below, pp. 111-114.

31 Sehling, V, 503.

32 Ibid.

33 Rietschel (58): "Thus he confers the name *ordo* and *ordinatus* on this action. But in truth this whole action in its development is only investiture and introduction into the office in question (So überträgt sich wohl der Name *ordo* und *ordinatus* auf diese Handlung. In Wahrheit ist aber doch auch die gesamte Handlung in ihrem Verlauf nur die Investitur und Institution in das betreffende Amt)." Rietschel pointed out that one should translate the lower-Saxon word *Ordeninge* as *Ordnung* rather than *Ordination* in Bugenhagen's comment that "Die Ordeninge nach der ersten Christen Gewohnheit geschieht mit Gebet und Auflegung der Hände" (Richter, I, 128). Drews, WA 38, 404, agreed with Rietschel's assessment.

34 Sehling, IV, 331-332; Cf. Richter I, 251ff.

35 Compare the description of the process for clergy assignment on the eve of the Reformation given by Karant-Nunn (7): "Patronage traditionally included three distinct privileges: when a pastorate fell vacant to select and present (*jus praesentandi*) a new man to the appropriate bishop; officially to call (*jus vocandi*) the candidate to his church; and upon confirmation by the bishop, to invest the nominee with the worldly appurtenances of his new position."

36 Sehling, IV, 332: "Darna up einen sondach schal de sülvige predicant vor dem

A Decade of Transition 137

altare, so idt eine stadt is, na der epistel mit upleginge der hende dorch de anderen predicanten, unde etlicke van der gemeene, unde den oldesten angenamen werden unde der kercken bevalen mit den ceremonien in der Lübeschen ordeninge vorvatet."

37 Lieberg, (188f.), observed that to say this was not to assume that Luther had the same view of the process as did Bugenhagen. It was clear from the letter to Myconius that Luther did not see the two of them in agreement or there would have been no need to call attention to the point. Lieberg believed that the act of establishing ordinations in Wittenberg was grounded in Luther's understanding of the vocation of legitimate pastors, and that he was a driving force in bringing it about.

38 Sehling IV, 332: "De överst so itzunder bereit in namhaftigen steden ordentlick beropen, examiniret und ingesettet sind, bedarfen keiner confirmation, sonder schölen alse confirmati geholden werden."

39 Rietschel, *Luther und die Ordination*, 60.

40 So Drews argued, WA 38, 407.

41 WA 38, 423–431 (LW 53, 122–126). For a different assessment see Paul Vetter, cited in note 1 above.

42 WA 41, 454–459; Drews demonstrated the correspondences in detail, and the argument for dating, WA 38, 412ff.

43 Sehling, I/1, 25; G. Rietschel, "Luthers Ordinationsformular in seiner ursprünglichen Gestalt," *Theologische Studien und Kritiken* (1895), 168ff.

44 Cf. Th. Kolde, "Zur Geschichte der Ordination und der Kirchenzucht," *Theologische Studien und Kritiken* (1894), 217ff.; where this edition was published for the first time (cited by Lieberg, 192, note 137).

45 Sehling, I/1, 459.

46 See Rietschel, *Luthers Ordinationsformular*, 168ff.; Drews, WA 38, 420; Kolde, 236ff.

47 Lieberg, 193.

48 The Latin version is based on the Wittenberg manuscripts ("R"); WA 38, 421ff.; cf. Sehling, I, 28.

49 WA Tr 5, 111-112.

50 See Drews, *Die Ordination*; and the study by Karant-Nunn, *Luther's Pastors*.

51 The second column below represents the account of the ordination of Benedict Schumann from Luther's *Table Talks*, WA TR 5, 111-112, rather than a distinct manuscript tradition (see Drews, WA 38, 418). It is included here as an important witness signifying both the stability and flexibility of Luther's liturgical thinking on ordination during the years 1535-39.

52 See G. Buchwald, ed., *Wittenberger Ordiniertenbuch I* (Leipzig, 1894). Sunday appears to have been the norm at least until 1540 according to the entries in the register.

53 WA 7, 22, 19ff. (LW 31, 346); WA 11, 411, 22ff. (LW 39, 309); WA 12, 173, 1-7 (LW 40, 11); 12, 191, 22-25 (LW 40, 37).

54 See Lieberg, 199.

55 The Latin version of the rite stated as part of the ordination prayer: "...we pray so that for these seeking confirmation of their call from this church...you might deign to increase your Holy Spirit (WA 38, 433: oramus ut hisce petentibus ab hac Ecclesia confirmationem suae vocationis ...spiritum sanctum... digneris largiri)." Thus the local congregation in Wittenberg (*ab hac Ecclesia*) was understood as the embodiment of the universal church before which the confirmation of call in ordination should occur.

56 Sehling, IV, 331-332. Cf. Richter, I, 251f.

57 PGD, ch. xiii, nos.13, 16 (Andrieu, *Pontifical* III, 369-370): "Tunc episcopus ad altare conversus flexis genibus incipiat ante medium altaris alta voce: Alleluia. Veni sancte spiritus (Require infra, de altaris consecratione), vel, si est infra octavam pentecostes, hymnum Veni creator spiritus.....Et si propter ordinandorum multitudinem necesse fuerit, cantetur sequentia *Veni sancte spiritus et emitte celitus*." Kleinheyer, *Die Priesterweihe*, noted that a hymn for the Holy Spirit at the anointing of the hands first appeared in German and French pontificals in the second half of the twelfth century. The *Veni sancte spiritus, reple* was used only in one pontifical, all others listing only the *Veni creator spiritus (202)*.

58 See WA 35, 448-449 (LW 53, 265-267) for Luther's version of the *Veni sancte spiritus, reple*; WA 35, 447-448 (LW 53, 263-264) for the *Nu bitten wyr*; and WA 35, 446-447 (LW 53, 260-262) for *Kom Gott schepfer*.

59 Consider, for example, his pastoral concern for keeping the elevation in the

A Decade of Transition

eucharistic prayer in spite of his vehement attacks on anything that hinted of offering or sacrifice. See especially WA TR 5, no. 5589, 265–267 and no. 5665, 308. Cf. WA Br 11, no. 4186, 257–259.

60 The text was as follows: "Deus, qui corda fidelium sancti spiritus illustratione docuisti: da nobis in eodem spiritu recta sapere; et de eius semper consolatione gaudere." Luther's German version is in WA 35, 554: "HErr Gott, lieber Vater, der du (an diesem Tage) deiner Gleubigen hertzen durch deinen heiligen Geist erleuchtet und geleret hast, Gib uns, das wir auch durch derselbigen Geist rechten verstand haben und zu aller zeit seines Trosts und Krafft uns frewen, Durch denselbigen deinen Son Jhesum Christum, unsern HErrn, Amen."

61 M. Andrieu, *Le pontifical romain au moyen âge* III, 381.

62 As Karant-Nunn's study documented. See especially 21–30.

63 WA 26, 50, 1–5 and 20–22 (LW 28, 282–283): "Cum tanta res sit ministerium ...opportet omnino esse validum, firmum et bonum, qui dicat: video errantes fratres non intelligere sanum verbum, fratres mei sunt, occurram in istum ignem, opponam me istis erroribus et iniquitatibus Satanae. ......Episcopus enim heist ein wechter, heimsucher, i.e. qui visitat, videndo visitat, circumspicit, qui doceatur, vivatur, apertis oculis considerat, ne irrumpat perversa doctrina aut ne sit...."

64 WA 26, 49, 14–16 (LW 28, 281): "...multos vagos et vaniloquos pseudoapostolos, qui ubique se ingerebant, referebant se urgeri spiritu, sapientia, talento...."

65 WA 25, 21, 8–11 (LW 29, 22–23): "Si Episcopus cogitat suam vocationem, videt se divino ritu, oraculo, iussu Episcopum, 2. habet in manu res et substantiam Christi. Quae? Est Euangelium et sacramenta."

66 The content of the sermon is known to us only on the basis of the eyewitness account in "Bericht über die Wahl und Einführung des Nicolaus von Amsdorf als Bischof zu Naumburg," in *Neuen Mitteilungen aus dem Gebiet historisch-antiquarischen Forschungen*, Bd. 2 (Halle, 1836), 155–228; and Sixtus Braun, *Naumburger Annalen vom Jahre 799–1613*. The text was also edited by G. Buchwald, WA 49, XXVII–XXXIX. See the comments by P. Brunner, *Nikolaus von Amsdorf als Bischof von Naumburg*, Schriften des Vereins für Reformationsgeschichte, No.179 (Gütersloh, 1961), 62–63.

67 Lieberg, 197; WA 38, 428, 25ff.

68 Lewis W. Spitz, "Luther's Ecclesiology and His Concept of the Prince as

Notbischof," Church History 22 (1953): 113-141.

69 Lieberg, 198.

70 Karant-Nunn, 58.

71 On the history of the gesture see, for example, C. Vogel, "L'imposition des mains dans les rites d'ordination en Orient et Occident," *La Maison-Dieu* 102 (1970): 57-72; P. Galtier, "Imposition des mains," *Dictionnaire de theologie catholique*, VII/2 (Paris: Librarie Letouzey et Ane, 1927), 1302-1425.

72 See, for example, WA 12, 191, 23f. (LW 40, 37): "By prayer and the laying on of hands let them commend and certify these to the whole assembly (...et orationibus ac manuum impositionibus universitati commendare et confirmare)"; WA BR 6, 44, 18ff.: "publicly before the altar with prayer and laying on of hands by the other ministers (...tum publice coram altari a reliquis ministris cum oratione et impositione manuum testimonum accipes et autoritatem coenae tractandae)"; WA 38, 228, 29ff. (LW 38, 187): "Die Apostel haben on Cresem allein die hende auffs heubt gelegt und gebettet uber die, so sie zum ampt berieffen odder sandten, wie Actuum am neunzeheden Capitel Sanct Paulus und Barnabas geschach und Sanct Paulus seinen Timotheon leret, Er solle nicht bald einem die Hende auff legen. (The apostles without chrism laid their hands on the heads and prayed over those whom they had called or sent out, as happened to St. Paul and Barnabas, Acts 19 [13:3] and as St. Paul instructs Timothy not to be hasty in laying hands upon someone [I Tim. 5:22])."

73 WA 52, 563-571.

74 WA 52, 569, 11-23: "Die Christen aber sollen wissen, zum Kirchendiener, Bischoff, Pfarrherrn, Caplan, oder wie mans nennen will, gehört mer nit, denn das er erstlich eines unergerlichen wandels sey, und ein guten verstand Christlicher lehr haben und die selbe sein klar könne von sich geben. Wo solchs ist, da darffs mer nit, denn das solche personen von der öberkeit beruffen, und ynen das predig ambt und ander Kirchendienst offenlich befolhen werden. Da mag man die aufflegung der hende mit brauchen und dabey betten und ist kein zweifel dram, solchs gebet, ob gleich der heylige Geyst nicht mehr sichtigklich kumbt, wirdt one frucht nit abgehen, sonder das aussrichten, darumb es geschieht, nach der zusagung Christi: Wo zwei oder drey im meinem namen versamelt sind, was sie den Vatter bitten, das wirdt er jnen geben. Also sollen die Christen ire Kirchendiener weyhen, so folgen sie der Apostel und ersten Kirchen Exempel." Lieberg, (209, note 239), commented that *mag man* could not be interpreted to mean that the action of laying on hands was an unnecessary addition, since the words referred also to *dabey betten*, and Luther clearly did not believe that prayer was dispensible (i.e., some kind of addition to what could otherwise occur without it).

A Decade of Transition 141

Cf. WA 6, 549, 21ff. (LW 36, 91), where Luther discussed laying on hands in confirmation. Lieberg also argued that when Luther said in the 1524 sermon on Acts 13: 1ff. (WA 17/I, 511, 5ff.), that the elements of an act of setting a person in an office were public, and said in the October 24, 1535 letter to Myconius that ordination consisted of public prayer and praise of God, laying on hands was understood to be included. The ordination rite itself as well as other remarks by Luther make it plain that Lieberg was correct in insisting on the indisoluble connection between prayer with laying on hands in Luther's understanding of how one received the office of pastor.

75 WA 52, 569, 22ff. Lieberg, (210), noted that Luther's comments on the early church debate about the act of call and ordination that took place between Cyprian and the Presbyter Felix are also applicable here; WA 2, 231, 2ff.

76 WA 43, 503, 26–27 (LW 5, 109): "Huc pertinet desciptio rituum, quibus usi sunt patres, sive in conferenda, sive in accipienda benedictione."

77 WA 43, 504, 3–5 (LW 5, 109–110): lines 3–5, "Sicut nos in nostris congressibus publicis ordimur a precatione aut gratiarum actione, et sicut oramus imponentes manus iis, qui ad functiones Ecclesiasticas ordinantur."

78 WA 43, 521, 16–19 (LW 5, 134–135): "Quando Deus tulit aliquam sententiam, non mutat aut re tractet eam, sicut homines solent. ...'Sine poenitentia autem sunt dona et vocatio Dei.'"

79 WA 43, 524, 32–33, 36–38; 525, 3–7 (LW 5, 140): "But this blessing is more than an empty sound of words or some verbal wish in which one person tells and wishes another person good things......this blessing of the patriarch Isaac states facts and is sure to be fulfilled. It is not a wish, it is the bestowal of a good thing......In Holy Scripture....there are real blessings. They are more than mere wishes. They state facts and are effective. They actually bestow and bring what the words say. We also have blessings of this kind in the New Testament through Christ's priesthood, which is our blessing when I say 'Receive the absolution of your sins.' (Neque vero haec benedictio inanis tantum sonus verborum est, aut verbalis quaedam imprecatio, qua alius alii bona dicit et comprecatur; ...Haec vero benedictio Patriarchae Isaac est indicativa et certa in futurum. Non est exoptatio, sed donatio boni.....In scriptura sancta autem sunt reales benedictiones, non imprecativae tantum, sed indicativae et constitutivae, quae hoc ipsum, quod sonat re ipsa largiuntur et adferunt. Cuiusmodo etiam nos in novo Testamento habemus per sacerdotium Christi, quod est nostra benedictio, cum dico: accipe absolutionem peccatorum tuorum)." Cf. WA 43, 526, 2–4, 6-8 (LW 5, 141–142).

80 WA 43, 599, 34–40; 600, 1–2 (LW 5, 248): "It is great honor and majesty, however, when one says: 'This is the Word of God.' I hear a man's voice. I see

human gestures. The bread and wine in the Supper are physical things. At ordination the hands of carnal men are imposed. In baptism water is water. For the flesh judges in no other way concerning all these matters. But if you look with spiritual eyes, namely at whose Word it is that is spoken and heard there...then you will understand that it is the house of God and the gate of heaven. (Magna vero dignitas et maiestas haec est, quando dicitur: Hoc est verbum Dei, audio hominis vocem, video gestus humanos, panis et vinum in coena sunt res corporales. In ordinatione fit impositio manuum carnalium hominum. In Baptismo aqua est aqua. Sic enim et non aliter iudicat caro de his omnibus, sed si aspexeris oculis spiritualibus illam additionem Nimirum cuius verbum illud sit.......ibi intelliges esse domum Dei et portam coeli)."

81 WA 43, 600, 19-26 (LW 5, 249): "Caro enim tantum defigit oculos in aquam, in panem, in vinum, in terram, ubi dormivit Iacob: sed spiritus debet videre aquam, manum, verbum Dei, et Deum in aqua. Caro tam acute videt, ut iudicet aquam esse aquam, et excludat Deum, sicut Sacramentarii et Anabaptistae faciunt. Discendum igitur est contra prospectum carnis non esse verbum simplex et inanem tantum sonum: sed esse verbum creatoris coeli et terrae. Sic impositio manuum non est traditio humana: sed Deus facit et ordinat ministros."

82 See p. 50, above; "ordination is a certain churchly rite, on a par with many others introduced by the church fathers...."

83 WA 26, 83, 5-7: "Ibi tractat aliquem ritum, de quo et supra: hoc donum habet ex impositione manuum. Eo tempore donabatur spiritus sanctus etiam visibiliter, quando imponebant, ut in Actis primitiva ecclesia. Non fuit aliud illa manuum impositio quam receptio et assignatio eorum, quibus commendabatur aliquid officii, Ut act. 13."

84 Lieberg, (210), argued that there were no concrete reasons which could validly be said to indicate otherwise.

85 Lieberg, (211). Lieberg noted that even Rietschel made the connection in saying that "ordination" and "laying on hands" were almost synonymous terms in the sixteenth century (cited page 211, note 249).

86 WA 43, 601, 23-28 (LW 5, 250): "Sed quandocunque ministro, hoc est, baptiso aut absolvo, debeo certus esse, quod meum opus non sit meum: sed Dei operantis per me. Baptismus est operatio Dei: quia non est meus, quamquam accommodo manus et os tanquam instrumenta. Sic quando absolvo te, aut voco ad ministerium, et impono manus, non dubitatis, quin Dei virtus sit, iuxta sententiam Petri."

87 See Schoenleber, "The Sovereign Word," who devoted his entire dissertation to making the case for seeing Luther's understanding of the sovereignty of the Word as the

A Decade of Transition 143

means by which to interpret his doctrine of ministry and ordination.

88 WA 52, 568, 22-28.: "Such a laying on of hands alone is not a sign of the public entrusting of the preaching office. One must also pray that God, through his Holy Spirit, will enlighten, guide, and lead the person chosen....through such laying on of hands and prayer the Holy Spirit comes...to the ordained servant of the church (Nun ist aber solches hand aufflegen nicht allein ein offenliches zeychen gewest des ubergebenen Predig ambts, Sonder man hat dabey gebetet, das Gott durch seinen heyligen Geyst solche erwelete person erleuchten, regirn, und furen wolle...Denn durch solches hendt aufflegen und gebett ist der heylig Geyst biss weylen sichtigklich uber die verordneten Kirchendiener kummen...)." Cf. WA Br 11, 156, 23ff.: "by the apostolic rite, the laying on of hands, we have declared (our witness concerning it) and we have entrusted to him the ministry of teaching the gospel and administering the sacraments (ritu Apostolico, impositione manuum declaravimus (testimonium nostrum de eo) et ei ministerium docendi Evangelium et administrandi Sacramenta commendavimus)"; and Enders 11, 42, 96ff. (cited by Lieberg, 213, note 253).

89 WA 26, 99, 18ff.: "Certainly the situation is full of danger, i.e., you should entrust an office easily to no one. Then the ministers have thus been ordained: there was a confirmation of ministers in the sight of the church (Certe periculosus status i.e. nemini facile concredas officium aliquod. Tum ministri sic ordinati: erat confirmatio ministrorum in facie ecclesiae)."

90 WA 53, 257, 6-9: "Aufflegung der Hende, die Segenen, bestettigen und bezeugen solchs, wie ein Notarius und Zeugen eine sache bezeugen, Und wie der Pfarrherr, so Braut und Breutgam segenet, ir Ehe bestiget oder bezeuget... ." On the issue of the Naumburg affair, see P. Brunner, *Nikolaus von Amsdorf*. See also Lieberg's analysis of the parallel to marriage voiced here (214).

91 Lieberg, (214), remarked that Brunner believed that only in 1542 did Luther include this sense of blessing in the action of laying on hands. But that is contrary to the evidence of the rite itself as well as the 1528 exposition of I Timothy (WA 26, 83, 6ff.), and other passages already discussed.

92 As noted above in the passage from the 1544 *Hauspostille* sermon: "Such a laying on of hands alone is not a sign... ." In an extended note Lieberg, (215, note 259) raised an interesting parallel from Luther's 1522 comments against Henry VIII. Luther there designated the laying on of hands in apostolic times as a "donatio visiblis spiritus sancti (WA 10/II, 221, 8f.)." Of course he was arguing against Henry's position that the laying on of hands in Timothy was the *sacramentum ordinis*.

93 WA 52, 569, 16-22: "Da mag man die auflegung der hende mit brauchen und dabey

betten, und ist kein zweifel dran, solchs gebet, ob gleich der heylige Geyst nicht mer sichtigklich kumbt, wirdt one frucht nit abgehen, sonder das aussrichten, darumb es geschicht, nach der zusagung Christi: wo zwey oder drey in meinem namen versamelt sind, was sie den Vatter bitten, das wirdt er ynen geben. Also sollen die Christen yre Kirchendiener weyhen, so folgen sie der Apostel und ersten Kirchen Exempel." Cf. WA 44, 307, 37f.: "Indeed we place our hands on the ministers and at the same time pour out our prayers to God (Ministros vero imponimus manus et simul fundimus preces ad Deum...)."

94 WA 12, 193, 33ff. (LW 40, 40): "Deinde, ubi sic oraveritis, nihil dubitetis fidelem esse quem rogastis, ut det quod petistis, aperiat pulsantibus, et inveniatur quaerentibus."

95 The question of what Luther considered the gift of the Spirit in ordination to be will be discussed further in the sections below. At this point it is worth reviewing Lieberg's brief summary of the views of Rietschel and others on the issue of blessing (216, note 262). Rietschel had argued (*Luther und die Ordination*, 53), that blessing (*Segnen*) was only "the expression of intercession which takes place in the same liturgical action of the congregation," and had ignored completely the aspect of it being a true spiritual gift. This was also the approach of E. Achelis, *Lehrbuch der Prakt. Theol.*, Bd. I, Leipzig, 1911, 139) who believed that laying on hands was for Luther only a "gesture of intercession for the person." J. Heubach, on the other hand, judged that for Luther the laying on of hands was "the imparting of the Holy Spirit and with it the gifts necessary for the exercise of the office," (*Die Ordination zum Amt der Kirche*, Berlin, 1956, 109). Brunotte's critique of Heubach was rejected by Lieberg because he, like Rietschel, ignored the blessing function of laying on hands with prayer in Luther's writings. Cf. also, Ralph Quere's "The Spirit and the Gift Are Ours: Imparting or Imploring the Spirit in Ordination Rites?," *Lutheran Quarterly* 27 (1975): 322–346.

96 Peter E. Fink, "The Sacrament of Orders: Some Liturgical Reflections," *Worship* 56 (1982): 482–502.

97 WA TR 5, 111–112 (LW 53, 123, note 1): "Zu dem sprach er: "Mein lieber Bruder Benedicte, Du bist verordnet von Gott, dass Du ein treuer Diener Jesu Christi zu N. sein sollt, seinen heiligen Namen zu fördern mit reiner Lehre des Euangelii, zu welchem wir Dich durch Gottes Gewalt rufen und senden, gleich wie uns Gott gesandt hat. Derhalben mache mit Ernst; sei fleissig; bitte Gott, dass er Dich in dieser hohen Vocation erhalten wolle, dass Du nicht durch falsche Lehre, Ketzerei, Secten, auch nicht durch Deine eigene Gedanken möchtest abfallen, sondern in Gottes Furcht, treuem Fleiss, stetem Gebet solchs möchtest ansahen und in Christo recht ausrichten." Das was das Häuptstück seines Gebets.

Darnach legte er die Hände auf ihn und betet kniend das Vater Unser uber laut. Da man nu aufgestanden war, hub er seine Augen und Hände gen Himmel, und sprach:

"Herr Gott, himmlischer, barmherziger Vater, der Du hast geheissen beten, suchen und anklopfen, auch zugesagt, Du wollest uns erhören, so wir Dich im Namen Deines Sohns anrufen: auf diese Deine Verheissung verlassen wir uns und bitten, Du wollest diesen Diener Deines Worts, Benedictum, in Deine Ernte senden; ihm beistehen; sein Amt und Dienst segenen; den Glaübigen die Ohren aufthun zum seligen Lauf Deines Worts, auf dass Dein Name gepreiset, Dein Reich gemehret und die Kirche wachse. Amen. Darum wünsch ich Dir, mein lieber Bruder, dazu Glück und Segen; dass Du wandelst in Gottesfurcht und Vertrauen an den Herrn!" Darnach sang man: "Nu bitten wir den heiligen Geist, etc." The ordination of von Amsdorf is discussed below.

98 Fink, "The Sacrament of Orders," 488.

99 Translation from the Revised Standard Version.

100 Th. Kolde, "Zur Geschichte der Ordination und Kirchenzucht," *Theologische Studien und Kritiken* 67 (1894): 217–244; see especially 237–238; Rietschel, *Luther und die Ordination*, 16 and his *Luthers Ordinationsformular*, 176.

101 Brunner, *Nikolaus von Amsdorf*, 74.

102 Peter Brunner, "Zur Lehre vom Gottesdienst der im Namen Jesu versammelten Gemeinde," *Leitourgia*, Handbuch des evangelischen Gottesdienst, Bd. 1 (Kassel: Johannes Stauda, 1954), 201ff. See also his *Von Amt des Bischofs*. In: *Schriften des Theologischen Konventes Augsburgischen Bekenntnisses*. Heft 9 (Berlin: 1955), 5–77.

103 See the analysis below, pp. 153–161.

104 LW 53, 263.

105 See WA 35, 447–448 for the German text; WA 35, 510 for the meolody. The translation quoted here is from LW 53, 264.

106 LW 53, 263.

107 Kolde, "Zur Geschichte der Ordination," 238.

108 Lieberg, 195, note 150.

109 LW 53, 78.

CHAPTER 4

EMERGING CONSENSUS: RITES FROM 1535–1570

The publication of Luther's rite in 1539 did not result in its immediate adoption throughout Germany. The Reformation had been in progress for twenty years and various methods for creating an evangelical clergy were underway. Gradually Luther's rite began to dominate, and coupled with the impact of his rite the mutual influence of many of the early efforts began to result in a relatively consistent pattern. In our chronological assessment the next stage of investigation leads to the rites of Hesse which followed the aborted effort of the 1526 Homberg Order discussed earlier.

As noted in the preceding chapter, the decade following the Homberg synod in Hesse was characterized by the emergence of a variety of brief Church Orders designed to speak to specific needs in the regulation of ecclesiastical life.[1] As in Saxony the means for establishing what those needs were was to provide for a visitation of the territory. This occurred in August of 1525 when Adam Krafft was appointed Visitor by Philip.[2] The Visitors were to report directly to the prince. In subsequent developments the jurisdictional power appropriated by the prince from the episcopal structures of the Catholic church was delegated to the superintendents, who were often also the Visitors. The office of superintendent eventually absorbed the duties of Visitor.

In Hesse the office of superintendent was established in 1531.[3] The territory was divided into six districts, each with a superintendent who exercised ecclesiastical jurisdiction over all within his area. Together with the "most learned and fit pastors" their gathering in a synod represented the highest ecclesiastical authority in the territory. The *Kirchendienerordnung* of 1531 and that of 1537 described the specific responsibilities of the superintendent, such as visiting all pastors in the district once a year.[4] They also described a significant limitation of the office. Unlike medieval bishops, the superintendent did not have sole authority to appoint or remove pastors: "Where a parish needs a preacher appointed, no superintendent has the authority alone to install such a pastor without the consent of the other superintendents, rather they should reach common consent...."[5]

Superintendents were chosen from among the pastors of the area in question. Three candidates were recommended by the pastors or by neighboring superintendents. The candidate chosen was then sent to the prince "with the appropriate documents and depositions" in order to be confirmed by him. If the prince disagreed with the choice he was free to select one of the other two candidates. A letter confirming the election was then provided by the prince. Pastors were also free to nominate candidates from territories other than their own.[6]

In addition these Orders described the function and support of pastors (*Pfarrherren*), the stewardship of pastoral and church property, the establishing of synods, etc. With such explicit regulation they come close to the modern concept of a church constitution. But they were disparate pieces, not yet collected into a coherent whole.

The decade 1527–1537 was one of intense religious and political ferment. It is difficult to appreciate the complexity of the task of reforming ecclesiastical structures without some knowledge of the larger cultural context. Yet analysis of that context is clearly beyond the scope of this study. With regard to the emerging Church Orders during this period in Hesse it may suffice to quote Hannelore Jahr's conclusions:

> The political and religious currents which permeated this decade are reflected in only a minor way in the Orders of these years. The influence of Zwingli is almost completely absent, while the work of Bucer is evident only in subsequent years. More interesting than evidence of any direct dependence of Hesse on individual reformers is the broader basis for Philip's religious politics. He stands as mediator among the protestant fronts, at first between Saxon Lutheranism and Zwingli...later joining the union efforts of Bucer, both against the Anabaptists as well as against the Lutheran position in the Lord's Supper controversy. Philip's place in this regard makes it clear that for the Hessen church and its Orders questions of doctrine are not in the foreground, but rather the external form of the church and the ways in which the church will take shape.[7]

Jahr's comments point to the unique situation of Hesse because of Philip's role in the larger Reformation movement. Significant is her accurate assessment of the juridical, ecclesiastical focus of the Church Orders in Hesse. Just as there is little doctrinal information so there is

Emerging Consensus 149

little liturgical material in the works of 1527-1537.[8] Yet the concern for church structure, "external forms," provides helpful insight into the issue of ordained ministry.[9]

Of particular interest is the way in which structures and lines of accountability took shape. The prince at first replaced the Roman bishop, but superintendents and the synod also took over what were formerly episcopal responsibilities. Some of this movement obviously affected the process by which one was ordained. For example, no pledge of obedience to a bishop was required in any of the ordination rites in Hesse. By 1537, however, ordinands were required to submit in writing to the synod that they would preach and teach no "new things" without the express approval of the synod. This was a forerunner of the kind of specific pledge to confessional loyalty that would emerge in Hesse a generation later.

Two Church Orders produced in 1539 provided more detailed descriptions of the liturgical issues connected with questions of ecclesiastical structure, the *Ziegenhainer Zuchtordnung*, and the *Kasseler Kirchenordnung*.[10] The former was written by a group of superintendents, pastors, and professors, including Martin Bucer. The Cassel Order in its longer Erfurt edition incorporated the material of the *Ziegenhainer Zuchtordnung*.[11] Jahr summarized the impact of Bucer's influence:

> In the two Orders of 1539... [Bucer] disconnects the question of discipline from the exclusively territorial jurisdiction of the governmental *Reformations-* and *Polizeiorndungen* and entrusts its exercise to the congregation and its agencies; the office of Elder comes into being. The introduction of the Bann and of Confirmation serve to sift out the community of true Christians. These elements are already present in the *Ziegenhainer Zuchtordnung*, their liturgical form is provided by the *Kasseler Kirchenordnung*.[12]

Why did Bucer affect reform in Hesse so directly? The Strassburg Reformation had influenced the developments in Hesse due to personal relationships such as that between Lambert of Avignon, who had authored the aborted 1526 Homberg Order, and Bucer, whom he had met in Strassburg. When the heterogenous structure of churches in Hesse was made more chaotic by the increased activity of Anabaptists, Philip looked for someone to bring order to the churches of his territory. As G. J. Van de Poll observed, "he considered Bucer the right man in the right place, and officially invited him to come to Hesse."[13] Bucer responded to the invitation, debated with leading Anabaptists in Marburg, and succeeded in doing exactly what Philip had hoped: restoring order and breaking the power of a separatist movement in Hesse.

The question of discipline (*Zucht*) was forced on the Hesse churches by the emergence and influence of the Anabaptists. In controversies with them Bucer proved to be the key for maintaining unity in the church there. According to W. Sohm, Bucer's efforts resulted in his winning over most of the leading Anabaptists to active participation within the Hesse church.[14] And from this point forward the element of "church discipline" (*Kirchenzucht*) remained a third *nota ecclesiae* in that territory. One element of importance in the organizational content of that "discipline" (which consisted for Bucer of the Bann, Confirmation, and the Office of Elder) is the office of Elder.

The model for the structure of Hesse's ministry was the *Strassburg Ordnungen*, and a specific parallel for the *Ziegenhainer Zuchtordnung* was Bucer's *Bericht aus der heyliger geschrift, 1534.*[15] Bucer's ecclesiology was part of a broader humanistic tradition alive especially in southern Germany.[16] The consequence of it was a fourfold distinction of ordained ministry: 1) the office of superintendent; 2) the office of presbyter, divided into elders and preachers; and 3) the office of deacon.

The later 1566 Church Order which drew heavily on the two 1539 works stated the distinctions more explicitly. In an opening section entitled "How Many or Which Servants are Necessary in the Christian Church" it explained:

> Those offices which are established for the Church by God in the New Testament: 1) The first are correctly called *episcopoi* in Latin...and called by us superintendent (Acts 20:28; I Tim. 3:1); 2) The second are called *presbyteri* or *seniores*, of which scripture describes two sorts. Some work in the word, or teaching and distribution of the Holy Sacrament, which one can call pastors [*hirten*] and doctors. The others are responsible for diligent regulation, that everything concerning the administration of the church be done faithfully (Acts 14:23; 15:4; 21:18); 3) The third are the deacons. Through them all the service in the community of God is accomplished, according to the command of Christ

Emerging Consensus 151

and the Holy Apostles (Titus 1:5; Acts 6:1-6; 7:54-59; I Tim. 3:12).[17]

The *Zuchtordnung* of 1539 discussed the same division although much less succinctly.[18] Its descriptive narrative contained no liturgical material, but this could be found in the Cassel Order of 1539.

Bucer's influence was again evident when the Cassel Order noted that there were three sacramental ceremonies: confirmation, marriage, and installation/ordination.[19] The description of the latter was brief but direct:

> The third sacramental ceremony is for those who will be ordained to the ministry for the first time. When they have a proper call, and have been examined and confirmed, they should be let into the church and have explained to them what they are to do in their office, according to St. Paul [I Tim. 3:1ff. and Titus 1:7ff.]. They then make their promise and to keep the same faithfully with divine help. The church prays for them, ending with a collect. Hands are laid on them to give hope in the divine Spirit and help in the name of the Lord. Thus they are placed in their office.[20]

The distinction made here between a sacrament and a sacramental ceremony continued the argument Luther and other Reformation leaders had made concerning the definition of a sacrament. But there was no question that the rite of ordination was understood as the way a person entered the office of ministry.[21] Significant was the ordering of the process, reminiscent of Bugenhagen's 1535 Pomeranian rite discussed in the preceding chapter: 1) call/election; 2) examination and confirmation (by an authority other than the congregation); and 3) a liturgical act including the congregation's prayer, the promise of the candidate, and laying on of hands.

The text of the presidential prayer from the Erfurt edition of the Cassel Order read as follows:

> Almighty and gracious God, heavenly Father, when your beloved Son, our Lord Jesus Christ, was raised to your right hand in his heavenly being, he at once began to provide for us here on earth apostles, evangelists, prophets, shepherds and teachers. These are his chosen ones who gather and teach, who through the command of his dear apostles are chosen and installed. They will dispense faithfully his holy Gospel and Sacrament, and will provide and accomplish all

pastoral care and shepherding. We ask you through the same, our great shepherd and bishop of our souls, your dear Son, that to these who have been chosen from your people for such service you might richly impart your Holy Spirit, which will illumine them at all times, lead and strengthen them, so that they may accomplish your lofty and holy service with real understanding and zeal; and that they might seek, find and bring to your dear Son all who are estranged from him or who have been led against him, that they might educate and improve all who are brought to him and who are still in his congregation. In this, preserve them from all of their own errors and frustrations, from all false slander and detraction, as well as from the powerful impediments to their service. All of this so that they may serve you and your dear church joyously, persistently, purposefully and blessedly, that your name might be ever more blessed and your kingdom spread on every side and be even more splendid. Through the same, your dear Son our Lord Jesus Christ, Amen.[22]

Frieder Schulz pointed out that the prayer contained a petition for the Holy Spirit and a development of the first three petitions of the Lord's Prayer, much like Luther's ordination prayer.[23] Here the petition for the Spirit was related exclusively to the ordinand rather than to the larger gathered community as well. Along with this specific emphasis on the gift of the Spirit for the office, one can discern a clear attempt to highlight right teaching, exemplary life, personal witness and the need to struggle against false teaching. As was the case in other prayer texts used at this point in the ordination rites discussed earlier, the prayer was both invocational and didactic. The mandate for this liturgical action was scriptural: "these are his chosen ones who gather and teach, who through the command of his dear apostles are chosen and installed." And the focus of their pastoral ministry, the content of their ordained position, was to "dispense faithfully his holy Gospel and Sacrament, and...provide and accomplish all pastoral care and shepherding."

The laying on of hands which followed the prayer was accompanied by a specific liturgical formula (*Vollzugsformel*). The imperative formula was an innovation at this point in developing Reformation rites for ordaining, although as noted in the preceding chapter the aborted 1526 Homberg Order had adopted the medieval Latin "*Accipe*" formula. The new formula was, "Take the hand and help of God, the Holy Spirit, who will teach, lead, and strengthen you that you may carry out your service fruitfully, through our Lord Jesus Christ. Amen."[24] This reflected a

Emerging Consensus 153

different theological emphasis but not necessarily a different understanding from that at work in rites where no imperative formula was used, as the discussion of prayer and blessing in Chapter Two indicated.

Luther's 1542 Episcopal Ordination

Luther's use of the 1535/39 rite was not restricted to presbyteral ordination. On January 20, 1542 he ordained Nikolaus von Amsdorf bishop of Naumburg in Saxony.[25] Records of the event, including a description of the ordination, an edition of Luther's sermon and a personal assessment by Luther, provide the opportunity for raising additional questions about the liturgical material explored thus far.[26] Peter Brunner's analysis of this 1542 ordination included investigation of the broader political and ecclesiastical issues. The focus here will be on the rite used and the explanations of it which Luther provided.[27]

Unlike presbyteral ordination which occurred within a regular Sunday or weekday liturgy, Luther's 1542 episcopal ordination of von Amsdorf was a self-contained event. It opened with the choir rendition of a motet by Ludwig Senfl, *Non moriar, sed vivam et narrabo opera Domini*.[28] The assembled community (which numbered over 5000 according to the reports) then sang the hymn, *Ein Kindelein so löbelich*, particular to the season of the church year.[29] At the conclusion of the hymn Naumburg's city pastor and superintendent, Nikolaus Medler, proceeded to the chancel and invited the community to prayer, including the saying of the Lord's Prayer. After reading I Timothy 3, the first reading in Luther's 1539 rite, Medler instructed the assembly concerning the appointment and placed von Amsdorf before them as a fitting person for the episcopal office. The community was then invited to express its approval of the appointment with "Amen."

Luther's hymn, *Nu bitten wyr den Heyligen Geyst*, was then sung by the choir with instrumental accompaniment as Luther moved to the central altar to deliver a sermon. In the 1539 rite this same hymn was used to bring the ordination to a close. Basing his remarks on Acts 20:28 (Acts 20: 28-31 was the second reading in the 1539 rite), Luther then delivered "a very powerful and comforting sermon" lasting "approximately a good half hour."[30] The sermon focused on exhortation and encouragement for the newly elected bishop. Luther was clearly mindful of both the delicate political situation into which von Amsdorf was stepping and the "burden" of the episcopacy. Given human weakness, Luther noted that it was a wonder that anyone was willing to undertake such responsibility, that is, "to watch over and tend Christian souls." He was particularly mindful of the temptation to power and glory that could seduce a person in this office.

As ordinator Luther remained in front of the altar at the end of the sermon. Von Amsdorf came forward and knelt on the highest step, facing Luther. Those assisting (the *Mitordinierenden*: Abbot Thomas Hebenstreit, Superintendent Georg Spalatin of Altenburg, Superintendent Nikolaus Medler of Naumburg, and Superintendent Wolfgang Stein of Weissenfels) also came forward and knelt on the step below the newly elected bishop.[31] At this point Luther intoned the antiphon *Veni Sancte Spiritus* with the choir and assisting ministers joining in and singing the hymn to the end. Luther then intoned the versicle (*Cor mundum crea in me Deus*) followed by the response (*Et spiritum rectum*) and Collect (*Deus, qui corda*). Spalatin's notes indicated that it was done in Latin and from memory.[32] The choir answered with a sung "Amen."

In the 1539 rite the Collect was followed by the readings. Here the readings had already been done and commented on by both Medler and Luther. Thus a briefer "charge" to the candidate could occur at this point concerning the responsibilities of the office. It closed with a question asking whether von Amsdorf would "faithfully minister to all the souls of the whole chapter (*Stifts*) and diocese (*Bistums*) of Naumburg; that he would administer and care for them by providing pure doctrine of the holy gospels and the blessed sacrament according to the institution of Christ the Lord, as well as supplying all other needs of the church.[33] The answer was a simple "Yes."

This brief charge made it clear that the responsibility of the episcopacy was preaching the word and administering the sacraments, as was the case for the presbyter/pastor. The task specific to the episcopal office was suggested by the words *vorstehen* and *versorgen*. The bishop was not only to teach, preach and administer the sacraments but also see to it that in his diocese this ministry was carried out properly by pastors.[34] The desire was to recover a traditional role of oversight, especially as the reformers understood this in biblical terms.

Luther and those assisting then laid on hands as Luther said the accompanying prayer. Unlike the 1539 rite, this service had used the Lord's Prayer at the opening, thus it did not appear here as part of the ordination prayer itself. Brunner argued that Luther's use of the Lord's Prayer and/or the longer elaboration of the petitions of the Lord's Prayer in the 1539 rite indicated that either was appropriate. Although this is probably true, one should not underestimate the importance for Luther of providing dominical foundation for liturgical actions which, as was argued earlier, at least bordered on the sacramental.

Like the 1539 rite's elaboration of the Lord's Prayer this ordination prayer was a free rewording based on the earlier models. If one compares the 1537 prayer used at Benedict Schumann's ordination, the prayer of the 1539 rite, and this prayer one can see that Luther had a "model" structure in mind but that content could be adapted freely.

Brunner correctly pointed out that it seemed to be characteristic of ordinations by Luther to conclude with a freely worded blessing after the laying on of hands and prayer. This blessing (*Segenen*) included the sense of both benediction and exhortation. When one compares the 1537, 1539 and 1542 versions:

> 1537: Ideo precor tibi benedictionem et successum, mi frater, ut verseris in timore et fiducia Domini (Therefore, my dear brother, I wish you moreover, blessing and success, that you may walk in the fear of God and trust in the Lord);

> 1539: Benedicat vobis dominus ut faciatis fructum multum (The Lord bless you that you may bring forth much fruit);

> 1542: Expecta Dominum, viriliter age, et confortetur cor tuum (Wait for the Lord, be strong, and let your hear take courage [Psalm 27:14]);[35]

it is apparent that there was no fixed formula but rather a biblically rooted image shared for the sake of what Brunner aptly termed "paracletic admonition."[36]

Following this concluding blessing an enthronement took place. Luther and those assisting led the bishop to the choir. The singing of the *Te Deum laudamus* accompanied the action as was the case in Durandus' pontifical.[37] It was noted that the *Te Deum* was executed by "three choirs," meaning those at the organ, the clergy, and the congregation. At the conclusion of the hymn a Collect was said, again in harmony with the *deroulement* in Durandus. In this case the Collect was said by Medler, Naumburg's city pastor and superintendent, who had opened the service. Thus, as Brunner succinctly put it, "with the Amen of the choirs the first ordination of an evangelical bishop on German soil came to a close."[38]

Although this ordination raises many provocative questions concerning an episcopacy in Lutheranism, the focus here is on the rite itself in comparison with the presbyteral rite. A structural outline reveals the relationship:

Presbyteral Rite of 1539	*Episcopal Rite of 1542*
	A. Choir: Motet, "Non moriar"
	B. Cong.: Hymn (for the season)
1. Prayer for the candidates and for the whole ministry.	C. Lord's Prayer
	D. Reading I Tim.3:1–7
	E. Address to the Community
	F. Choir: "Nun bitten wir den Heiligen Geist"
	G. Sermon (on Acts 20:28)
2. Choir: *Veni Sancte Spiritus*	H. *Veni Sancte Spiritus*
3. Versicle: Create in me...Resp.: And renew a right spirit...	I. Versicle: Create in me...Resp.: And renew a right spirit...
Collect: *Deus qui corda*	Collect: *Deus qui corda*

4. Readings:
  a. I Tim. 3:1–7
  b. Acts 20:28–31	

5. Address by Ordinator	J. Admonition to the Candidate Answer: Yes
6. Promise of the Ordinand	
7. Laying on hands with the Lord's Prayer	K. Laying on hands with prayer
8. Ordination Prayer	

Emerging Consensus 157

9. Reading/Charge: I Peter 5
10. Blessing (with the sign of the cross) of the ordinands
11. Song: "Now Let Us Pray to the Holy Spirit"
12. Singing of the Lord's Prayer by the Ordinator
13. Communion

L. Blessing

M. Enthronement (Choir: *Te Deum laudamus*)
N. Collect

The structure of the two rites varied in terms of the ordering of parts, yet it is apparent that the 1542 episcopal rite paralleled the 1539 presbyteral rite. The variations were due more to the differing contexts, the latter occurring within a normal liturgy, the former being an independent rite. The most significant variation was the concluding enthronment. In fact only the explanation to the gathered community at the opening and the enthronement at the end revealed that this was an episcopal rather than a presbyteral ordination. Brunner explained:

> The dogmatic content of this is clear: the episcopal office of Nikolaus von Amsdorf is in essence the same as the pastoral office. Presbyterate and episcopate are one ministry of the Word...The particularity of the episcopacy resides first in the spatial extension of the church for which the bishop is responsible. More importantly, it lies with the special responsibility which the bishop has to see to it that the bishopric in his care has properly called pastors for the preaching office. With regard to ecclesiastical structure there is no difference between the office here given to the elected bishop of Naumburg and that conferred in the Wittenberg ordination rite.[39]

Luther provided his own justification for and explanation of this action in a 1542 work entitled, *Exempel, einen rechten christlichen Bischof zu weihen*.[40] Since this was one of the few places where Luther explained his liturgical theology, the remarks should be considered carefully.

He identified what he had done as a consecration (*Weihe*): "...I know better than the pope and his people how to consecrate a bishop. Because at such a consecration it was not I alone who laid on hands, but also the following bishops...."[41] But the *Weihe* was understood primarily as the act of laying on hands: "How can such a thing be, that the bishop of Naumburg allowed himself to be consecrated or have hands laid on him by such hostile heretics and apostates of the papal church."[42] Brunner pointed out that earlier in this work Luther had expressed the equivalency of the terms *Weihe* and *Ordinatio* by saying:

> Moreover we poor heretics have committed a great new sin against the infernal unchristian Church of the most infernal father the pope. In the chapter of Naumburg we have ordained and consecrated a bishop without chrism, as well as without butter, lard, bacon, tar, grease, incense, coals, and whatever makes it even holier, [we have done it] against their wishes, but not without their knowledge.[43]

Luther made the same point in a letter to Jacob Propst written on March 26, 1542: "I wonder that you have not heard the news, that the heresiarch Luther ordained Dr. Nikolaus von Amsdorff as bishop of the church of Naumburg on St. Fabian's day."[44] As Brunner noted, in all of these comments Luther was referring to the liturgical act of ordination.

The significance of this is again made apparent by the contrast and comparisons which Luther employed. It was the Roman consecration with "chrism, butter, lard, tar, grease" to which he objected. By interpreting his episcopal consecrating as ordination Luther made the polemical point that proper ordination and improper Roman consecration were very different things. The German *Weihe* corresponded to the Latin *consecratio*. Durandus' pontifical titled the rite for episcopal consecration *De examinatione, ordinatione et consecratione episcopi*.[45] *Ordinatio* was the inclusive term in the pontifical for all clerical ordinations up to the presbyteral office while *consecratio* was used of episcopal consecrations only. By interpreting his episcopal consecrating as ordination Luther indirectly pleaded the case he had made at other times that the presbyterate and episcopate were identical.

Luther also raised again the issue of Roman acceptance of bishops consecrated by heretics, thus pointing to the objective quality of ordination which made it "valid" in the same way that baptisms done by heretics or simonists were still considered valid.[46] The key to proper understanding of the role of bishop, to be a servant and not to "lord it over the people," was the unity of church and bishop in the mutual promise. The act of ordaining was critical in establishing this relationship:

> Because it is a matter of whether the church and the bishop are united, and whether the church listens to the bishop and the bishop teaches the church. And so it has happened [in Naumburg]. The laying on of hands, the blessings certify and testify like a notary and witness attest a secular thing; or like the pastor who blesses the bride and bridegroom to certify and testify to the marriage which they have undertaken and publicly proclaimed. It does not matter whether the pastor is an angel or a devil, by virtue of the office the bride is blessed.[47]

It was essential for Luther that the action occur publicly in the context of the community's worship. That fact, along with the congregation's participation and especially its public acclamation of the election, assured that the office was understood within the context of the community as the church and never apart from it.

Furthermore it was the laying on of hands that confirmed and attested this unity. The comparison of ordination and marriage revealed Luther's conviction that a public act was a necessary component of the mutual relationship. But the unity did not begin and end with the specific local community in the case of ordination. The collaboration of other "bishops" from neighboring cities assured that this was an act of the whole church. The election and consecration were thus recognized as legitimate, universally "valid," for this was not an independent or geographically restricted act.

The confirmation of the election of a bishop was, of course, an issue of ecclesiastical jurisdiction. Normally the election would be confirmed by the pope through the proper channels within the Roman Curia. Such channels were obviously not operative in this case. As Brunner explained:

> The decentralization of church administration, the relative independence of the church in a given territory, the abandonment of the juridical character of the whole church in favor of a spiritual brotherhood with its visible signs, all of this played a role in the radical reorganization which the Naumburg episcopal ordination signalled in a symbolic way.[48]

It was the whole of the election and ordination process that legitimated the action for Luther. As the rite itself showed, the election process, the assent of the candidate and community, and the laying on of hands with prayer were the constitutive elements of an episcopal (and presbyteral) ordination. The argument concerning the validity of ordinations done by heretics also reinforced the point that for Luther it was not the person (ordinator) who set the candidate in office but rather the means by which it was done (*Weise der Einsetzung*).[49] The centrality of a liturgical definition within Luther's theological reflection on the nature of ordained ministry is once again readily apparent.

In spite of all the polemical battles of the second quarter of the sixteenth century in which Luther attacked, and was attacked by groups with concerns as varied as Catholics and Anabaptists with regard to his understanding of ministry in the Church, he never abandoned the liturgical act of ordaining as the center of his theological reflection and ecclesiastical practice. He resolutely maintained the ritual act in which, by which and through which a person was called to and publicly recognized as being placed in the specific office of leadership in the Church known as the *ministerium verbi*. No matter how much the context changed, the terms of the debate shifted or the points of argument were altered, Luther relied on the worshipping community to provide the focus around which issues and questions about ministry revolved.

To say this is not to claim unbroken continuity with medieval Catholic liturgical traditions. Luther changed dramatically the ritual content of the medieval rite of ordination represented by Durandus' *Pontifical*. But there should be no question that he retained liturgical continuity which embraced elements of both content and structure. One must simply admit that evangelical ordination rites were self-consciously understood as ordination rites. They were inevitably seen, therefore, as having some kind of relationship to what had been done under that name in the past. The evangelical rites were not experienced in a vacuum. To use an image drawn from contemporary semiotics and structural criticism, intertextuality was at work here. The reformed rites were replacements for the medieval rites, but they were not creations of a completely new theological or liturgical event.

Luther's reshaping of the rite reconstituted its implicit core: participation by a gathered community, reading of scripture, and use of specific word and sign (prayer for the gift of the Spirit with laying on of hands). Yet to say that Luther reshaped the rite and produced a standard for subsequent liturgical development is to fail to recognize the foundation laid by Bugenhagen, especially in his 1529 Hamburg rite.[50] In spite of Rietschel's assessment that the latter was a rite for installation and not ordination, its structure and content clearly provided a model for Luther's ordination rite six years later.

Considering the complexity of the medieval rite, it is not mere coincidence that both Luther and Bugenhagen opened their ordination service with "Come Holy Spirit" sung by the congregation, closed it with "Now Let Us Pray to the Holy Spirit," also sung by the congregation, and made laying on of hands with prayer a central ritual focus, with others previously ordained being the ones to lay on hands. Thus one must credit Bugenhagen as much as Luther with whatever genius one attributes to the simplicity and directness of early Reformation ordination rites.

One must note also that Luther's use of the liturgical act of ordaining indicated his conviction that there was but one office of the *ministerium verbi*. To be sure, there could be different roles played out within that one office, but the liturgical action revealed an inherent equality among the pastor of a congregation (the 1535/39 rite), the bishop overseeing many congregations (the 1542 episcopal ordination), and the deacon assisting in the life of the community (the 1525 ordination of Rörer). The focus in all cases was on the fact that through this liturgical act one was ordained into an office which served the whole church.

The 1542–44 Rites of Bugenhagen

It has already been stated that Bugenhagen adopted Luther's rite in the church orders he produced after 1539. His rites for Wolfenbüttel (1543) and Hildesheim (1544) were clear examples of this.[51] The Wolfenbüttel rite ("Wo erwelede edder gevorderde predicanten apenbar anthonemende sind") explained that the elected preacher was to be sent to the superintendent to be examined. If found worthy, the candidate was to be ordained before the altar by the superintendent during a weekday eucharistic liturgy:

> The elected preacher shall be sent to the superintendent, whoever is proved ready, and he shall be examined. If he is worthy he shall be ordained before the altar by the superintendent, on a weekday, after the sermon and the latin litany (after which all shall be exhorted from the pulpit to pray).[52]

Immediately after the sermon of the day, the litany was sung, followed by the *Veni Sancte Spiritus*, and versicle *Cor mundum crea in me, Deus*.[53] The remainder of Luther's 1539 rite was retained unchanged.

This arrangement was also used in the 1544 Hildesheim Church Order, "Wo erwelede edder gevörderde predicanten antonemende synt"[54] Again Luther's 1539 rite was adopted. One important distinction in Hildesheim, however, concerned where the ordination occurred:

> After the examination, on a weekday after the sermon, the elected and called candidate shall be commended to the people from the pulpit, in his church, and admonished to pray.[55]

Here, in contrast to Wolfenbüttel where the candidate was sent to the superintendent to be examined and ordained (that is, not in the candidate's own church or before the congregation that had called him), Bugenhaen had the ordination occur "*yn syner kercken.*" In spite of the fact that Bugenhagen adopted Luther's rite, he was not willing to give up his conviction that ordinations not be centralized.

A variation in the Hildesheim rite in comparison with Wolfenbüttel was a note that the litany prior to the singing of *Veni Sancte Spiritus* was to be done in German rather than Latin ("Darup late men singen die düdesche letanie").[56] The use of this litany is the consequence of the ordination occurring in the midst of a weekday communion liturgy.

The 1547 and 1559 Württemberg Rites

Unlike Wittenberg and Saxony which were the home of Luther, Melanchthon, Bugenhagen and others who began and led the Reformation, or the territory of Hesse which was guided by a prince unswervingly committed to the cause of reform, Württemberg was a late-comer to the cause of the Reformation and initially had no native reformers of any stature. The evangelical movement took hold there not

Emerging Consensus 163

as the result of continuous ferment among leaders such as those listed but rather as an almost overnight transition when Duke Ulrich won the territory from the Austrians in 1534 with the help of Philip of Hesse, and subsequently declared it to be Lutheran.[57] The significance of this became clear in the early stages of the reform movement as different groups vied for prominence.

Erhart Schnepf was the representative of a more strictly "Lutheran" perspective, along with Johannes Brenz, pastor in Schwäbisch-Hall. Ambrosius Blärer, influenced by Bucer and by the Swiss reform movement, provided a more strictly "Reformed" perspective (albeit the labels are anachronistic at this point). Most of the evangelical pastors for Württemberg were supplied by the southern areas of Germany and by Switzerland (thirty-nine of them at the outset of the Reformation there). Only ten were of Lutheran persuasion, men recommended by Brenz, Luther, and Melanchthon.

Although Lutheran supporters feared that the Blärer/Bucer camp might gain a foothold, for example in their eucharistic theology, the Lutheran party, even though small in number, eventually gained the upper hand. Blärer was restricted in 1538 and some of his supporters moved out of the area. After the Smalcald Wars a strong group of leaders emerged in Württemberg including Brenz, Johannes Isenmann of Schwäbisch-Hall, Martin Frecht of Ulm, and Matthias Alber and Johannes Schradin of Reutlingen. Under their leadership the early confessional battles disappeared.[58]

It is difficult to demonstrate how, under the strained legal, economic and political conditions, the need for evangelical pastors was met in the decade following Duke Ulrich's victory. The largest number among the first generation were Catholic clergy who embraced the Reformation cause, sometimes by choice, sometimes under duress. Many former monks could also be found among the "new" clergy. As was the case in Saxony and Hesse, the need to develop an evangelical process for ordination was not addressed as long as the Reformation churches were able to draw from a supply of already ordained Catholic clergy (or in the case of Württemberg, were supplied with evangelical pastors from other areas). But this important history is secondary to the liturgical focus being pursued here.

Frieder Schulz argued that the Württemberg rite of 1547/1559 represented one of three major types (with Wittenberg and Hesse representing the others) because it was conceived of as a local installation or introduction into the "parochially restricted preaching office."[59] He viewed the Wittenberg rite, on the other hand, as representing a distinct type because it conceived of ordination as a general introduction into the preaching office of the whole church.

Schulz recognized that "a close material connection" existed between these two ways of understanding the rite but maintained that they were in fact distinct. He also noted that later redactions of the Württemberg rite (after 1559) absorbed elements of Luther's 1539 rite, thus clouding the distinction. The differing liturgical contexts which served as further justification for Schulz's argument will be discussed below. At this point it is necessary to evaluate the rite itself.

A Württemberg ordination rite appeared for the first time in the 1547 *Synodalordnung*.[60] The Dean of the area was in charge of the "ordination" of new pastors and deacons. It was stated clearly that what was being done was not a "papist consecration or ordination."[61] This clearly stated distinction, in terms of specific contrast with the Roman rite, along with that indicated by the local Dean being the ordinator, supports Schulz's contention that this act, even though introducing a person into an office of ministry for the first time, was conceived of differently than in the rites of Wittenberg and Hesse.

Few comments are made in the 1547 *Synodalordnung* describing the context for the action. It was stated simply that on a determined day the Dean, accompanied by an additional person to serve as an official witness for the ceremony, proceeded to the church with the pastor or deacon who was to be installed. The congregation assembled and the service began with the singing of *Nun bitten wir den Heiligen Geist*. A sermon on the ministry of the Word was then delivered by the Dean or the person who was there as official witness. The sermon was directed to the congregation concerning the origins of and reasons for the office. Its purpose was specifically said to be for instruction on these points. The Creed was sung following the sermon.

The rite proceeded with the Dean, as installer, going to the altar after the singing of the Creed and calling forward the candidate, who then

Emerging Consensus 165

knelt before him. The Dean addressed a short admonition to the community attesting that the candidate was properly chosen, called and capable of fulfilling the office. In other words this constituted a formal presentation of the candidate. The Dean then said the following prayer "in a bright, clear and understandable voice":

> Almighty God, Heavenly Father you have instituted the worthy office of preaching through your beloved Son, Jesus Christ, so that poor humanity might be comforted and helped. You have also stated and promised that those who believe and are baptized will be blessed. Because we know that our corrupt and awful flesh is troublesome and dangerous, we pray your special help and gracious assistance to protect this dear and worthy treasure from the greatly depraved and wrathful enemy, which we would not be capable of doing in our miserable, weak, and earthly vessels. We ask you in your boundless grace and mercy, that you would not leave or abandon us, but would hold us in your divine hand. We especially pray for your servant, N., who has been sworn to preach the Holy Gospel, that he may remain steadfast against all onslaughts of the Devil, steadfast in your healing, useful and necessary command until the end of the earth in your sacred kingdom. We pray that we may never be deprived of your heavenly comfort, through Jesus Christ your Son, our Lord, who with you and the Holy Spirit lives and reigns, one God forever. Amen.[62]

The prayer made it clear that the office of preaching was instituted by Christ. It expressed the need for God's continuing grace to make the bearing of such an office possible. It commended the candidate by name to God's care. Its purpose was thus both didactic and epicletic. It is also clear that the rite presumed earlier stages in the vocational process to have occurred. The candidate had already "been sworn to preach the Holy Gospel." The examination, with its emphasis on "right teaching," was considered an integral part of the "confirming" process which had in the medieval Catholic tradition been borne by patrons and bishops. But it was this liturgical action which in turn served both to validate that "confirmation" and specifically place the person in the office.

The opening prayer was followed by a reading of John 20:21: "The Lord said, 'As my Heavenly Father has sent me, even so I send you.' And when he had said this he breathed on them and said, 'Receive the Holy Spirit. If you forgive the sins of any they are forgiven; if you retain the sins of any they are retained.'" This formula, sandwiched between two prayers which in form and content paralleled traditional "ordination prayers" accompanying the laying on of hands, was an indirect way of making a claim which the Roman rite had made with its imperative formula based on the same text. In this action the gift of the Spirit for the "office of the keys" was related to the one being installed/ordained in this particular office in the community. To note that it was done "indirectly" is not, of course, an unimportant point.

The reading of the text, providing scriptural warrant for the present action, was in turn followed by another prayer which served explicitly as an invocation of the Spirit on the candidate.[63] Its concerns echoed the prayer which preceded the reading except for its clear epiclesis. The Lord's Prayer was then used to conclude this central, euchological focus of the rite. On the one hand this echoed Luther's rite, yet on the other it communicated a different emphasis. The stress here was on the Lord's Prayer as a concluding communal action and affirmation rather than as a presidential prayer of ordination, the function it had in Luther's rite. And none of these prayers was said in conjunction with the laying on of hands.

It was expressly stated that "after the praying or singing of the Lord's Prayer, the Dean shall turn toward the altar with his back to the congregation," and as ordinator then "place his right hand on the bare head of the new pastor or deacon and say":

> Dear brother, we have gathered in the Holy Spirit, have called out and prayed to God our Heavenly Father through Jesus Christ our Lord and Savior on your account. We do not doubt that He has heard us according to his divine promise, and that He will grant our petitions. Accordingly, by command of the Almighty and by command of our gracious Prince and Lord, who is the right and God-given magistrate, I ordain, confirm and certify you as servant and pastor of this congregation. All of this with the earnest command that you would energetically and faithfully administer this with all honesty and without anger, as you must give account on that day before the judgment seat of our Lord Jesus Christ, the true judge, in the name of the Father and of the Son and of the Holy Spirit. Amen.[64]

This was not a prayer and so represented a shift from the traditional connection of a prayer for the Spirit with laying on of hands, or the laying on of hands being done in silence. The gesture was here attached

Emerging Consensus 167

to a word of assurance and exhortation addressed to the candidate. In the midst of it stood the strong declarative formula, "I ordain, confirm and certify you"; a declaration made, it should be noted, on the basis of the command of the prince. No other assistants (ordained or not) were said to be involved in this action. In other words a juridical emphasis overshadowed any theological investment in the gesture of laying on hands.

It is perhaps fair to suggest that the juridical character of the act of ordaining stood out most in this Württemberg order. Yet it contained elements of prayer and liturgical action in the midst of a word service which, though minimal, reveals its reliance on the core traditions regarding what it meant to ordain. To conclude the service the congregation sang the *Te Deum laudamus* in Latin, or *Grates nunc omnes* in German. Once again the congregational participation betrayed a fundamental conviction of the Reformation movement that ordained ministry was an ecclesial reality, a congregationally centered calling. One is led to suggest that, for the framers of this rite, if the presence and prayer of the community were not present then neither episcopal action nor ritual gesture (laying on hands) made any difference. To conclude the rite the Dean spoke the Aaronic benediction from Numbers 6.

Only presbyters and deacons were discussed in this 1547 Order, although the role of a "*Superattendent*" was mentioned earlier in the Order with regard to the installation of a Dean into that office.[65] Yet the 1559 *Württemberg Summarischer Begriff*, which adopted most of the 1547 rite's prayers, broadened the application of the rite to include it use for installing/ordaining "Pastors, Preachers, Deacons, and Subdeacons."[66] It also provided a fuller description of the process for selecting and ordaining candidates, raising issues which help to clarify how the situation in Württemberg was understood at the time.

A concern for continuity remained as the 1559 Order made clear:

> ...we order, command and desire that in our principality and all our protectorates and related authorities, regions, cities, villages and townships, present and former pastorates, preaching places, diaconates and subdiaconates, former ones and ones currently maintained, should all remain unchanged. For that reason it is our prescribed decree that there shall be respect and vigorous supervision in the performance of church services. Such ministries, as soon as they are vacated,

shall be invested *de iure Patronatus*, no matter who or from what class he may be. Positions shall be taken speedily and without delay by God-fearing, energetic, learned and experienced servants and ministers of the aforementioned Augsburg (and our) Confession and church, according to the following orders.[67]

As in the Orders in Hesse and Wittenberg, so here also the desire was to provide well-trained ministers. No church worker was to be called without first presenting testimony concerning his birth, background, conduct and teaching. Once approved, the candidate was to be examined by appointed theologians, privately and in Latin.[68] Then they were examined publicly by three appointed theologians on the basis of delivering a sermon. The details of the whole procedure were then spelled out in detail.[69]

Once approved and called the candidate was to be ordained with the rite provided. It was titled "The Manner in which a new minister [*kirchendiener*] may be commended, introduced and installed by the Superintendent of his church."[70] The rite followed that of 1547 with a few exceptions, such as the superintendent being the ordinator rather than the local Dean. It added the reading of I Timothy 3, drawn from Luther's rite and one from Ephesians. The latter's incipit is recorded as "So care for yourselves and for your flock." Since this text is not in Ephesians, it could be that the reading of I Peter 5 from Luther's rite was intended here. The reading of John 20:21-23 was retained.

The prayer from 1547, "Almighty God, heavenly Father, you have instituted...," was placed after the readings rather than before. Also it was noted that one could use the ordination prayer, "Merciful God, heavenly Father," from the Mecklenberg rite, which was the ordination prayer of Luther's rite. The remainder of the ordination followed the 1547 rite completely. A structural outline of the 1559 rite provides easy comparison with Luther's 1539 Wittenberg rite:

Luther 1539	*Württemberg 1559*
Prayer	"Now Let us Pray to the Holy Spirit"
"Come Holy Spirit"	
Collect	Sermon
	Creed
	Short Address

Emerging Consensus 169

Readings:	Prayer
I Timothy 3:1-7	Readings:
Acts 20:28ff.	John 20:21ff.
	I Timothy 3:1-7
Address	Ephesians [?]
	Ordination Prayer
Laying on Hands	Lord's Prayer
Prayer	Laying on Hands
Charge	Exhortation
"Now Let Us Pray to the Holy Spirit"	Blessing
Communion	"*Te Deum laudamus*"
	Blessing

The 1547/1559 Württemberg order departed significantly from the structure of the Wittenberg and Hesse rites, yet gave evidence of maintaining certain key emphases of evangelical ordination: the centrality of scripture readings with a sermon or address based on them; prayer for the gift of the Spirit; congregational participation, especially through singing of hymns, and the visible sign of laying on hands, albeit here with a unique focus, more juridical than epicletic. As noted earlier, after 1559 the Württemberg rite absorbed elements of Luther's rite and therefore lost some of its distinctive character.[71] Similarly, in churches where Luther's rite was used the Württemberg order was adopted for use in installations. This reinforced a distinction between the two: Luther's Wittenberg rite being understood as a general act of ordination into the office of ministry, the Württemberg rite being understood in a more restricted sense as a local or parochial rite of installing.

Most of the differences in the structure of the Wittenberg and Württemberg rites can be attributed to the larger liturgical context within which they occurred. In Wittenberg the ordination was part of the evangelical mass. In Württemberg it was part of the customary high German liturgy. Thus, as Schulz explained,

> the sermon and sung Creed, opening and closing hymn with closing blessing, and also the (sung) Our Father, as the conclusion of the ordination prayer, are permanent parts of the normal service. Since the sermon deals with the preaching office, a special address after the readings is dispensed with. So also the question to those being installed is missing. For that reason a presentation

which gives public notice of the proper call and suitability of the "new pastor" precedes the actual act of ordination, after an introductory prayer is said.[72]

The issue here is how ordination to the church's preaching office functioned as an introduction/installation in a specific pastorate, and what constituted the "legal" dimensions of the relationship of the pastor with that specific community. In other words, was the act of ordaining in Württemberg seen as the concluding portion of a juridical (and only secondarily theological) process, or was it rather a spiritual event in the ongoing liturgical life of the community?

Perhaps one should not create such an either/or distinction, but the point of the juridical elements overshadowing the theological was not lost on the framers of the Württemberg rite. It was not simply the appearance of the *Vollzugsformel* with its legalistic focus, but also the fact that the superintendent appeared for the rite along with "the district magistrate [*Amtmann*] of the same region" (the latter choosing the day and time for the ordination!) that gave the Württemberg order its distinctive character. Thus the central action of laying on hands with prayer here functioned in a way quite unlike its use in Luther's rite, where other pastors joined in what was clearly a liturgical and theological gesture, not a juridical one.

Subsequent developments in Württemberg and neighboring areas, such as the *Grafschaft* of Hohenlohe, often took quite individualistic turns depending on the circumstances peculiar to the given territory or city.[73] The issue of the relationship between "ordination" in the church and "investiture" or "installation" in a specific, local congregation under the control of a given prince or other ruler, remained controverted. The Württemberg family of rites contributed its juridical solution to this facet of the ongoing debate concerning what constituted evangelical and catholic ordination.

The Rites of the 1566 Church Order of Hesse

The limitations inherent in speaking of an emerging consensus in Reformation rites during the period 1535–1570 are made obvious by the

Emerging Consensus

issues raised in the first major Church Order for all of Hesse, the *Kirchenordnung* of 1566. The General Synod of 1559, caught up in questions of ecclesiastical order, tried to clarify questions on the basis of already existing Orders in the territory. The Synod resolved to retain the *Ziegenhainer Zuchtordnung* 1539 and to expand the *Kasseler Kirchenordnung* of the same year "according to the needs of the territory."[74] This evidently proved to be an insufficient means to bring about the unity toward which the church in Hesse was moving.

The Synod of 1560/61 charged Andreas Gerhard Hyperius and Nikolaus Rhodingus with the task of producing a single Church Order from the earlier materials. A new Order was finally produced in 1566, but its actual origins are not clear. Its content stemmed from a variety of sources.[75] Beyond dispute is the fact that the 1566 Order stood at the end of forty years of reform efforts in Hesse. And it included a section describing in detail the procedures for ordaining superintendents, presbyters, and deacons.[76]

The opening comments concerning the office of superintendent are revealing:

> (How the superintendent is to be chosen)
> Because we have no clear form expressed in the Holy Scriptures for the election of a superintendent, according to which one might judge use in all places and times, we attempt here as much as it is possible to follow the example of the ancient and pure church and take care only that everything in the church proceed in an orderly way. For that reason, when a superintendent is to be elected for an area a synod is called together, to which other superintendents from neighboring areas are called, so that everything is attended to and executed by them, and so that they might together consent in the election of the new superintendent.[77]

A number of principles emerge here. First, scripture was the norm for present practice. When a specific basis for action could not be found in scripture, evidence from early Christian writers provided sufficient warrant for ecclesiastical procedures. In other words there was a self-conscious desire not to continue certain aspects of medieval Catholic tradition. Second, election of a person to an office had to be done by the gathered community as represented by an official, public synod. Third, those already in office had a special role to play in the process of adding someone to their number.

The procedures outlined for the calling and leading of the synod clarified a few additional points.[78] The new superintendent was to be selected from among those already ordained in the presbyterate (that is, elders or preachers), either from among those present or a candidate from outside the district in question, although still within the territory: *aus einem andern zirk dieses fürstentumbs*. When a candidate was chosen the lesson, I Timothy 3:1-7 was read. One of the superintendents offered a brief sermon outlining what was expected of someone in this office. All then knelt and sang, "Come Holy Spirit," after which the superintendents present joined in prayer.[79] The description of the Synod continued with additional legislative matters, finally ending with a benediction.

After this process of election was completed the ordination could occur. Insofar as titles indicate theological intent the office of superintendent was considered an "order" even though those elected to it were already ordained presbyters. The Church Order headed its description with the words, *Von der ordination des superintendenten*. The prince was to publish written approval of the newly elected person and provide written notice to all pastors in the area (*zirk*) he was to serve. On the Sunday preceding the day designated for the ordination the location of the celebration was to be announced after the sermon and prayer in the morning liturgy of all churches. All were encouraged to fast and pray for the event.

On the day of the ordination all gathered. The liturgy was presumably the normal service of the day. It was not stated specifically that it was a eucharistic celebration.[80] The prince's decree approving the candidate was read from in front of the altar and one of the superintendents announced the ordination according to the will of the prince (equivalent to the presentation of the candidate). One of the superintendents or pastors present then read the lessons: Matthew 28:18-20 and I Timothy 3:1-7. This was followed by an extended exhortation on the responsibilities of a superintendent with regard to doctrine, the sacraments, obedience, the selection of teachers and pastors (the task of examining and ordaining them), visitation, calling synods,

Emerging Consensus 173

and education.[81]

The exhortation concluded with the request for the candidate's promise to fulfill the obligations:

> These are the responsibilities, dear brother in Christ Jesus, which belong to the office of superintendent according to the word of God and the clear witness of the apostles as recorded in scripture (I Tim. 3:1-7). So we ask you now in the sight of God, our Lord Jesus Christ and his heavenly host, and before this gathering whether you solemnly vow and promise to keep these obligations with all possible diligence.[82]

The candidate then answered with an extended affirmation of the responsibilities to be undertaken.[83]

One of the superintendents, presumably the one who had been leading the rite thus far, in turn exhorted the gathered community to live up to its responsibilities. All then knelt for prayer, the prayer being the concluding Collect from the 1539 Cassel Order.[84] The two superintendents flanking the candidate then stood, while the congregation remained kneeling along with the candidate, and laid hands on the candidate as the following prayer was spoken:

> O Lord God, heavenly Father, you alone create and send able servants of the church and empower them. We humbly ask you that you would enlighten the heart of this your servant with the Holy Spirit. Likewise guide and direct him with your mighty hand, so that that he may faithfully carry out his office to the honor of your name and to the edification of all faithful people in the church of your Son; through the same Jesus Christ, our Lord. Amen.[85]

Again the focus of the prayer was an invocation of the Holy Spirit for the work of the office of ministry. The request was for the sake of the office, although the person in it was obviously the specific object of the prayer's intention.

The congregation and newly ordained superintendent then stood. The newly ordained turned to face the congregation and the presider said the commendation:

> And so we commend you now, beloved brother, that you would faithfully nurture, govern, lead and preserve from harm this congregation of the Lord,

> redeemed with the blood of Christ, which has been entrusted to you by the Holy Spirit. At all times set the believers an example in speech and conduct, in love, in spirit, in faith and purity. Be constant in reading of scripture, in preaching, in teaching. Do not neglect the gift you have, which was given you by prophetic utterance when the elders laid their hands upon you. Practice these things, so that all may see your progress. Take heed to yourself and your teaching; hold to that, for by so doing you will save both yourself and your hearers (I Timothy 4:12–16).[86]

This commendation, like the prayer, rooted its focus in the moral conduct of pastors, here specifically in the scriptural command to be an example of righteousness. Ethical conduct was a recurring theme within these rites because it voiced a basic Reformation concern to improve the respectability and status of pastors. Thus the issue of status, although not tied to the theological issue of the grace of justification, was not abandoned by the reformers. "False teachers" (especially Anabaptists and Enthusiasts) were evidently a source of trouble in many areas. Without clergy whose lifestyle and ability to teach were above reproach the Reformation cause was jeopardized.

The reformers were aware, however, that pastors did not stand alone in the task. Thus the members of the congregation were also addressed with an exhortation concerning their responsibilities:

> We commend to you all this ordained superintendent, and admonish you, as much as we can, that by God's will you would accept and keep him as the true and faithful shepherd of your souls; that you would honor, love and esteem him for the sake of his work and his effort, be at peace with him, follow and be faithful to him, regardless of the class or order to which you may belong, be it sacred or secular; at all times remember that he must keep watch over your souls, and must give account for them, so that he may do this joyfully, and not sadly, for that is of no advantage to you (Heb. 13:17). (The superintendent may further add anything fitting and appropriate).[87]

The issue of status, or at least respect, emerged in this commendation in the form of class recognition. All were to submit to the authority of the superintendent; none could claim to be above it. Yet again the focus was on the office, "for the sake of his work," rather than on the person. That the ordaining superintendent could make additional comments if the situation called for it indicated the flexibility which existed in the rite at

Emerging Consensus 175

this point. Fixed formulas were not essential for the integrity of the action to be maintained.

To conclude the rite the whole community joined in the singing of Psalm 19. The Order continued with a section describing the necessity for proper record keeping (listing all information about the one ordained in the *Kirchenbuch*). One can outline the structure of the rite as follows:

> Reading the Prince's Approval of Candidate
> Presentation of the Candidate
> Readings:
> > Matthew 28: 18-20
> > I Timothy 3: 1-7
> Admonition to the Candidate
> Question and Reply
> Prayer
> Laying on of Hands and Prayer
> Commendation to the Candidate
> Commendation to Community
> Psalm 19
> Benediction

The process describing the "Election and ordination of the pastor or elder" followed that for superintendents.[88] Some confusion existed concerning the ordering of ministry. It was noted earlier that developments in Hesse were influenced by Bucer's interpretation of the New Testament evidence for a four-fold office. The framers of the 1566 Order were aware that this understanding was not universal in the Reformation movement:

> So that a contemporary person might understand the office of elder and judge accordingly, one must know above all that the name presbyter or elder is a common name which may comprise all of those who are in church office with the exception of the deacon. When seen correctly, therefore, one may divide all servants of the church after the superintendent into either presbyters or deacons. Presbyters are those who teach God's word, distribute the sacrament, and determine what is necessary for the maintenance of discipline and good church order. Deacons, on the other hand, manage the property of the church and distribute it. Spiritual property, called by the apostle the mysteries of God (I Cor. 4:1) is dispensed and distributed by the presbyters. Corporal or temporal things such as the church may have are distributed by the deacon.[89]

Even with such a clarification the text stated explicitly that the form and manner in which they were elected was not consistent.[90] The process for examination and election was then described in detail. The description of the rite followed.

The Order stated that ordinations for Hesse were to occur in Marburg. Candidates were to present themselves there on the day following their examination and approval. It was not indicated that this was a Sunday. The community gathered and a superintendent announced that the ordinand had been properly called, elected, presented, examined and approved for the preaching office (*predigampt*). Reading of scripture followed: Matthew 28:18-20; Titus 1:5-9; II Timothy 3:14-4:5. The readings were a departure from Luther's rite which had I Timothy 3:1-7 and Acts 20:28-31. The ordinands were then led to the altar and exhorted concerning the responsibilities of office.[91]

The structure and content of the exhortation paralleled that for the superintendent described above, except that it was less full and eliminated those responsibilities peculiar to the office of bishop such as calling synods, examining pastors, and ordaining. At its conclusion the candidates were asked:

> Is it the desire of each of you, before the face of God and our Lord Jesus Christ and his chosen angels (I Tim. 5:21) and this congregation to promise to keep this constantly and faithfully?[92]

The ordinands answered with a promise which followed immediately on the question quoted above:

> Then the ordinands answer individually: that they recognize this is a difficult office which they wish to undertake, but because they have been called to this and rely entirely on the prayers of the whole church and the gracious help of a generous God, they promise to do all that is in their power.[93]

Although the promise focused on the ecclesial dimensions of the office it required no pledge of obedience. The focus was on the fact of being called, needing the help of the congregation and of course the grace of God to carry out the tasks of ministry. Implicit here was the abiding concern of reformers to inhibit any sense of personal aggrandisement in

Emerging Consensus 177

the ordinand. Ordination was always to servanthood, not to a position of rank or status.

As in the rite for ordaining superintendents, a word of admonition was then directed to the gathered community. It concluded with the same Collect.[94] The laying on of hands followed. The superintendents present along with all other servants of the Word and elders (that is, ordained presbyters) joined in this action as the ordinands knelt. An ordination prayer accompanied the gesture:

> O Lord God, heavenly Father, you alone make able workers of the church and you alone give power and strength; we ask you from our hearts...etc. (see the prayer for ordaining superintendents).[95]

The same prayer being used for both superintendents and pastors again indicated a desire to level hierarchical distinction in terms of the power of the office, even though distinctions in responsibility and authority were still apparent.

The ordinands then stood before the presiding superintendent as he addressed them with the commendation:

> Now I commend to all of you and to each of you the Church. You are set over it as shepherds and teachers, so that you may faithfully and energetically direct, lead and keep God's flock, purchased by Christ with his own blood, commended and placed before you by the Holy Spirit (Acts 20:28). Each one of you attend, that you are examples to the faithful in word, in behavior, in spirit, in faith and in purity (I Tim. 4:12), as you have already been admonished.[96]

The key words for the newly ordained were shepherd and teacher. The primary task of the office of ministry was to proclaim the Gospel through word and deed. Aptness to teach and uprightness of life were considered essential to this task, even more so in light of the sad state of the clergy. Sloth, indifference and incompetence were not to be tolerated. Only later, of course, did doctrinal standards (the Lutheran Confessions) become a means by which the "purity in teaching" was assured.

The community was then admonished concerning the office, its scriptural warrant, and its purpose. The whole community sang Psalm 19 (or some other song, *oder sont ein christlichen geseng*), after which the presiding superintendent pronounced the benediction.

A structural comparison of this rite with that for ordaining superintendents reveals their similarity:

Superintendent	Preacher
Reading of Prince's Approval	
Presentation	Presentation
Readings:	Readings:
Matthew 28: 18-20	Matthew 28:18-20
I Timothy 3: 1-7	Titus 1:5-9
	II Timothy 3:14-4:5
Admonition to Candidate	Admonition to Candidate
Question and Reply	Question and Reply
Prayer	Prayer
Laying on of Hands	Laying on of Hands
Prayer	Prayer
Commendation (Cand.)	Commendation (Cand.)
Commendation (Cong.)	Commendation (Cong.)
Psalm 19	Psalm 19
Benediction	Benediction

The rites were identical with the exception of minor variations in content appropriate to the description of the respective responsibilities of each office.

Immediately after the reminder about recording the pertinent details of the ordination in the *Kirchenbuch,* the Order continued with a description of the installation service for the newly ordained. A separate rite was made necessary by the centralization of ordination at Marburg. A preacher still had to be officially, liturgically placed in office in the specific congregation that had called him. The Order explained that the superintendent, presumably of the district in which the calling congregation was located, gathered with the newly ordained, neighboring pastors and the congregation. Before the sermon the superintendent announced to the congregation that he had a written order (*befelch*) concerning their future pastor. The appointed texts for the day were then read after which two texts "about the office of preacher" (*von ampt eines predigers*) were also read, Titus 1:5-9 and I Thessalonians 5:12f.

The presiding superintendent was to preach a two-part sermon, the first part on the appointed texts for the day, the second on the special texts in which he was to discuss the office of pastor and what God expected of the congregation. The presider and new pastor then proceeded to the altar ("to the place where the Lord's Supper is held"). The new preacher/pastor was commended to the congregation and reminded again to carry out the responsibilities of his office energetically. The new pastor responded with a promise to do so with God's help (*er wöl alles mit Gottes hulf tun*). The superintendent then admonished all (*den eltesten, diacon und der ganzen gemein*) to work together.

It should be noted that the installation described here had no structural correlation with the rite for ordination. There was no central act of laying on hands and prayer, no participation by others already ordained. The superintendent of the area in which the congregation was located simply introduced the new pastor and publicly reminded all present of the mutual responsibility to be undertaken.

The ordination of elders was correlative to the ordination of preachers/pastors in some ways.[97] They were to be chosen from within the congregation, the form and manner of their election based on Acts 14:23. A person for this office did not need to be as well educated as a person for the preaching office, although he was to lead a good, upright life. How many elders a congregation should have was not clearly stated in scripture and so was an open question depending on the size and needs of the congregation. Once elected the person had to be examined before all the other ministers of the congregation on a specified day.

Elders were to be ordained like deacons, even though the offices were different, that is with prayer and laying on of hands (based on Acts 6:1–6). The ordination could be done by either the superintendent or the pastor in concert with one or two other ministers.[98] No information concerning the day or time for the ordination was given. The ordinator, usually the pastor of the congregation rather than the superintendent, first gave a short address (*Vorrede*) in which he discussed the nature of the office based on the text Acts 20:28–31. He then gave an extended exhortation outlining the responsibilities of the office (diligence, true and faithful teaching, striving for unity, enforcing the Bann, etc.). The exhortation concluded with the question to the candidate:

> For that reason I desire to know from you now, before God and our Lord Jesus Christ and all of the exalted angels, and the congregation here gathered, if you wish to diligently carry out and maintain these things.[99]

The ordinands were then to answer in turn with the extended promise used for the ordination of a preacher.[100] The ordinator invited all to kneel and pray:

> Almighty, eternal God, heavenly Father, your beloved Son promised to remain with us always, to the close of the age (Mt. 28:20). In the same way he left humanity many kinds of gifts, among which were your help, counsel and power to ordain and preserve the Church. We humbly pray that you would grace, teach and sanctify the heart of these your servants with the Holy Spirit, that they, filled with wisdom and salutary counsel, may faithfully and constantly govern your Church and its pastors and elders. Allow the spiritual fruits to be full and overflowing to all the faithful, through the same your Son, Jesus Christ, our Lord, etc.[101]

The prayer, as might be expected, asked for the gift of the Spirit, but with much less clarity about the nature of the office itself. Governance was the only task mentioned specifically for the elder. Otherwise the prayer, as a general invocation of the Spirit for the blessing of spiritual fruit, had no special character to identify its applicability to the office of elder.

The ordinator and all other ordained ministers present then laid their hands on the candidate as the same formula used for the ordination of a pastor/preacher was spoken. The newly ordained elders then stood in the midst of the community as a commendation was addressed to them:

> Thus we commend to you this church in which you have been chosen as elder. Govern and keep salutary this flock of the Lord, which he has redeemed with his blood. That you may carry out all these things, be watchful of everything pertaining to them, be helpful to the servants of the Word in all things. When they advise, behave wisely and in an upright way. In your admonitions, be moral, in your punishment, remember love. When you judge or condemn, cast off all human affectation. In every matter which comes before you deal according to the rule of God's word. There should be nothing weightier than the

Emerging Consensus 181

honor of God and the education of the faithful. Finally, you should behave in all things as if you were not only before humans, but as if you would have to give account before God's judgment seat.[102]

The community was then addressed and reminded to show goodwill toward the elders in all they did. All joined in singing Psalm 23, followed by the benediction. Again, the names of those ordained were recorded in the *Kirchenbuch*.

One can now add a third column to the structural comparison of the rites for ordaining:

Superintendent	Preacher	Elder
Reading of Approval		
Presentation	Presentation	Introduction
Readings:	Readings:	Readings:
Matthew 28: 18–20	Matthew 28:18–20	Acts 20:28–31
I Timothy 3: 1–7	Titus 1:5–9	
	II Timothy 3:14–4:5	
Admonition to Candidate	Admonition to Candidate	Admonition to Candidate
Question and Reply	Question and Reply	Question and Reply
Prayer	Prayer	Prayer
Laying on of Hands	Laying on of Hands	Laying on of Hands
Prayer	Prayer	Prayer
Commendation (Cand.)	Commendation (Cand.)	Commendation (Cand.)
Commendation (Cong.)	Commendation (Cong.)	Commendation (Cong.)
Psalm 19	Psalm 19	Psalm 23
Benediction	Benediction	Benediction

Again one can see the structural correlation, a correlation reinforced by the use of identical formulas at certain points in the rite. This correlation manifested an underlying theological premise: these offices shared somehow in a common foundation. Or, to use more traditional language, they represented one order of leadership within the church and not a hierarchical division according to status.

When one turns to the section on deacons (*Von der erwelung und ordination der diacon*), the usual citation of scriptural foundations for the office appears first, in this case Acts 6:1–6.[103] That text, according to the Church Order, defined deacons as those who were entrusted with the care (*sorg*) and attention (*aufsehen*) of church property so that both other ordained ministers and the poor of the congregation were properly cared for. Pious and reputable men (*fromme, aufrichtige menner*) were to be chosen on the basis of the recommendations of the pastor, or all the elders, some from the council (*Rat*) or with permission some from the congregation. The number to be chosen again depended on the needs of the place. The biblical mention of seven people was not considered prescriptive. Those chosen had to serve a period of probation in order to prove their suitability.

No description of a rite was provided in spite of the fact that the title of the section indicated that deacons were to be ordained. It was simply stated that when those elected had completed their period of probation and were ready to be ordained they were to be admonished concerning the duties of their office. An "address" similar in structure to that in the ordination of superintendents, preachers/pastors, and elders was provided. In the former rites this address/exhortation occurred just prior to the prayer and laying on of hands. It ended with the question to the candidates concerning their willingness to undertake the office just described. That was also the case here. The exhortation concluded with the words:

> These are the foremost offices of the deacon in God's church, according to the Holy Scripture. For that reason I wish to know from you, before God and his holy angels, that you answer and affirm to keep all of this faithfully.[104]

But unlike the other rites the description ended here. What the reply was to be was not stated (assuming perhaps a simple "yes" rather than a more extended affirmation as appeared in the preceding rites). This first section of the four-part 1566 Church Order concluded with a description of how ministers were to be removed from office, and under what circumstances.

The 1569 Rites of Wolfenbüttel

It was not until the 1568 visitation in Wolfenbüttel conducted by

Martin Chemnitz, superintendent for the city of Braunschweig, and Jacob Andreae, provost and chancellor of the University of Tübingen, that the Reformation took hold there. The 1543 work discussed above was negated by the return to Catholicism in 1547 under Heinrich, who ruled until his death in 1568.[105] As a result of the visitation Chemnitz and Andreae put together the 1569 Church Order. The model for its *agenda* section was the Lüneburg Order of 1564, and for its legislative section the Württemberg Order of 1559.

A pattern that repeated itself throughout Germany, a pattern already noted in the analysis of the Württemberg rites above, was the borrowing of Luther's 1539 rite for ordinations and the use of a local or other borrowed rite for installations. That is the pattern adopted here. The ordination rite was introduced with the words, *"Folget die form der ordination, durch D. Martinum Luther gestellet."*[106] And indeed Luther's rite was then printed in its entirety. The introductory comments simply noted that a superintendent was to perform the ordination. Immediately following the ordination rite the Church Order included a rite for installation entitled *"Auf welche weiss ein neuer kirchendiener von den superintendenten seiner kirchen commendirt, eingeleibt und installirt werden soll."*[107] The rite was to be used for installing either a pastor or a deacon. The content was that of the 1547/1559 Württemberg Order's rite for installation, with some additions.

As has been evident in all the preceding Reformation approaches to the act of ordaining or installing discussed earlier, the first words of this installation rite indicated that the community was to gather. The liturgy was apparently understood to be an independent act, not occurring within the context of some other service. The congregation was to begin the rite with the singing of *"Nun bitten wir den heiligen Geist."* The superintendent (or an adjunct, presumably appointed to take his place) was then to preach a sermon which addressed both candidate and congregation concerning their mutual responsibility. The congregation then sang the creed as the superintendent and pastor or deacon being installed went to the altar.

With the pastor or deacon kneeling before him, the superintendent then directed a brief admonition to the congregation reminding them of their call of this minister and of their task to pray for him. This was followed by a presidential prayer ("Almighty God, heavenly Father, you have instituted the worthy office of preaching. . ."). Three readings were then done: John 20:28-31; I Timothy 3:1-7 and Acts 20:28-31 (the Württemberg rite had only the first two of these). One of two prayers was then to be said, the second was the ordination prayer of Luther's rite, the first was the one which had followed the readings in the Württemberg rite:

> O merciful God, heavenly Father, you have comforted us in a fatherly way through the Apostle Paul, saying that it pleases you to save us through the scandalous preaching of the cross to those who believe. We ask you earnestly that you would now give your servant, N., called to your office of preaching, your divine grace and Holy Spirit. In the power of this, he will be strengthened against all temptations of the devil. With your healing and unerring word may he feed your flock, dearly purchased with the precious blood of our Lord Jesus Christ, your Son. All of this, to the praise and glory of your Holy Name and the advancing of your kingdom; through Jesus Christ your dear Son. Amen.[108]

As has been demonstrated in preceding discussion of similar texts, the focus of the prayer was on the gift of the Spirit for the person to have strength to fulfill the tasks of ministry, especially preaching and teaching.

Given the fact that similar prayers occurred in both the "ordination" and "installation" rites, each asking for the gift of the Spirit, it is not accurate to argue from an external doctrinal perspective that the gift here was a personal possession of grace. One cannot legitimately fix a point of "reception" of the Spirit, or of grace for the office, within the rite itself. Again, it was the whole vocational process, and specifically the ecclesial context for the liturgical facet of it, that constituted the identification of the clergy. Any quantitative understanding of the Spirit would make nonsense of the repetitive nature of these two rites, occurring in such close temporal proximity.

At the conclusion of the prayer, the congregation, or where present a choir, then sang the Our Father. At this point the superintendent was to turn toward the altar, facing away from the congregation, place his right hand on the head of the one being installed and say the exhortation drawn from the Württemberg rite. The rite then ended with the singing of the *Te Deum* or *Grates nunc omnes* and the final blessing of the

Emerging Consensus 185

superintendent.

Significant here was the firm separation of a rite for ordaining and one for installing, along with the fact that Luther's 1539 rite had become the preferred, even standard form for ordination. But the actual content of these two rites makes it difficult to differentiate them. Only the context and prior knowledge of what the specific event was intended to do would reveal that these rites, which looked very much the same, were accomplishing two different things. In both cases a superintendent, the evangelical equivalent of a Catholic bishop, presided at the rite so that who ordained did not necessarily comunicate the distinction.

The liturgical consensus that emerged in these years tended to blur any ritual distinction between ordination and installation. The question is whether that betrayed a theological position which the reformers themselves had not clearly articulated, that 1) without apostolic succession in a narrow sense, which automatically qualified the ritual act of a bishop who was in succession as a once for all time "ordination" into the priestly estate, and 2) with an emphasis on the essential participation of the congregation in confirming those who were called to be its pastors, were ordinations and installations, even if separated in time and place, in fact the same act? A further question is whether subsequent installations, after the first which might simultaneously be called the ordination, were in essence reordinations, since the relationship of specific pastor and specific congregation always demanded reconstituting the promise between them.

The evidence of the preceding chapter on the first decade of transition revealed that the reformers began to make the necessary changes in ecclesiastical life to effect reform only after visitations were underway late in the 1520's, and as it became clear that Catholic bishops were not going to embrace the cause of reform. When princes or electors began to use political and military power to enforce adoption of reform, the initial method of bringing about change in local churches was simply to use those who had already been ordained as priests who were willing, by force or persuasion, to accept evangelical teaching. Basically this meant that the priest had to agree to preach on Reformation teaching and support any action against the existing Catholic hierarchy.

During that period the means for accepting those priests who agreed was to confirm them in their new role, usually by means of approval from whatever political power was behind the reform—such as the local magistrate, the prince, or the elector. Bugenhagen advocated confirmation of the new calling by means of an installation; that is, a public liturgical action. But this confirmation was not defended as an ordination if the person had already been ordained. In the midst of this confirming or installing the reformers continued to press and hope for bishops who would be willing to adopt the reforms. Only after this failed to occur, and after the presentation of the *Augsburg Confession* in 1530 and its eventual rejection, did the reform movement find itself pushed beyond provisional methods for securing an evangelical clergy.

Thus the way by which the Reformation moved into the cause of ordaining was, so to speak, through the back door. Because installations, which were in effect skeletal versions of ordination, had been in use for bringing already ordained Catholic clergy into the Reformation fold, it was quite understandable that they be adopted as the means to ordain when that became necessary. That is undoubtedly why Bugenhagen's 1529 Hamburg rite provided the basic structure for Luther's ordination rite, and it explains the commonality that existed among the Reformation churches when their ordination rites finally emerged.

The consensus that developed in the subsequent decades discussed in this chapter centered on the relationship between these installations and the new evangelical need to ordain in the absence of Catholic structures. What the rites reveal is the struggle to unite theological and juridical expressions of what the rite was accomplishing. Thus one finds the use of the *Vollzugsformel* reemerging to clarify and emphasize that the person ordaining had both the right and authority to do so. The use of similar rites to ordain people as deacons, presbyters, elders and superintendents, particularly in Hesse, also reveals the tension experienced by Reformation churches in whether and how to articulate a distinction among different "orders" in the church's ministry. That issue has never been resolved by churches of the Reformation traditions. What help the liturgical witness might give in leading to some resolution is discussed in the following chapter.

NOTES

1 For example, the *Stipendiatenordnung* 1529 was concerned with scholarships for educating pastors; the *Kastenordnung* 1530 regulated the distribution of goods; the *Kirchendienerordnung* 1531 established the number and jurisdiction of superintendents; the *Kirchenordnung* 1532 described worship. For the texts of these various Orders see Sehling, VIII, 66-100.

2 Sehling, VIII, 15.

3 See the *Kirchendienerordnung* 1531; Sehling, VIII, 71-74.

4 See, for example, the descriptions of the 1531 Order, Sehling, VIII, 71-72; or the 1537 Order, Sehling, VIII, 92ff.

5 Sehling, VIII, 95: "Wo ein pfarr mit einem predicanten zu bestellen, sal kein superintendens fur sich selbs allein macht haben, einichen pfarhern dahin zu setzen on der andern superintendenten verwilligung, sonder sollen sich die superintendenten einhelliglich miteinander...."

6 See the description of this process in the *Kirchendienerordnung* 1537, section 3 (Sehling, VIII, 93).

7 Ibid., 20.

8 The *Kirchenordnung* 1532, ibid., 75-79, described worship life in Hesse but contained no liturgical texts.

9 A paraphrase of instructions in the *Kirchendienerordnung* 1537 included under the title "On the Call and Displacement of Pastors" reveals the kind of concerns being treated at this point. KO 1537, section 6 (Sehling, VIII, 95-97): "Superintendents do not have the power to install pastors according to their own wishes. They must have the permission of other superintendents...when a person is found to be pastor his name and a letter of commendation will be sent to the prince, and upon the prince's approval the candidate will be decided on at the next synod. When he is approved at the synod he shall acknowledge his faith and doctrine in writing and promise not to introduce new things without the knowledge and consent of the synod, upon penalty of loss of parish. He shall be installed [*bevolen und commendirt*] by two neighboring pastors with appropriate sermon, prayer and dignified reverence as a pious, learned and faithful servant of God. If he is found wanting by the synod, he shall be commended to further study and examination. ...It is the will of the prince that no governor (or other

bureaucrat) may dismiss a pastor, chaplain, teacher, treasurer or similar church worker at will, but must allow that authority to remain with the superintendent."

10 See A. Ockeley, *Die Kirchenordnungen von Ziegenhain und Kassel 1539* (Marburg, 1939).

11 For a discussion of the editions of the Cassel Order see Jahr's comments (Sehling, VIII, 21).

12 Sehling, VIII, 21.

13 G. J. Van de Poll, *Martin Bucer's Liturgical Ideas* (Assen: Van Gorcum and Company, 1954), 130. Van de Poll explained in a note on this relationship: "As early as 1529 the Landgrave [Philip] had started a correspondence with Bucer; both worked together to bridge the differences between Lutherans and the Swiss party..." (130, note 6).

14 W. Sohm, *Territorium und Reformation in der hessischen Geschichte 1526-1555* in *Veröffentlichungen der Historischen Kommission für Hessen und Waldeck*, 11, 1 (1915), 162ff.; as cited in Sehling, VIII, 102, note 7.

15 R. Stupperich, *Bibliographia Bucerana*, in *Schriften des Vereins für Reformationsgeschichte*, No. 43; as cited in Sehling, VIII, 103.

16 See, for example, J. Courvoisier, *La notion d'eglise chez Bucer*, 1933; especially 37ff., and 97ff.

17 Sehling, VIII, 189: "Welche ämpter Gott im neuwen testament in der kirchen angerichtet. (1) Die ersten werden genennt episcopi, welche...auf lateinisch recht und wol superintendentes, das ist aufseher (Actor.20,28; I Tim. 3,1) nach unserem teutschen können genennt werden. (2) Die andern werden genennt presbyteri oder seniores, welcher zweierlei die schrift anzeigt. Etliche arbeiten im wort oder lehre und austeilung derer heiligen sacrament, welche man sonst hirten und doctores, das ist lehrer, nennen mag (1.Cor. 12,28; Ephes. 4,11). Denen andern aber stehet zu fleissiges aufsähens, dass alles, so die regierung der kirchen belangt, treulich versähen werde (Actor.14,23; 15,4; 21,18). (3) Die dritten sind die diacon. Durch diese wird aller dienst in der gemeine Gottes und so viel müglich nach dem befehl Christi und derer heiligen aposteln bei uns verhandelt (Tit.1,5; Actor.6:1-6; 7:54-59; 1.Timot.3,12)."

18 Ibid., 102ff.

19 Bucer taught that the three sacramental ceremonies were the laying on of hands in confirmation, the blessing of marriage, and the laying on of hands in the installation of

Emerging Consensus 189

ministers. See Sehling, VIII, 124, note 33.

20 Sehling, VIII, 127: "Die dritte sacramentlich ceremonien ist zu brauchen an denen, die zum kirchendienst erstlich verordent werden. Dieselbigen sollte man, wann sie nun genungsam nach rechtmessigem beruff verhöret und beweret sein, in der kirchen fürstellen und ihnen vermöge ihres ampts aus dem heiligen Paulo mit ernst fürhalten und erkleren, darauf ihre zusage nemen, demselbigen vermittelst göttlicher hülf getreulich nachzukommen, und demnach die kirche für sie bitten lassen und alsdann sollich gebet mit einer collecten summiren und ihnen also die hende auflegen, sie damit götlichs geistes und hülf im namen des Herren zu vertrösten und sie in ihr ampt einzusetzen." No further explanation is given concerning the liturgical context for this "sacramental ceremony." The content of the prayer, specifically the closing collect noted, is provided in the Erfurt edition of the Cassel Order. See below for the translation, and note 22 for the German text.

21 The later 1566 Church Order of Hesse cited Augustine's definition (*Accedat verbum ad elementum et fit sacramentum*) and Luther's explanations of what constituted a sacrament. There was no "element" to which the Word could come in these sacramental ceremonies. Thus the 1566 Order stated concerning the laying on of hands (Sehling, VIII, 290): "Therefore we do not use the laying on of hands as a sacrament of the New Testament, but rather as a very ancient ceremony from the fathers and servants of the church, used before and after Christ, when they wanted to indicate that one person among other Christians shared the gifts of the Holy Spirit...What is the laying on of hands...other than a prayer over a person? (Derhalb gebrauchen wir uns nit der uflegung der hende als eines sacraments des neuen testaments, sonder als einer sehr alten ceremonien von den vättern und kirchendienern, beide von und nach Christo gewonlich gebraucht, wann sie begerten, dass einem in sonderheit vor andern christlichen gaben des hei. Geists mitgeteilet würden. ...Was ist die uflegung der hende anders...dann ein gebet uber den menschen?)."

22 Sehling, VIII, 127: "Almechtiger gütiger Gott, himlischer vater, als dein lieber Son, unser Herre Jhesus zu deiner gerechten in das himlisch wesen erhöbet, hat er alsbald angefangen, uns hie uf erden zu geben aposteln, evangelisten, propheten, hirten und lerer, seine erweleten damit in ihm zu versameln und zu erbauen und den seinen durch seine liebe aposteln bevohlen, bei allen seinen gemeinden zu welen und setzen, die sein heilig evang. und sacrament getreulich ausspenden und alle seesorg und hirtendienst versehen und verrichten. Wir bitten dich durch denselben unsern erzhirten und bischoff unserer seele, deinen lieben Sohn, du wollest diese, die von deiner gemein zu solchem dienst erwelet sein, deinen heiligen geist reichlich mitteilen, der sie allzeit erleucht, für und sterk, damit sie diesen deinen so hohen und heiligen dienst mit rechtem verstand und eifer allezeit fruchtbarlich verrichten, suchen, finden und brengen zu deinem lieben Son all, die nach von ihm entfrembdet oder wider von ihm abgefüret seind, erbauen und bessern alle, die zu ihm gebracht und in seiner gemein noch halten. Hiezu beware sie

vor allen eigen felen und ergernusse, vor allem falschen verleumbde und verkleinerung, auch vor alle gewaltigen hindernusse ihres dienstes, uf dass sie dir und deiner lieben kirchen in allem lustig, bestendig, geflissen und seliglich dienen, damit dein nam immer mehr geheiliget und dein reich allenthalben erweitert und herrlicher werd, durch denselbigen deinen lieben Son unsern Herrn Jhesum Christum, Amen."

23 Schulz, *Evangelische Ordination*, 43. Schulz also noted that the point of the prayer was the equipping and building up of the congregation through various ministries. The biblical passage to which it was linked was Ephesians 4:8, 10-11. Along with the ministry of preaching and sacraments, care of souls and pastoring were specifically mentioned. This was all in accord with Bucer's conceptions of office. The prayer used here can in fact be found in a Latin version of Bucer's *De ordinatione legitimae*, 258f.

24 Sehling, VIII, 127: "Nim hin die hand und hülf Gottes, den heiligen Geist, der dich lehr, für und sterk, deinen dienst fruchtbar zu verrichten durch undern Herren Jhesum Christum, Amen." Compare the formula used at the laying on of hands in the rite of Confirmation: "Nimm hin den heiligen geist, schutz und schirm vor allem argen, sterk und hülf zu allem gutem, von der gnedigen hand Gottes des Vater, Sohns und heiligen Geistes, Amen" (Sehling, VIII, 126).

25 The definitive study is that of Peter Brunner, *Nikolaus von Amsdorf als Bischof von Naumburg* (Gütersloh: Verlaghaus Gerd Mohn, 1961).

26 The sources are listed by Brunner, 159. For information on the ordination the following are especially pertinent: "Berich über die Wahl und Einführung des Nicolaus von Amsdorf als Bischof zu Naumburg." In: *Neue Mitteilungen aus dem Gebiet historisch-antiquarischer Forschungen*. Bd. 2 (Halle, 1836), 155-228; Sixtus Braun, *Naumburger Annalen vom Jahre 779-1613* (Naumburg, 1927); Georg Spalatin, *Annales Reformationis oder Jahr-Bücher von der Reformation Lutheri* (Leipzig, 1718). Luther's analysis, *Exempel, einen rechten christlichen Bischof zu weihen*, is in WA 53, 231-260.

27 The following summary is based entirely on Brunner's investigation, along with Buchwald's edition of notes on Luther's sermon in WA 49, xxvi-xxix, and Luther's "Exempel" cited in note 26..

28 On this composition see Hans J. Moser, WA 35, 535-538, and O. Clemen, WA Br 5, no. 1727, 635-640. This performance at the Naumburg ordination is the first known for this work (as noted by Brunner, 61).

29 According to Strodach and Leupold in LW 53, 37, note 67, this song was "a pre-Reformation Christmas hymn to the melody 'Dies est laetitiae.'" See Julian, *Dictionary of Hymnology*, 325. For the text and melody of this hymn, see Wilhelm Bäumker, *Das katholische deutsche Kirchenlied*, I (Freiburg: Herder, 1886), 286-289.

30 WA 49, xxvi–xxix: "Darauff hatt der her D. Martinus Luther fur dem Altar stehend eine sehr gewaltige undt trostliche predigt gethan aus dem 20 Capittell der Apostell geschichte (xxvii, 1–3)...Aus diesem Text hatt D. Luther angezogen Erstlichen die grosse beschwerung eius Bischoffes (xxvii, 7–8)...Hatt also D. Luter hier mit seine Prediget, die ungeferlich eine gutt halbe stunden gwehert, beschlosen, undt vor dem Altar also stehen blieben (xxix, 4–5)."

31 Brunner, 63; cf. WA 53, 257, 16–19.

32 Brunner, 64.

33 Cited by Brunner, 64: "...aller Seelen des ganzen Stifts und Bistums Naumburg treulich und wohl pflegen wollte, ihnen mit Versorgung der reinen Lehr des heiligen Evangelii und der hochwürdigen Sakrament nach Einsetzung Christi des Herrn, desgleichen auch mit Versehung aller anderen der Kirche Notdurftigkeit wohl vorstehen und versorgen woltte." Brunner noted that "chapter" and "diocese" were tautologous. Chapter probably referred to the area in which the Naumburg bishop had secular authority, diocese referring to the whole of the bishopric (ibid., 64, note 54).

34 Brunner, 64.

35 For the 1537 text see WA Tr 5, no. 5376, 112, 12–14; for 1539 see WA 38, 431, 21–23; and for 1542 see the sources cited by Brunner, note 36.

36 Brunner, 65. Brunner cited a letter which Luther had written to von Amsdorf soon after the ordination on February 3, 1542 (WA Br 9, no. 3709, 609, 12): "Ceterum debes meminisse, quod tibi manum imponens dixi: 'Expecta Dominum, viriliter age et confortetur cor tuum' (But you ought to remember what I said to you at the laying on of hands: 'Wait for the Lord, be strong, and let your heart take courage')." Brunner clarified: "...that the blessing was spoken after the laying on of hands is made clear by the Naumburg report where it is immediately after the mention of laying on of hands with the accompanying prayer: "And [Dr. Martinus] after that admonished the bishop that he be faithful and courageous in his office" (NM 2, 184). This "exhortation" consisted of the words of the psalm as the quoted letter demonstrated" (Brunner, 66, note 58).

37 PGD, ch. xiv, n. 62 (Andrieu, *Pontifical* III, 391): "Tunc consecrator stans ante cathedram incipit excelsa voce hymnun *Te Deum laudamus* (Then the consecrator standing before the throne begins the hymn *Te Deum laudamus* with voice uplifted)."

38 Brunner, 67.

39 Ibid., 69.

40 WA 53, 231-260.

41 WA 53, 256, 18-20; 257, 13-15: "…ich…besser weis einen Christlichen Bischoff zu Weihen, weder der Bapst sampt alle den seinen….Denn bey solcher Weihe ist gewest und hat die Hende auff gelegt Nicht allein Ich, Sondern auch diese folgende Bischove…."

42 WA 53, 256, 10-13: "Obs auch zu verantworten sey, das sich der Bischoff zur Neumburg solche Feindselige Ketzer und der Bepstlichen Kirchen Apostatos hat lassen Weyhen oder die Hende aufflegen." Cf. the comments in the Smalcald Articles, cited above, Chapter 2, p. 70.

43 WA 53, 231, 1-8: "Wir armen ketzer haben abermal eine grosse sünde auffs neu begangen wider die hellische unchristliche Kirche des aller hellischten Vaters des Bapsts, das wir einen Bischoff im Stifft Neumburg Ordinirt und Eingeweihet haben on allen Cresem, auch on butter, schmaltz, speck, ther, schmer, weirauch, kolen, und was der selben grossen heligkeit mehr ist, dazu wider iren willen, doch nicht on ir wissen."

44 WA Br 10, no. 3728, 23: "Nova te miror non audisse, scilicet D. Nicolaum Amsdorffium Episcopum esse Naumburgensis Ecclesiae ordinatum ab Häresiarche Luthero, die S. Fabiani."

45 PGD, ch. xiv (Andrieu, *Pontifical* III, 374): "De examinatione, ordinatione et consecratione episcopi."

46 See WA 53, 257, 1-5.

47 WA 53, 257, 4-11: "Denn es ligt daran, ob die Kirche und der Bischoff eines sind, Und die Kirche den Bischoff hören und der Bischoff die Kirche leren wolle. So ists geschehen. Aufflehunge der Hende, die Segenen, bestettigen und bezeugen solchs, wie ein Notarius und Zeugen eine Weltliche sache bezeugen, Und wie der Pfarrherr, so Braut und Breutgam segenet, ir Ehe bestiget oder bezeuget, das sie zuvor sich genomen haben und offentlich bekand; Es sey nu der Pfarrherr ein Engel oder Teuffel, weil das Ampt geschehen, So ist die Braut gesegenet."

48 Brunner, 72-73.

49 Ibid., 75.

Emerging Consensus 193

50 See Appendix II for a translation of Bugenhagen's rite in the 1529 Hamburg Church Order.

51 For the rite of the 1543 Wolfenbüttel Church Order see Sehling VI/1, 69–71; for the 1544 Hildesheim rite see Sehling VII/2b1, 868–870.

52 Sehling VI/1, 69.

53 For the Latin litany see WA 30, III, 36–40; for Luther's German litany see WA 30, III, 1–28.

54 Sehling VII/2b1, 868.

55 Ibid.

56 Ibid., 869.

57 Martin Brecht, "Herkunft und Ausbildung der protestantischen Geistlichen des Herzogtums Württemberg im 16. Jahrhundert," *Zeitschrift für Kirchengeschichte* 80 (1969), 163–175.

58 Ibid., 165.

59 Schulz, *Evangelische Ordination*, 4.

60 Richter, II, 94–95.

61 Ibid., 94: "Es solle auch des decani offitium sein einem jeden newen Pharrer einzulaiten und der Kürchen desselbigen Ortz zu commendieren, wie man deshalb wol mog Christenliche Ceremonias, Benedictiones et preces zuesamen tragen, welches anstatt der alten papistichen Wyhin und ordination möchte geprucht werden, Namlich wie hernachvolgt, 'Vf nachwolgend weis solle ein newer Pharrer oder Diacon vom Dechan eingeleibt und Installiert werden.'"

62 Ibid.: "Almechtiger Ewiger got himlischer vater, du hast je selbs dem armen menschlichen Geschlecht zu Wolfart Trost und hilff das hochwürdig Predigambt des heiligen Evangelii durch Jesum Christum dein geliebten Sun geordent und eingefetzt, auch dabey zugesagt und versprochen, das welcher glaubt und gestaufft würd, selig sein soll. Dieweile uns aber unsers ver derpten und sündigen fleischs halb beschwerlich und geferlich sein will solchen so teuren und weerden schatz wider den anlauff des tausentlüstigen und grimmigen Vheinds ohne dein sonderliche hilf und gnedigen Beistand in unsern so elenden schwachen und irdischen gefetzlin zu bewaren, So piten Wir dich

hertzlichen, du wellest uns durch dein grundtlos gnad und Barmhertzigkhait inn nöten nit verlassen, sondern mit deiner göttlichen hand ober uns halten und sonderlich ober disen deinen diener, N., welchen jetzund das hailig Euangelion zupredigen bevolhen ist, damit solcher dein so heilsamer, nutzlicher und notwendiger Bevelhe bis zu end der Welt in deiner hailigen Christenhait wider alle gespenst des Bötzwichts sein fürgang hab und Wier des himlischen Trosts nimer beraubt werden durch Jesum Christum dein geliebten Son unsern Hern, welcher mit dir und dem hailgen gaist lebt und regiert gleicher Gott hochgelobt in Ewigkhait. Amen."

63 Ibid., 95: "O merciful God, heavenly Lord and Father: you have comforted us in a fatherly way through the Apostle Paul, saying that it pleases you to save us through the scandalous preaching of the Cross to those who believe. We ask you earnestly for that now, that you would give your servant, N., called to your office of preaching, your divine grace and Holy Spirit. In the power of this, he will be strengthened against all temptations of the Devil. With your healing and unerring Word may he feed your flock, dearly purchased with the blood of our Lord Jesus Christ, your Son. All of this to the praise and glory of your Holy Name and the promotion of your kingdom, through Jesus Christ your dear Son. Amen (Ach gnediger Gott himblischer Herr und Vater, der du uns durch deinen heiligen Apostel Paulum väterlichen getröst und zugesagt hast, das es dier O himlischer Herr und Vater wol gefall durch die töricht Predig des Creutz seelig zu machen alle die so daran glauben, So piten Wir dich nun auf sollichs gantz ernstlich, das du deinen Diener, N., hiezugegen, welchen du zu diesem so seligen und hochwürdigen Predig-Ambt berüffen hast, mit Deiner göttlichen Gnad begaben und deinen hailgen geist geben und mittailen wellest, durch welches krafft er gestergkt wider alle Anfechtung des teufels besteen und dein geliebte Herd durch das blut unsers Herrn Jesu Christi deines sons teur erkaufft und erworben mit deinem heilsamen und ungefälschten Wort nach deinem göttlichen Wolgefallen waiden mög zu Lob und breis deins hailgen Namens und fürderung der ganzen Christenhait durch Jesum Christum deinen geliepten Son. Amen)."

64 Ibid.: "Lieber Brüder, dieweil Wir nun im hailgen gaist versamelt Gott unserm himlischen Vater durch Jesum Christum unsern Herrn und Hailand ober dich angeruffen und gebeten haben und deshalb nit zweifeln er werde uns lut seiner göttlichen Zusagung gnediglihn erhört und gewert haben, Demnach so ordne, confirmier und bestetige ich dich aus bevelch des Almechtigen und unsers gnedigen Landsfürsten und Herrn als der ordentlichen und von Got gegebnen Magistrats zu ainem Diener und seelsorger diser gemein hiezugegen mit ernstlichem bevelch, das du solcher Erlichen und on alle Ergernus mit höchstem vleis und trewen vorsteen wöllest, wie du dann vor dem Gerichtsstül unsers Hern Jesu Christi an jenem Tag Red und Antwurt geben must, dem Rechten Richter im Namen des Vaters und des Sons und des hailgen geists. Amen."

65 Ibid., 94: "Von Ambt eins Dechan und was Ime bewolhen sein wolle. So also dieser decanus erwellt und geordnet solle er anfengklichs dem Superattendenten vor dem

Emerging Consensus 195

gantzen Capitel stipulata manu verhaissen und zusagen, das er in seinem Ambt vlessig und trew sein welle... ."

66 Ibid., 198: "Wie alle Pfarren, Predicaturen, Diaconaten und Subdiaconaten, besetzt werden sollen."

67 Richter, II, 198: "Demnach ordnen, bevelhen und wöllen wir, wa in unsers Fürstenthumbs, auch desselben zu und eingehöriger Schirms verwandter Oberkeit und Gebieten, Stetten, Flecken und Dörffern, von althers eigne gestiffte Pfarren, Predicaturen, Diaconaten und Subdiaconaten, gewesen unnd erhalten worden, Das dieselben fürthin noch also unabgengig bleiben. Derhalben unsere verordnete Räth, zu verrichtung der Kirchediensten, ir fleissigs auffsehens, achtung und Superintendentz haben sollen, damit solche *Ministeria*, so offt die vacieren, es habe gleich *de iure Patronatus* dieselben zuürleihen, wer oder wes Stands der seie, jeder zeit fürderlichen und onverlengt mit Gotsfürchtigen, eifferigen, gelerten und erfarnen Dienern unnd *Ministris*, obgedachter Augspurgischen, und unser Confession, Kirchen, unnd nachgesetzer derselben gleicher fernerer Ordnungen gemess bestelt, und kein unversehen gelassen werden."

68 Ibid., 199.

69 Ibid., 199–202.

70 Ibid., 202.

71 Schulz, 4, noted that the Württemberg rite adopted the readings from I Timothy 3 and Acts 20, along with the ordination prayer from Luther's rite.

72 Ibid., 5.

73 See, for example, Sehling, XV, for an analysis of the development of the Church Orders of Hohenlohe.

74 Sehling VIII, 25. The brief historical comments here are again based on the work of Jahr in her introduction.

75 See the discussion by Jahr, ibid., 26–35.

76 "Das erste Teil: Von denen dienern, welche im kirchenampt vonnöten sein"; Sehling, VIII, 188–212.

77 Ibid., 190; citations from Cyprian, Cassiodor, Theodoret, and Jerome follow.

78 See Sehling, VIII, 191-193 for the discussion of synodical procedures.

79 Ibid., 192. The text of the prayer is given, but since it is not part of the rite for ordination it is not included for analysis here. Jahr noted that it was not from the Hesse tradition and was probably newly formulated. It was not taken up in any of the later Agendas.

80 Ibid., 193: "Wan aber der gottesdienst nach gewonlicher weis verrichtet, ohn das gebet, sollen sie allesampt an dem ort, da man pflegt des Herren abendmal zu halten, sich ordentlich nidersetzen, also dass der ein superintendens zur rechten seiten, der ander zur linken, darnach der neu superintendens, so zu ordinieren ist, sampt den beruffenen pastoribus ihre session nemen (When the worship service has run its course in the usual way, before the prayer, they all together are seated in an orderly way in the place where the Lord's Supper is usually held, one superintendent on the right, the other on the left, and after them the new superintendent to be ordained, together with the called pastors in session)."

81 The exhortation is three pages long; Sehling, VIII, 194-197.

82 Ibid.,197: "Dies seind nun die stuck, geliebter bruder in Christo Jesu, welche gehören zum ampt eines superintendenten nach der lehr Gottes und klaren zeugnis seiner lieben aposteln, wie man in ihren schriften findent (I Tim.3, 1-7). Derhalben begeren wir nun von euch vor dem angesicht Gottes und unsers Herrn Jesu Christi und seiner auserwelten engeln und dieser ganzen versamlung, dass ihr uns angelobet und zusaget, diesem allem, so euch vorgehalten, möglichs fleiss nachzukommen."

83 Ibid.; see section 5.

84 Cited above, pp. 151-152, and note 22.

85 Sehling, VIII, 198: "O Herr Gott, himlischer Vatter, der du allein tuchtige diener der kirchen machest und sendest und ihnen kraft und macht verleihest, wir bitten dich demütiglich, du wöllest das herz dieses deines dieners mit deinem heiligen Geist im namen J. C. erleuchten und ihn mit deiner gewaltigen hand also leiten und füren, damit er sein befolen ampt zu deines namens ehr und auferbauung aller gleubigen in der kirchen deines Sohns treulich verrichten möge durch denselbigen deinen Sohn Christum, unsern Herrn. Amen." Frieder Schulz, *Evangelische Ordination*, noted that "this brief prayer about the gift of the Holy Spirit for the ordinand for the building up of the faithful in the church of Christ has the function of a collect, spoken in connection with the laying on of hands, and is peculiar to the Hessen tradition (44)."

86 Ibid.: "So befalen wir euch nu, lieber bruder, alle kirchen dieses zirks, dass ihr die gemein des Herrn, mit dem blut Christi erlöset und euch nu vom heiligen Geist vertrauet, mit aller treu und grosser sorg weidet, regirt, furet und unverletzt bewaret und stellet euch allenthalben zum vorbild den gleubigen im wort, im wandel, in der liebe, im geist, im glauben, in der keuscheit. Haltet an zu aller zeit mit lesen, mit ermanen, mit leren. Lasst nicht aus der acht die gabe, die euch gegeben ist durch die weissagung mit handauflegung der eltesten. Solchs wartet, damit gehet umb, auf dass euer zunemen in allen dingen offenbar sei. Habt acht auf euch selbst und auf die lehre, beharret in diesen stücken; denn wo ihr solchs tut, werd ihr euch selbst selig machen und die euch hören (1. Tim. 4, 12–16)."

87 Ibid.: "Wir befehlen nun euch allesampt diesen ordinierten superintendenten und vermanen euch, so viel an uns ist, dass ihr nach dem beflech Gottes (1. Thess. 5, 12f.) ihn als den rechten and treuen hirten euer seelen wöllet annemen und halten, ihn ehren, lieb und wert haben unb des werks und seiner mühe willen, und seid friedsam mit ihm und wollet ihm allesampt, wes stands und ordens ein iglicher ist, er sei im kirchenampt oder uber weltliche regiment gesetzt, folgen und gehorchen und euch allezeit erinnern, dass er wachen muss uber euer selen, als der davor rechenschaft geben soll, auf dass er solchs mit freuden tue und nit mit seufzen, dann das ist euch nit gut (Hebr. 13, 17). Und was dergleichen der superintendent vor gut ansehen wird, das zu dieser vermanung will dienlich sein, mag er wieter hinzusetzen."

88 Ibid., 199–209.

89 Ibid., 199: "Auf dass aber ein itzlicher recht verstehen möge das ampt der eltesten und darvon urteilen könne, muss man vor allen dingen wissen, dass der nam presbyteri oder eltesten ein gemeiner nam ist und mag von allen denen, so im kirchenampt sein ausgenommen die diacen, wol verstanden werden; dann so mir recht betrachten, so mag man wol alle diener der kirchen nach dem superintendenten, welchen ich ausneme, in presbyteros und diaconos teilen, also dass diejenigen presbyteri seien, welchen die lehr Gottes wort, die austeilung der h. sacrament und was zu erhaltung der disciplin und guter ordnung dienlich, befohlen wird, diaconi aber, welche die güter der kirchen zu verwalten und auszuteilen haben und kurzlich darvon reden zureden [sic]. Von den presbyteris werden dispensirt und ausgeteilet geistliche güter, oder wie es der apostel [1. K 4,1] nennt, die geheimnis Gottes. Von den diacen aber die leibliche oder zeitliche güter, so der kirchen zustehen."

90 Ibid., 200: "Die form und weise aber, dieselbigen zu erwelen, wird nit in allen kirchen bei uns gleich gehalten." The process for examination and election can be found on 201–203.

91 Ibid., 204: "...soll der superintendens die ordinanden, so auf der seiten des altars stehen, da man pflegt das abendmals zu halten...."

92 Ibid., 205: "Beger derwegen von euch vor dem angesicht Gottes und unsers H. Jesu Christi und seiner auserwelten engeln (1. Tim. 5,21) und dieser ganzen christlichen versamlung, ob ihr auch versprechen wollet, dies also stetig und treulich zu halten."

93 Ibid., p. 205: "Sie erkennen wol, dass ein schwer ampt sei, darin sie sich begeben wollen, dieweil sie aber doch darzu beruffen und sich auf das gebet der ganzen kirchen und die gnedige hülf des gütigen Gottes genzlich verlassen, verheissen sie, alles zu tun, was in ihrem vermögen ist."

94 Namely, "O Almighty gracious God, heavenly Father...", originally from the 1539 Cassel Order. See Appendix III, p. 260, for the translation.

95 Sehling, VIII, 206: "O Herr Gott, himlischer Vatter, der du allein tüchtige diener der kirchen machest und allein kraft und macht gibst, wir bitten dich von herzen, etc." ["etc.," is explained with the words "as was said in the ordaining of the superintendent"]. The prayer from the rite for ordaining superintendents is in Sehling, VIII, 198. See the translation p. 173 above, and original text, note 85.

96 Ibid., 206: "Nun befehle ich euch allen und einem iglichen insonderheit die kirchen, uber welche ihr als hirten und lehrer gesetzt werdet, auf dass ihr die herde Gottes, welche Christus mit seinem teuren blut erworben und euch vom heiligen Geist bevohlen und zugestellet, mit aller treu und grossen fleiss weidet (Act. 20,28), regiret, füret und erhaltet zu der ewigen seligkeit. Und sehe sich ein iglicher wol für, dass er ein vorbild sei den gleubigen im wort, im wandel, in der lieb, im geist, im glauben, in der keuscheit [1. Tim. 4,12], wie ihr zuvor ermanet seit."

97 Ibid., 207–209.

98 Ibid., 208: "...und dies soll entweder der superintendens, was er daselbst visitiret, oder sonst irgents ein pfarherr sampt einem oder zweien dienern des worts verrichten."

99 Ibid., 209: "Derwegen beger ich nun von euch zu wissen vor dem angesicht Gottes und unsers Herrn Jesu Christi und aller auserwelten engeln, sampt der ganzen gemein, hie zugegen, ob ihr solchs alles auch fleissig ausrichten und halten wollet."

100 Ibid., 205: "Sie erkennen...etc." See above, p. 176, and note 93.

101 Ibid., 208: "Almechtiger, ewiger Gott, himlischer Vatter, nachdem dien geliebter Sohn, unser Herr und hoherpriester Jesus Christus verheissen, er wolle allezeit bei uns

bleiben bis an ende der welt [Mt 28,20], und hat gleichwol den menschen mancherlei gaben verlihen, under diesen aber euch hulf, beistand und gewalt, die kirchen recht zu ordiniren und zu erhalten, so bitten wir demütiglich, dass du dieser deiner diener herzen mit deinem h. Geist begnadigest, lerest und heiligest, uf dass sie mit weisheit und heilsamen rat jederzeit gefasst lustig und von herzen diese deine kirch smapt den pfarherrn und eltesten, so im wort arbeiten, treulich und bestendiglich regieren, damit man die geistliche frucht an allen gleubigen volkomlich und uberflüssig spüren möge durch denselben deinen Sohn Christum unsern H. etc."

102 Ibid., 209: "So befehlen wir euch diese kirch, in welcher ihr zu eltesten seid erwelet worden, dass ihr die herde des Herrn, so er mit seinem blut erlöset, und vom heiligen Geist euch vertrauet ist, wol regiret und gesund behaltet, und dass ihr solchs alles verrichten möget, so seid vorsichtig, habt fleissig acht uf alles, was sich zutregt, seid den dienern des worts in allen dingen behüflich. Wan sie ratschlagen, so handelt weislich und ufrichtig, in vermanungen seid sittig, im straffen allezeit ingedechtig der liebe. Wan ihr urteilt oder richtet, so legt alle menschliche affect von euch; alles, was ihr oder andere vorbringet, das handelt nach der regel des göttlichen worts. Es soll euch nichts heftigers angelegen sein, dan Gottes ehr und die erbauung der gleubigen. Endlich solt ihr euch also in allen dingen halten, als die nicht allein vor den menschen, sondern auch vor dem richterstul Gottes jederzeit rechenschaft geben müssen."

103 Ibid., 209-211 for the description of the office of deacon.

104 Ibid., 211: "Dies seint der diacon in der gemein Gottes vornemste empter, welche in der heiligen schrift angezeigt sein. Darumb beger ich nun von euch vor dem angesicht Gottes und seiner h. engeln, dass ihr wollet angeloben und zusagen, solchs alles treulich zu halten."

105 See Sehling VI/1, 3-11 for an historical summary of the Reformation in Wolfenbüttel.

106 Ibid., 188.

107 Ibid., 189.

108 Ibid., 191 (see note 63 above for the German text and translation of the Württemberg original): "Ach gnediger Gott, himlischer Herr und Vater, der du uns durch deinen heiligen apostel Paulum veterlichen getröst und zugesagt hast, das er dir, o himlischer Herr und Vater, wolgefalle, durch die thoricht predigt des kreuzes selig zu machen alle die, so dran glauben [1. K 1,21], so bitten wir dich nun auf solches ganz ernstlich, das du deinen diener N., hie zugegen, welchen du zu diesem so seligen und hochwirdigen predigampt beruffen hast, mit deiner göttlichen gnaden begaben und deinen heiligen Geist geben und mittheilen wöllest, durch welches kraft er gesterket, wieder alle

anfechtung des teufels bestehen und deine geliebte herde, durch das blut unsers Herrn Jhesu Christi, deines Sohns, theur erkauft und erworben, mit deinem heilsamen und ungefelschten wort nach deinem wolgefallen weiden möge zu log und preiss deines heiligen namens und fürderung der ganzen christenheit durch Jhesum Christum, deinen geliebten Son. Amen."

CHAPTER 5

THE END OF AN ERA: CONCLUSIONS

The first sixteenth-century efforts to produce reformed ordination rites resulted in a new theological understanding of ministry but did not create a new theological datum. In the transition from medieval Catholic ecclesiastical life to an evangelical church polity sufficient continuity existed in the first few decades of reform to recover and insure the recognizability of the liturgical center of the *ministerium verbi*. One can argue, however, that a shift occurred in the way that center was explained.

On one point the reformers and the medieval Catholic hierarchy agreed completely: the medieval rite of ordination admitted the ordinand to a sacrificial priesthood. The reformers would have nothing to do with such a view of ordained ministry. Yet the liturgical evidence does not support the polemic that has typically characterized the movement from Catholic to evangelical as radical and discontinuous. Two points must be borne in mind when such an assertion of continuity is made. First, this investigation has been limited to the first generation reforms in Germany among Lutherans. Secondly, the statements would not hold true for the so-called "radical Reformation" churches.[1]

In the early efforts of reformers like Luther and Bugenhagen the case for liturgical continuity can clearly be defended and, as was discussed in Chapter Two, a case can also be made for a degree of doctrinal continuity if one sorts out the polemics. For Luther to argue against anointing and what he considered to be secondary or improper ritual effusion in the ordination rite was not the same as arguing that ordination and the ministry to which it admitted a person were irrelevant. In making a case for liturgical continuity, of course, much depends on the kinds of questions asked and on decisions made regarding what degree of comparability in form and content constitutes genuine continuity.

The gradual overlaying of early reform efforts with accumulations of doctrinal debris from the Reformation and counter-Reformation debates in the years of the Council of Trent and beyond have made it difficult to see what the reform of ordination looked like in the critical transitional years after 1525. Thus the comments of Paul Bradshaw, while not inaccurate, characterize a perspective on the events of these years which is influenced more by subsequent development than by the actual reforms of the second and third quarters of the sixteenth century:

> The primary purpose of the ministry of the churches of the Reformation was seen as the preaching of the Word, and as a consequence all sacrificial and sacerdotal language and imagery disappeared from ordination rites. This radically different concept of the ministry from that of the medieval Church generally also led to the rejection of any sort of continuity with it and to a denial of the validity of its orders.[2]

Unquestionably, sacrificial and sacerdotal language disappeared from the rites. There was also a denial of any hierarchical distinction among orders. There was not, however, a denial of the validity of medieval Catholic ordination but rather only a denial of the validity of the understanding of priesthood associated with it.

The reformers never demanded that those already ordained as priests be reordained. Almost all of the early Reformation pastors, including Luther and Bugenhagen, were in fact priests whose entry into an evangelical ministry was not by reordination based on a denial of previously celebrated rites but rather by a confirmation of the person's willingness to embrace Reformation teaching. Their very availability for this was clearly understood to be on the basis of their having already been admitted to the church's ministry. They were now asked to do what they had been ordained to do, but had rarely done because of the corruption of the office of the *ministerium verbi*.

Liturgical events such as ordination do not occur in a vacuum. They are supported by an attendant structure which influences the way in which they are experienced and understood. In a sacramental system that could generate indulgences, private masses, stipends, and benefices having nothing to do with the actual work of ministry as the reformers understood it (rightly characterized by Bradshaw as focused on the "preaching of the Word"), hierarchical distinction, priestly status and quasi-magical power could easily be said to be given by the ritual act of ordination. For the sacerdotal role a person played as a consequence of the rite indicated such. But it was not the ritual act alone that made such an interpretation possible. That is why here, as in other areas of liturgical reform, Luther could argue for the maintenance of traditions which had been purged of "false teaching."

As these transitional years came to a close, the Reformation movement did not build on the emerging consensus discussed in the preceding chapter by proceeding to the adoption of a uniform process for training, examining and ordaining candidates for ministry. Yet the mutual influence of the rites in the various Church Orders did result in recognizable patterns, especially after the appearance of Luther's own rite and its gradually being adopted as a model throughout Germany. Two final examples of the ritual development in Reformation churches can lead into a summary discussion of the interrelationship of the reforms and their connection with medieval traditions.

The 1574 Rite of Hesse

The 1574 *Agenda* of Hesse represented the final stage of the early Reformation movement in that territory, and signaled the start of a new period. It was already one step beyond the first generation of ferment that produced the Lutheran church. As Hannelore Jahr observed:

> Just eight years after the emergence of the Church Order of 1566 the Agenda was completed. And yet these two Orders belong to two different generations, and not only with respect to language. The Agenda is shaped by a generation which itself did not experience the original awakening of the Reformation movement and has moved into its place those for whom Luther has already become an idealized figure of the past. In the Agenda a generation takes the lead which opposes the medieval heritage in an almost zealous way, yet lacks the progressive leadership of a single, great prince.[3]

In spite of the political reality to which Jahr accurately spoke, the development of the rite for ordination retained the structure and content familiar from the materials considered in the preceding chapters for the churches of Hesse.

The process for examining and electing a pastor was described briefly.[4] When the person chosen for a parish had not been ordained previously (that is, had not been called from one position to a new one) the superintendent or a pastor appointed by him, with two or three neighboring pastors for witnesses, arranged to ordain the candidate. The ordination began with a sermon "of one-half to three-quarters of an hour" on evangelical doctrine. The context was a liturgical gathering of the whole congregation as subsequent references make clear.

The ordination rite began when the ordinator moved before the altar, flanked on each side by the designated pastors/witnesses. All faced the congregation with the exception of the ordinand, who faced the ordinator. The whole community then sang *Veni Sancte Spiritus*.[5] At the conclusion of the hymn the ordinator addressed the congregation with an explanation of the nature of the pastoral office and call. Three appointed texts were read, Matthew 28:18-20; Titus 1:5-9; II Timothy 3:14-4:5.[6]

Customary for the Hesse rites, an extended exhortation addressed to the ordinand then followed. It included: 1) a reminder that the office was rooted in the command of Christ; 2) a list of authoritative teaching to which one must subscribe—scripture, the three creeds, the *Augsburg Confession*, and the *Apology to the Augsburg Confession*; 3) a statement of the pastor's responsibility for proper administration of the sacraments; 4) an admonition about obedience to superiors; 5) a discussion of the need for providing catechetical instruction for children, visiting the sick, teaching young and old, etc.; 6) an injunction to lead a moral and exemplary life. The exhortation concluded:

> These are the principal tenets, dear brother in Christ, which a pastor or servant in the church of the Lord Jesus Christ must do in his office. I now ask you before God and Jesus Christ, the holy angels, and this Christian congregation, if you are resolved to promise faithfully and energetically to carry this out.[7]

These principal tenets, especially the recognition of the *Augsburg Confession* and its *Apology* as normative, were of course much more specific than had been the case in the preceding rites in Hesse, and clearly moved the rite away from the earlier focus on biblical foundations for each prayer and action undertaken.

The ordinand gave an extended response:

> I recognize that this is a difficult office to which I wish to commit myself. But because I have been rightly called and rely entirely on the prayers of the Christian church for God's gracious help, which he promises to all of his called servants, I swear and promise here and before God faithfully to accomplish with God's help all that my office demands, with all my power.[8]

The unique contribution of this promise was its emphasis on the reliance on the congregation's prayer for the ordinand to fulfill the work of his ministry. The connection between office and community was considered essential. This emphasis was apparent when the ordinator then invited the whole congregation to pray as he said an ordination prayer, although done before laying on of hands.[9] The prayer again summarized the tasks to which the person was called and asked for the gift of the Spirit to fulfill them.

At this point the Agenda introduced an element new to Hesse into the rite: a declaratory *Vollzugsformel* to accompany the laying on of hands. With the ordinand still kneeling before the altar the ordinator and other pastors laid on hands while the formula was spoken:

> I now declare and certify you on behalf of God's church, upon your promise, a servant of the church and a teacher of the holy Gospels, in the name of the Father, and of the Son, and of the Holy Spirit. Amen.[10]

This was followed by a second prayer, which along with the prayer preceding the laying on of hands functioned as a presidential prayer of ordination in the traditional sense, asking God for the gift of the Spirit for the office undertaken. But here the two prayers framed a specific liturgical action and accompanying formula. Thus one is left with the impression that the core of the ordaining act was the declaration, although one must be cautious not to isolate it over against the other elements of the rite, especially the prayers which surrounded it. A commendation, similar to that in the 1566 rite was then addressed to the newly ordained and to the congregation. The singing of the *Te Deum laudamus* (in Latin or German), or another hymn of thanks or praise concluded the rite.[11]

Adding a structural outline of this rite to the earlier rites for Hesse discussed in Chapter Four produces a clear picture of the stability of the ritual tradition in that territory, even though the addition of the declaratory formula in this rite revealed a shift of accent.

Preacher	Elder	Pastor (1574)
		Sermon on the Office
		Veni Sancte Spiritus
Presentation	Introduction	Presentation
Readings:	Readings:	Readings:
Matthew 28:18–20	Acts 20:28–31	Matthew 28:18–20
Titus 1:5–9		Titus 1:5–9
II Timothy 3:14–4:5		II Timothy 3:14–4:5
Admonition to Candidate	Admonition to Candidate	Admonition to Candidate
		1. Doctrine, Scripture and Confessions
		2. Sacraments
		3. Discipline
		4. Pastoral Care
		5. Behavior
Question and Reply	Question and Reply	Question and Reply
Prayer	Prayer	Prayer
Laying on of Hands	Laying on of Hands	Laying on of Hands
		Declaratory Formula
Prayer	Prayer	Prayer
Commendation (Cand.)	Commendation (Cand.)	Commendation (Cand.)
Commendation (Cong.)	Commendation (Cong.)	Commendation (Cong.)
		Blessing
Psalm 19	Psalm 23	Te Deum Laudamus
Benediction	Benediction	

The use of the *Veni Sancte Spiritus* and the *Te Deum* was probably due to Luther's influence since the former appeared in his own ordination rite and the latter was well-known as one of his favorite hymns. But it was in an entirely new section of the Agenda that Luther's influence was seen most dramatically. His ordination rite was adapted for use as the "form for installing a pastor or church servant and commending him to the congregation when he has already been ordained and in the preaching office for some time."[12] This is exactly the reverse of what occurred in Württemberg where Luther's rite supplanted the indigenous evangelical

The End of an Era

rite for ordinations, while the local rite was then used for installations of those already ordained. This is evidence for the fluid way in which reformers treated the issue of what, from a liturgical point of view, constituted the distinction between the two acts.

Again, a sermon about the office of pastor/preacher began the rite. The *Veni Sancte Spiritus* was sung as the new pastor and installing superintendent proceeded to the altar. The superintendent spoke to the congregation attesting the election and ordination of the new pastor while expressing the hope that he would preach the gospel and administer the sacraments in a faithful and diligent manner. The congregation was also admonished to obey the pastor in things concerning care of their souls. The superintendent then prayed one from among a number of Collects listed earlier in the Agenda.[13] Readings followed: John 20:21-23, I Timothy 3:1-7, Acts 20:28-31, the latter two having been taken over from Luther's rite. The prayer from Luther's rite, *Barmherziger Gott*, was also then said but without a laying on of hands. The superintendent commended the new pastor to the congregation and the congregation to the new pastor, using the commendation from the Agenda's ordination rite. The rite concluded with the *Te Deum laudamus* or "some other song of praise."

Two things are noteworthy here: 1) the rite was basically Luther's 1539 ordination rite with some material from the Agenda's own rite inserted (the commendation); 2) the laying on of hands was omitted. It is significant that the installation service made a point of both recalling the ordination rite and yet clearly distinguishing itself from it.

The Hesse churches made clear contributions to the developing understanding of the significance of ordination in the Reformation movement. This is apparent even in the one point which all ordination rites shared, a central prayer or prayers for the gift of the Spirit. In the medieval Roman rite, for example, the focus of the prayer for the gift of the Spirit was on the power it bestowed to celebrate the mass, specifically to offer the sacrifice of the mass. In Luther's Wittenberg rite the Spirit was invoked so that the Word might be preached rightly, especially against Anabaptists and Enthusiasts. The Hesse Orders envisioned the gift of the Spirit as being primarily for the service of the ordained in the community, that is for their role as care givers

(*Seelsorge*) and shepherds (*Hirtendienst*). Although one should not take such focused distinctions too far, they do capture the spirit of the prayers in each rite.[14]

In comparison with Luther's rite, the Hesse rites are distinguished by the choice of readings, the content of the prayers, and especially the lengthy and explicit exhortations. Furthermore, the participation of the community, clearly central for Luther in his understanding of the whole calling and ordaining process, also played a decisive role in the shape of the Hesse rites from 1526 on. This participation was manifest not only in the songs and prayers of the congregation, but also in the specific exhortations addressed to them. One cannot miss the point in these rites that the office of ordained pastoral ministry was mutually entered into by ordinand and congregation.

The 1566 Church Order's classification of the offices of ministry is also worth noting. As Niebergall aptly summarized:

> What the Church Orders of 1526 and 1539 only intimated, the Order of 1566 developed openly in that it distinguished different ordinations, not in principle perhaps, but at least in form; namely that of superintendent, pastor, community elder, and in a certain sense also deacon and "Opfermann." The 1574 Agenda, on the other hand, recognized only the ordination and installation of a pastor. Thus here the tendency to reductionism, defining the pastoral office as the normal and only office of the church, is apparent....[15]

This ambivalence even in Hesse (the 1566 Order lasted only eight years before being supplanted by the 1574 Agenda) touches on one of the most confusing elements of Reformation history with regard to ordering ministry: the inability to decide what constituted essential offices for the church's life.

Almost immediately, for example, the minor orders disappeared from conversation in Reformation territories. They were simply not discussed. With regard to the traditional major orders of deacon, presbyter and bishop one finds a tendency toward embracing Luther's equating of the latter two, while the role of deacon remained ambiguous. The overlapping of the role of deacon and elder in the Hesse churches compounded the confusion. By the time of the 1574 Agenda, the focus on ordination into the presbyterate (to use the traditional terminology)

The End of an Era 209

clouded the fact that superintendents were in fact still functioning as overseers and that deacons and elders continued to serve Hesse churches.

In the ordination rite itself, the Hesse church's insistence on a specific vow by the ordinand stood in contrast to Luther's rite. The vow made it clear that the ordinand had to rely on the grace of God and the intercession of the community in order to fulfill the responsibilities of the office. The 1574 Agenda had the clearest expression of this promise, but its significance was already implicit in the 1539 Cassel Order. The theological implication of this emphasis was that the mutuality of office and community was considered unassailable. The power which enabled persons to fulfill the responsibilities of the office was not solely their own but rather lay outside them, and in an ongoing way—the congregation's prayers were needed not just in the rite of ordination but throughout one's ministry.

The use of an *Ordinationsvotum* was also a contribution of the Hesse tradition. The 1526 Homberg Order had used the imperative formula of the Roman rite, but it was not adopted subsequently by any of the Orders in Hesse. In the 1539 Cassel Order the votum was connected with the preceding prayer for the gift of the Spirit. It indicated that the Spirit was for the instruction, direction and strengthening of the ordinands, who needed the "hand and help of God" which was now being promised to them. Similarly in the 1566 Order, although there was no votum, the prayer spoken at the laying on of hands was linked with the preceding prayer. Only in the 1574 Agenda did the votum become more clearly juridical, representing an ecclesiastical act. As Niebergall explained,"the votum was now no longer related to the preceding intercession of the community but rather to the promise of the ordinand."[16] But even here the formula was embraced on either side by ordination prayers which indicated that the focus of the action was the prayer for the gift of the Spirit for the office of ministry.

The 1580 Rite of Albertine Saxony

The distinction between installation and ordination was contextually determined. If one were not aware of attendant circumstances most of the ritual structure and content would not be able to bear the distinction.

The simple fact of how the act was titled, that is, whether it was called an installation (*Einsetzung, Einweisung, Investitur, Introduction, Installation*) or an ordination (*Ordination, ordinatio*) was one of the ways in which the distinction was made. But there were also some internal ritual variations between them as the preceding analyses have shown.

The 1580 rite of Albertine Saxony identified the two as ritually synonymous. The rite was introduced with the words: "The general manner in which a new church servant should be ordained, and installed and commended by his superintendent in the prescribed church."[17] A single rite followed, that of the 1559 Württemberg *Summarischer Begriff*, with the addition of a reading and the ordination prayer from Luther's rite. Luther's ordination prayer was listed as an option, to be used instead of the presidential ordination prayer of the 1559 Württemberg rite. It was stated specifically that this rite was for ordaining/installing deacons and pastors, and that it could occur on any day chosen by the superintendent doing the ordaining and installing. A comparative outline clarifies the relationships:

Luther's 1539 Rite	*1559 Württemberg Rite*	*1580 Saxony Rite*
Prayer		
	"Now Let Us Pray to the Holy Spirit"	"Now Let Us Pray to the Holy Spirit"
Veni Sancte Spiritus Versicle		
	Sermon	Sermon
	Creed	Creed
	Short Admonition	Short Admonition
	Prayer	Prayer
Readings:	Readings:	Readings:
	John 20:21ff.	John 20:21ff.
I Tim. 3:1–7	I Tim. 3:1–7	I Tim. 3:1–7
Acts 20:28–31		Acts 20:28–31
Address by Ordinator		

The End of an Era 211

	Ordination Prayer	Ordination Prayer
Promise of Ordinand		
	Lord's Prayer	Lord's Prayer
Laying on Hands	Laying on Hands	Laying on Hands
Lord's Prayer	Exhortation	Exhortation
Ordination Prayer		
Charge (I Pet. 5)		
Blessing/Sign of Cross		
"Now Let Us Pray to the Holy Spirit"	Te Deum laudamus	Te Deum laudamus
Lord's Prayer		
[Communion]	Blessing	Blessing

The 1580 rite clearly followed the Württemberg pattern. Although ordinations were not restricted to Sunday they usually took place on that day in the midst of a eucharistic liturgy. The fact that the rubrical description in this 1580 rite noted that it could occur on any day chosen by the superintendent may indicate that its use was primarily as an installation rite. It was to be done in the congregation which had called the candidate. That pattern, of course, had been Bugenhagen's desire from the beginning.

Frieder Schulz provides a helpful explanation:

> The contemporary co-existence of a general introduction into the service of the Gospel by means of an unrepeatable act of ordination and a repeatable installation (which looks back to the first act) in a specific location (a specific pastorate) is the result of historical development. In the 16th century they are simultaneous: the centralized ordination (understood to take place in a regular congregational liturgy) and the ordination to the first place of service. Here the connection between the office and the congregation is most clearly expressed, whereas the centralized ordination or ordination in a home congregation illustrates the universally significant mission character of the act, without the unavoidable limitation to the historically contingent parish-model and the pastoral image rooted in it.[18]

The variety of ways in which ordaining and installing were handled, as has been demonstrated in the preceding chapters, modifies Schulz's opening comment, but his distinction is well taken. In other words the initial act of ordaining someone into the ministry of the whole church was simultaneously their installation into the service of the congregation which called them and had made their ordination possible, and vice versa. With centralized ordinations the confusion that arose was whether the "artificial" congregation in which the ordination occurred, it not being the community which the newly ordained person would actually serve, represented not only the whole church but also that specific community to which the person had been called. If a separate act of installation in the congregation to be served took place did it hint at a different ecclesiology?

In one case the unity of the church was affirmed on the basis of its extra-local reality; the church was more than a federation of disparate, local congregations. Thus one could not construe subsequent installations in new communities as a repetition of ordination. On the other hand, the parochial model indicated that the emphasis was on the autonomy of the local congregation. Although it was sometimes difficult not to see installation as a repetition of ordination, the rites often being quite similar, the act of ordination was considered valid for the whole church. Subsequent installations were never described as reordinations.

A final example of maintaining the distinction can be seen in Wittenberg itself. Luther's rite had been published there in 1539, and ordinations for much of Saxony had been occurring in Wittenberg since the 1535 decree of the Elector. But the "Constitution und artikel des geistlichen consistorii zu Wittenberg. 1542" described how pastors were to be installed in that territory after the ordination had taken place:

> "On the investiture or installation of a pastor in the parish."
> The installing of a pastor and preacher should be done by the neighboring superintendents, one or two of them, before the community, in the parish which is in need of the pastor. First the sixth chapter of I Timothy should be read, from "teach and urge these duties" [I Tim. 6:2b] to the end of the chapter. Then the pastor or preacher should be commended to the community, as God had directed Moses to do with Joshua, as is said in Numbers 27, with the imposition of hands.[19]

The End of an Era

The reading from I Timothy 6 was new, but it elaborated themes about proper conduct with which the Wittenberg ordination rite was also concerned in its use of I Timothy 3. The action as described was rather minimal. This was due to the fact that such an installation within the area of Saxony near Wittenberg would have occurred very soon after the ordination itself, with many of the same people present in both cases. The concern here is simply to underline again the distinction between ordaining and introducing a pastor into a specific congregational relationship, for this pointed to the theological conviction that ordination was a distinct and universally significant act.

The Case for Ritual Models

Frieder Schulz argued that three different models for ordaining emerged in the sixteenth century.[20] Schulz's belief that three basic types of evangelical ordination rites developed early in the Reformation on which all later orders were dependent was rooted in his theological evaluation of the structure and content of the rites on the one hand, and the context within which they occurred on the other. It was also connected with the simple fact of which rites ended up having the most influence in subsequent development.

Confusing chronology as well as the complicated interdependence of the various Church Orders (more than 130 were produced) render suspect any claims to definitive interpretation. Yet Schulz did correctly point to a surprising commonality which existed among the rites:

> Especially conspicuous is the dominant place of the selected scripture readings, to which a homiletical-parenetical explanation of the responsibilities of office, based on the apostolic word, is connected (being in fixed or free form) either before or after the readings themselves. After this foundation and explanation of tasks, the response and accompanying action of the gathered community follows, asking for God's Spirit and blessing for the ordinand through corporate song and prayer. The personal gift of God's word, along with prayer for confirmation of the one being taken into this ministry, is a consequence of the act of laying on hands. The succession of these individual parts is not interchangeable since an objective, necessary theological relationship exists.

> These parts, held in common by all the Orders, represent the Reformation basis of ordination.[21]

Given this structure, which he thought revealed the basic functions of the act of ordaining for the reformers, Schulz then distinguished three "families" as represented by rites produced in Saxony, Hesse and Württemberg. He charted the relationships of these rites to reveal his assessment of the basic structure.[22] What was the heart of the distinctions?

Luther's 1535/39 Wittenberg rite was interpreted by Schulz to be a general introduction into the preaching office. In other words it was an act of the universal church and did not function simultaneously as an introduction into a specific parish, even though it was necessary for a specific parish to have called the candidate as a prerequisite for the ordination. The centralization of ordination at Wittenberg after 1535 helped to make this clear, as did Luther's retaining the practice of having only previously ordained people involved in the laying on of hands. Yet the form of the concluding charge to the newly ordained in Luther's rite, drawn from I Peter 5, revealed the installing character of the act since it was a specific parish to which one had been called and for which one was made responsible.

The Württemberg rite, in contrast, was an order of installation according to Schulz. It introduced a new candidate into the pastoral office in a specific community. In other words the rite was "parochially restricted."[23] Scripture and prayer still dominated the structure, as was true in Luther's rite. And this installation accomplished the same end as the Wittenberg rite: ordaining someone in the sense that it constituted the means of entry into the office of ministry. When a pastor subsequently moved to a different parish this rite was not repeated. Instead the new pastor was presented to the congregation by the superintendent and one prayer was said (the first from the 1547/1559 Order). Later, however, when Luther's rite was adopted as the ordination rite in Württemberg its native rite (1547/1559) was used as a separate service for installation.[24]

Some of the differences between the Wittenberg and Württemberg rites can be attributed to the different liturgical contexts in which they

The End of an Era

occurred (the former in an evangelical mass, the latter in a high German service). Thus, for example, the Württemberg rite had a sung creed after the sermon. But a critical difference was the use of a *Vollzugsformel* at the laying on of hands, set in the midst of other prayers. Schulz considered this to be the defining characteristic of the Württemberg rites:

> The introductory portion [of the prayers within which the *Vollzugsformel* occurred] recalls the preceding action in good Reformation fashion: gathering "in the Holy Spirit," "divine promise," prayer and exhortation for the new pastor. The concluding portion represents a short admonition to true service in view of being accountable before the tribunal of Christ. Without the middle part [the *Vollzugsformel*] one could see the whole thing as a short remonstrance toward the conclusion of an installation.[25]

What the *Vollzugsformel* did, said Schulz, was to shift the meaning of the rite. A laying on of hands bound up with an imperative formula such as "I ordain" could only be interpreted as a juridical formula.[26] In other words, an installation of the Württemberg type combined a secular (juridical) and religious act, analogous to the way in which marriage involved the pastor in a secular and religious act. The danger in this was that the theological focus could be overwhelmed by the juridical.

Like the Württemberg rites from which they borrowed, the Hessen rites functioned as an installation, but in a slightly different way according to Schulz. Here the ordination functioned simultaneously as a first installation, even though the context was a centralized ordination in Marburg, akin to the use of Luther's rite in Wittenberg. Ordination was thus accomplished as an act separate from, yet related to the introduction into one's first pastorate. The Hesse rite retained Luther's shaping of the action as a movement from appointed readings, to admonition, to questioning the candidate. Also, as in Luther's rite, the prayer followed immediately after the ordinand's answer.

Like Württemberg, however, the Hesse churches opted for a *Vollzugsformel* in 1539 and 1574 (the 1566 Order did not have such a formula). The formula was not connected with an admonition as in the Württemberg rite, but Schulz believed that it still represented the "characteristic proprium of the act of ordination."[27] Of course the influence of Martin Bucer colored the Hessen tradition most in its early adoption of his four-fold division of ordained ministry. Yet by the time of the 1574 Agenda the use of an ordination rite was restricted to one pastoral office.

In terms of ritual experience the most noteworthy aspects of the Hesse rites were the lengthy commendations to both candidate and congregation. These served to highlight the mutuality of the liturgical action—ordinand, ordinator, and congregation being bound in ecclesial partnership. The length and didactic tone of the commendations were formidable. Also embedded in the 1574 rite was the first appearance of confessional subscription as constitutive of ordination. One would not be wrong to point out the similarity between the vow of obedience to the bishop in the medieval Roman rites and such Lutheran demands for obedience to confessional documents.

Schulz evidently considered Luther's rite to be the clearest expression of evangelical reform of ordination. The Hesse and Württemberg rites suffered in his analysis because of the presence of the *Vollzugsformel* at the center of the liturgical action, and because of their mixing of the issue of ordination and installation. In both cases, especially the former, the risk was narrowing the significance of the act of ordaining:

> The Hesse *Vollzugsformel* forms a distinct parallel to the Württemberg formula. A "high church" legal act in Hesse is equivalent to the territorial act in Württemberg, which is foreign to the evangelical concept of Lutheran ordination rites, and stands in danger of ritually restricting the liturgical event of ordination to the *Vollzugsformel*.[28]

Apart from the question of whether Schulz read more into these early formulas due to subsequent development than is justifiable, one can question why he considered Luther's rite to embody "Reformation understanding of ordination" better than the others. It is apparent from the emergence of the very families Schulz described that one cannot speak of any single Reformation understanding of ordination.

Schulz was more accurate in his evaluation of the choice of scriptural texts. He rightly pointed out the central significance of the readings in all the evangelical rites of ordination.[29] Luther's desire to equate the office of bishop and pastor/presbyter was reinforced by his choice of I

Timothy 3:1-7 as the first reading, while his concern for the teaching and guardian role of the pastor in an era when "false preachers" abounded was manifest in his use of Acts 20:28-31. But as had been indicated, these readings were also part of the medieval tradition in ordinations.

The 1547/1559 Württemberg order retained a closer affinity to its Roman predecessors by using the John 20:21 text to explain the spiritual gift given in ordination and the centrality of the power to forgive sins as constitutive of the office of ministry. The Hesse Orders modified Luther's pastor/bishop identification by adopting Bucer's image of the pastor as "elder, working in the Word." The use of Matthew 28:18-20's "great commission" made the connection. But the Hesse rite's use of Titus 1 and II Timothy 3 also revealed concerns similar to Luther's: the desire to assure that pastors were good examples in their leading of irreproachable lives, and also good teachers who could combat heresy.

With regard to scriptural texts chosen, the styles of sermons, admonitions, or commendations, and the different ways in which pastoral responsibilities were sorted out in each of the families, Schulz demonstrated the ritual traditions did indeed represent distinct variations on a theme. The problem is whether Schulz described the theme adequately or uncovered the heart of the reform efforts with regard to ordaining.

The evidence presented here leads to the conclusion that if one is to speak of models for ordaining there were only two. One was rooted in the centralization of ordinations, usually in university cities where the examinations could be done by the theological faculties, and the other was rooted in a congregational model where the rite occurred in the community which had called the new pastor (and by so calling, of course, made the ordination possible).

The reason these two patterns can be spoken of as different models is because of the liturgical role of the community in evangelical rites. The heart of the evangelical reform of ordination is to be found there. Private ordinations were as out of the question for Luther, Bugenhagen, Melanchthon and others as were private masses. The role of the community, especially the community's prayer, was so essential as to constitute, to use the medieval Catholic terminology, the evangelical equivalent of the "form and matter" of ordination. That is why Melanchthon could speak of the office of ministry as a sacrament in the *Augsburg Confession*. And the communities present in these two models are different, as the ecclesiological issues discussed earlier indicated.

It does not seem legitimate to characterize the rites according to the use of the *Vollzugsformel*. Even Schulz's point about the juridical emphasis being made paramount by the use of such a formula must be qualified by the euchological context in which it occurred. And it is clear that although the ritual gesture of laying on hands was considered central—it was almost universally retained for both ordinations and installations—it was not considered to be the "sacramental moment" of the rite.

It is impossible to choose any specific point in the Reformation rites and claim it as essential either to carrying out the rite itself or to the validation of a person's ministry. For every generalization about the universal use of some aspect of the ordination process there are irrefutable critical exceptions. This restriction on making any unilateral claim includes the venerable practice of laying on hands, the use of a presidential ordination prayer, the singing of a particular hymn, or the use of scriptural readings. But lack of uniformity does not indicate an absence of unity. The boundaries of recognizability and acceptability may have been fluid, but they were not formless.

These rites never stand in isolation. How they were experienced was influenced by social, economic, political and ecclesiastical factors which shaped and reshaped how the church ordered its life. Chapter One traced how that was true as well for the medieval development of the ordination rite up to Durandus' pontifical.

The Issue of Continuity

At one level the evidence argues for continuity between medieval Catholic and emerging Reformation practice in the process of ordaining clergy. Yet at another level the consequences of the reforming efforts have been described as an ecclesiastical revolution. How can such seemingly contradictory positions be maintained simultaneously? Part of the answer must be rooted in the recognition that the ritual data yields different results depending on the framework within which questions are asked of that data. If one looks at the rites from the perspective of how they are experienced by those present at their performance, or from the perspective of the opinions of theologians of the period, people like Luther and Bugenhagen, or from that of the concerns of contemporary liturgical study, different evaluations will result.

It was noted in Chapter Two, for example, how Luther's reforms of the mass produced radical alteration of the eucharistic prayer from the perspective of a theological assessment of its text. Yet from the perspective of the actual experience of the eucharistic liturgy by the community present those alterations would have been completely unnoticed because the canon was spoken silently by the priest. Thus Luther's changes mark discontinuity at one level and continuity at another. From the perspective of contemporary liturgical study of that ritual history, Luther's changes have been viewed as radical by some and conservative by others depending on the doctrinal weight given to the specific content of the sections of the prayer which he altered or excised.

A parallel to this example drawn from revisions of the eucharistic prayer of the mass is the ordination rite's use of the laying on of hands and an ordination prayer. This central focus, visually and theologically, of laying on hands with prayer by the bishop in the medieval rites (even in light of the ritual profusion which obscured it) was clearly retained by Luther. But, as in the eucharistic prayer, its textual content was changed dramatically. Thus on the level of ritual experience continuity existed since the central gesture with some kind of prayer was retained. But at the theological level the content of that prayer was shifted. Contemporary liturgical study, of course, has revealed the historical stability of the medieval prayers. People in Luther's day, however, would have been unaware of the antiquity of that euchological content. Thus to change it, without changing the fact that prayer was said, would have made little experiential difference. It is only the gift of hindsight that enables interpreters today to say that these changes mark a clean break with a long and venerable medieval euchological tradition.

The question of continuity between the medieval and evangelical rites cannot be answered on the basis of the extant texts alone. At the level of direct literary relationships there is almost no continuity. Not one of the medieval Roman prayers, exhortations or formulas was taken over by any of the Reformation rites. The old Roman core of invitatory, collect, and ordination prayer was abandoned, as were the accumulated prayers and formulas discussed in Chapter One. But the ritual function of many of these elements was retained.

For example, the opening dialogue, allocution and exhortation in Durandus' rite served to verify the worthiness of the candidate and to provide scriptural foundation for the act about to be undertaken. In the evangelical rites discussed earlier that same function was fulfilled, at the same point in the rite, by an address of the ordinator to the community. The themes of these admonitions varied, and in some cases we do not have texts to reveal what was said as, for example, in Luther's rite which simply stated, "If they are worthy, the congregation after due admonition by the preacher, shall pray for them." Specific content varied, but the functional equivalence was unmistakable.

Similarly, Durandus' exhortation provided biblical justification for the act of ordaining: Moses choosing the seventy elders, and Jesus sending out the seventy-two disciples. Pauline imagery concerning the variety of gifts within the church was also employed ("And one body of Christ is composed of many members, each with its own value"). Luther's rite used the biblical story of God sending laborers into the harvest. The images were obviously different and so, consequently, were the implications of their emphases for how one was to understand the office of ministry—different, but not radically unrelated.

The laying on of hands has usually been argued to be the central ritual act of ordination. This is partly because it is biblically verifiable and partly because it has been universally associated with ordaining in the western church's extant rites since the time of Hippolytus. With the exception of the minor and short-lived objection of Bugenhagen to this gesture as already discussed, all the Reformation rites retained it. And, as might be expected, they linked an ordination prayer or prayers to it. In most cases there was a presidential prayer, in some a declaratory formula surrounded by ordination prayers. The gesture itself was never described as essential, but rather was always understood in light of the

The End of an Era

invocation prayers which surrounded it. It was the invocation of the Spirit for the ordinand, the church and its ministry that defined the liturgical center of ordination. The imposition of hands focused the ritual moment, but it did not define it. In all but the 1535 rite of Bugenhagen for Pomerania, which advocated that a layperson participate in the laying on of hands, the Reformation rites stated that those already ordained were the ones to perform this ritual gesture.

Durandus' rite moved from the first laying on of hands to a series of ritual actions and formulas which were completely abandoned by the reformers: vesting, anointing, and the *traditio instrumentorum*. These were discussed earlier in the analysis of Luther's objections to the confusion of priesthood and ministry. But parts of the post-communion complex of ritual actions in Durandus' rite were not lost completely. The use of John 20: 21ff. appeared in a number of evangelical rites, and the vow of obedience to the bishop was eventually replaced by the pledge of the ordinands to subscribe to and abide by the *Augsburg Confession* and its *Apology*. This was a consequence of the Reformation emphasis on right teaching. Even where the official Lutheran Symbols were not mentioned, doctrine was the abstract, conceptual lord of the church rather than the bishop. Ordinands were always admonished concerning their primary responsibility to preach the word rightly. Closing exhortations, or extended blessings, freely worded and commending the newly ordained as they now undertook their tasks were also evident in Reformation rites as in Durandus' pontifical.

A more specific ritual example of how complicated the issue of continuity or discontinuity can be is provided by the Reformation use of *Veni Sancte Spiritus*. In the medieval tradition this was not an ordination hymn but rather the sequence for Pentecost. As a general invocation of the Spirit it did not specify ordained functions in any sense. As was discussed in Chapter One, a hymn to the Holy Spirit was added to the medieval ordination rites in the twelfth century, but it was the *Veni Creator Spiritus* not *Veni Sancte Spiritus*. The latter was used along with the former only when ordinations occurred on the Ember Saturday of Pentecost. In any case the purpose of the hymn in the medieval rites was simply to accompany the action of the anointing of the hands.

Luther put the hymn at the opening of the rite, using the *Veni Sancte*

Spiritus. Given his attack on the practice of anointing, was Luther's choice here a sign of his desire to replace unction with prayer/hymnody to the one Spirit who vivifies all functions and ministries within the church? If so, his choice of the *Veni Sancte* over the *Veni Creator* makes sense since the latter was the ordination hymn of the medieval pontifical tradition while the former was a more general hymn used at other times (specifically, Pentecost). His additional appropriation of the proper Pentecost Collect, not present in the pontifical ordinations, reinforces this theological interpretation because of its text's reference to "the same Spirit." On the one hand Luther's use indicates discontinuity since the hymn in the pontifical accompanied a subsidiary rite of anointing while in his own rite it had a primary place. Yet on the other hand retaining prayer for the Spirit for the sake of the event, ordaining someone, reveals functional continuity.

The liturgical context for the ordination rite was retained, or perhaps one might argue, it was recovered. It occurred within a eucharistic liturgy, usually but not always in the same place within that liturgy both in the medieval Catholic and evangelical rites—in the midst of the readings or near them, after a sermon. For the reformers the congregation had to be present and participating, and the congregation was constituted by the laity. Medieval ordinations could and did theoretically affirm this same point, but the actual role of the community had been attenuated as the church was understood more as the clergy than as clergy and laity together. This attenuation of the significance of the laity was not the case in the evangelical performance of the rite. Even the tension between Bugenhagen and Luther on whether the rite should occur in the congregation which had called the ordinand, or in a central location where the congregation was not the one that would actually be served by the person(s) being ordained did not compromise this point. The congregation not only had to be present, but also had to offer its prayer as an essential component of the rite.

How to interpret the role of the congregation is raised by the ritual example of the relationship of the use of the litany and old Roman Kyrie in the medieval rite to the use of the hymns "Now we pray we to the Holy Spirit," remembering that the latter appeared in almost every Reformation ordination and installation rite, and *Veni Sancte Spiritus*.

These are mixed in a variety of ways as the preceding analysis has shown. In all cases for the Reformation rites they represent the prayer of the people and push the point of realizing that the community's action is a central proprium of the rite. Yet here the reformers were recovering what present day liturgical study has revealed to be the intent of the ordination rites from the beginning. Is this recovering, therefore, revolution or in fact genuine recovery and for that reason continuity?

The biblical texts chosen for the rites also varied significantly, but at least here one can state that the texts associated with the ordination of presbyters and bishops in the medieval rites were the ones used by Bugenhagen and Luther in their rites. The issue for the reformers, of course, was the conflation of the texts so that one could make clear the unity of the presbyteral and episcopal office. Again purely at the level of textual repetition one can argue for continuity. Because the texts were used so differently, however, and commented on at length, one can also say that their use was new.

Obviously, the case for discontinuity can be made. Much of the ritual content of the medieval rite disappeared. That cannot be disputed. But is it not worth considering that the liturgical center, even though ritually and ceremonially carried out with significantly different images, was not obscured? What the reformers in fact accomplished was the recovery of the liturgical center, ordination and installation were quite literally the work of the people. But the ecclesiology of Luther and Bugenhagen was not restricted to viewing the local congregation as the only expression of the church. Attention to broader ecclesiastical realities, including the use of university theological faculties, the Visitors, superintendents, and even the princes (as "emergency bishops") was clearly part of the theology of the church for the Lutheran reformers.

The Question of Structure

It has often been difficult for liturgical scholars to escape an approach in liturgical analysis that leads to a focus on specific moments in rites as central. An example of this with regard to ordination is represented by the comments of W. Jardine Grisbrooke:

> The great majority of ordination rites comprise, so far as the specifically ordinatory material is concerned, three main parts: the ordination itself is preceded by introductory rites, and followed by explicatory rites. The latter are later developments than the former, although, as is well known, in some cases, notably that of the unreformed Roman rite, their development and character was such that there were times when one or another part of them was not uncommonly held to be necessary for validity—times when, in other words, they became confused with the ordination itself.[30]

What is "the ordination itself?" The question of validity is inevitably reductionistic, and in the end liturgically unhelpful. If churches are to take both their diversity and their unity seriously the issue in liturgical study must be recognizability and integrity, not validity. Searching for definitions of validity also tends to isolate liturgical action from the broader context in which it occurs.

Further on in his discussion of ordination Grisbrooke argued for clarification of the form and matter of ordination, stating that "to judge simply from the rites themselves, in more than one of the unreformed rites it was not at all obvious exactly when the ordination had or had not taken place."[31] He was speaking of recent contemporary reforms in various traditions. The issue of reductionism was evident when Grisbrooke concluded that "in none of the new rites is there any possibility of confusion in identifying either matter or form from the rite itself, quite apart from any authoritative statements which may accompany it. In every case the compilers of the rite have settled for one clear laying on of hands accompanied by the ordination or consecration prayer."[32]

What is useful in this explanation is the proper attention to what the rite itself communicates apart from statements which are external to it. But the focus Grisbrooke advocates here may be misplaced. Much more is made of this ambiguous ritual gesture (it is, after all, used to bless, in healing, in baptism, and a variety of other ways) than is merited by the larger ritual complex within which it occurs. The gesture is clearly biblical, traditional, and helpful in communicating what is going on in ordination, but only because it is part of a larger whole which defines it and without which it cannot function.

The same caution can be raised with regard to Frieder Schulz's definition of the requisite components of evangelical ordination described earlier. The presupposition behind assertions like those of Grisbrooke and Schulz is that the Reformation rites can be reduced to essentials. If one adheres to a descriptive approach, an explication of the parts of any liturgical rite is both legitimate and helpful. The problem is not in then comparing various rites but rather when one goes on to create a liturgical abstraction in order to provide a normative model for judging the specific rites being compared.

Can one say anything normative about the Reformation rites for ordination? And if so does their normativity bear any relationship to answers given to the same sorts of questions with regard to medieval Catholic ordination? The liturgical issue here is how rites and their interpretations stand in mutually critical correlation, and how they then judge one another. If the medieval bishops claimed to be ordaining people to ministry in the church, defined in terms of the power of order for sacrificial action on behalf of the whole community, and reformers claimed to be ordaining people to ministry in the church, defined in terms of ministry of the word understood primarily as preaching the gospel, were they both doing a recognizably similar thing in the actual act of ordaining? This investigation leads one to answer yes if the question is framed in terms of the recognizability and integrity of the ritual action within the larger vocational process. But one cannot summarize the preceding descriptive analysis in any shorthand way. It is sifting through the evidence itself that leads one to judge its message and its continuity with the traditions of the church it sought to reform.

The dilemma for the early reformers was a profound one. As the Reformation was embraced radical swings of the pendulum often characterized the reactions of churches. Where bishops or patrons had controlled the economic life of their dioceses, and controlled the appointment of the ordained, magistrates who found themselves suddenly free of such control in the sweep of the Reformation were quick to abandon existing patterns:

> There is evidence to suggest that after the Catholic bishops' sway over the parish clergy had come to an end, *Amtmänner* and *Schösser* had appointed, dismissed, and inducted pastors. In some places there may have been no one else to do it. The practice became entrenched and was difficult to eradicate. ...Few other

instances of outright appointment by magistrates are to be found after the initiation of new procedures, however.[33]

The power of such appointment was obviously taken to heart, usually for economic reasons. But there was little concern for the gospel in all this, or as Luther put it, for right teaching. And without some kind of ecclesiastical control, many wandering, self-appointed preachers continued to create serious problems for churches.[34]

In the end, then, which in terms of time was not very long, the reformers realized that both extra-local authority and local prerogative had to be combined. The evangelical stress on call provided the latter, while centralized ordinations, or ordinations done in concert with neighboring superintendents or pastors, with the approval of the prince or elector, provided the former. What the medieval church had accomplished on the basis of a unified episcopal structure the reformers accomplished on the basis of a more fragmented but, nonetheless, integrated liturgical and juridical structure. And when in either case a person was said to be ordained, the liturgical justification for the assertion was the same.

The point of much of the Lutheran and Roman Catholic polemical argument on questions concerning what constitutes ordained ministry and what the appropriate means are by which one becomes a part of it turn on interpretive, doctrinal formulations rather than on liturgical description. Ironically, Lutherans, especially in the nineteenth century, wanted to stress that the origins of Reformation understanding of ministry were always to be appreciated in terms of preaching the gospel, and therefore stood in sharp contrast to the ritually, sacramentally rooted priesthood of Catholicism. Yet it was exactly the proper liturgical center that the reformers recovered in their development of ordination rites. Abandoning liturgy was never advocated by the proponents of the magisterial Reformation.

It is this doctrinal/liturgical interplay that causes such consternation in the church's assessment of itself. As Paul Bradshaw has noted:

> ...the doctrinal and liturgical elements are inseparably linked and cannot be treated independently. Liturgists cannot beg doctrinal questions, any more than dogmatic theologians can ignore liturgical data. In some areas of doctrine and

liturgy we have now, thankfully, passed beyond Reformation controversies and found our common ground elsewhere. In ordination, however, the Reformation period still highlights the relevant questions which we need to ask, even if in the end the solutions which we have yet to seek cannot be found there.[35]

The question of doctrinal and liturgical influences can indeed only be answered on the basis of the cultural circumstances which are generating the questions. Bradshaw correctly reminds us that in the case of ordination and ministry the Reformation period yields provocative material for interpreting the stumbling block this issue has been in contemporary ecumenical conversation.

Open Questions for Ecclesiology

One cannot dismiss lightly the ecclesiological implications of the changes made by the sixteenth-century Reformation in the medieval church's inherited patterns of daily church life. The manner in which the whole vocational process was carried out raises questions of how to assess continuity or the lack of it. In the medieval system, for example, bishops were to be elected by the clergy and people in keeping with patristic precedent and ecclesiastical legislation. Those elected were to be confirmed in office by the pope as Latin patriarch. In actual practice in many countries the king nominated the candidate, the chapter of canons actually elected (not always the person nominated), and the primate and/or neighboring bishops (at least three) ordained. The pope confirmed the election and ordination.

Luther restored the local congregation's right to election, the call of a congregation being the prerequisite for ordination in the evangelical process, the neighboring pastors' role in ordaining, and the association of the local church and its ministers with the wider church. Yet his emphasis on the role of the prince in overseeing and providing for the welfare of the church within his territory to the exclusion of any role for the bishops and the pope was a radical departure from medieval tradition.

If one stresses the necessity of the traditional medieval role of bishops, particularly of being in succession, and the pope, then Luther's reforms mark discontinuity with the prevailing patterns. But if one stresses things like the election by the congregation or the liturgical action of clergy and laity a picture of continuity emerges. The participation of other ordained persons in presbyteral ordination was, for example, a *sine qua non* of all medieval presbyteral ordinations. Thus the reformers' emphasis on it indicated affirmation of the tradition. The replacement of the confirming power of the bishop and pope with an examination and confirming process controlled by university theological faculties, the superintendents and the prince shifted the locus of power, but did it radically alter the use of power?

The ecumenical consensus of the western church prior to the Reformation clearly affirmed that only bishops could ordain to the major orders. Non-episcopal ordinations were so exceptional as to make their occasional appearance confirm that broad ecumenical consensus. Luther encouraged the princes to usurp the juridical prerogatives of the bishops, yet he never advocated any liturgical role for the princes. The fact that bishops, understood in the medieval tradition to be *de iure divino* and essential to the structure and mission of the church, were omitted does reveal the sharpest break with the previous processes and theology if one focuses on the point of episcopal succession. Luther's theological position that presbyters and bishops constituted one order reveals, however, that he did not abandon the liturgical and theological role of the bishop in the process of ordaining. He never advocated that the laity lay on hands, or that the prince as *Notbishof* in the juridical sense function similarly in a liturgical or theological role. One never finds princes preaching or presiding. Again, depending on one's focus, either continuity or discontinuity can be stressed.

Luther's and Bugenhagen's reemphasis on the role of the community was consistent with the intent of patristic and medieval ordination practice. For, as stated earlier, ordinations were held on one of the great Vigils of the year, *coram ecclesia*, in the presence of the community's head, the bishop, surrounded by his presbytery and assisted by his deacons. It is true that the focal point changed insofar as the presiding and ordaining official was not a bishop in apostolic succession but rather one of the presbytery functioning as *primus inter pares*. But again, apart from the prior knowledge that the presider was a bishop, or apart from

The End of an Era 229

the vestments which ceremonially would have indicated such, the ritual event would have looked similar. And it should be remembered that the reformed rites themselves did not eliminate a distinction between clergy and laity. Thus it is at the level of theological reflection more than ritual experience that distinctions between medieval and evangelical ordination appear.

Such analysis leads one finally to the question of whether the new rites were radical because they were not mere simplifications of an elaborate ritual process but rather the products of a new theology of the church and a new historical situation that denied both pope and bishops as integral to the liturgy of ordination. The congregational focus of Bugenhagen might lead one to make such an assertion. For the point would then be that it is in fact the assembly that validates the act of ordaining apart from any extra-local authority in the church. Yet such a radically congregational ecclesiology simply is not supported by the preceding evidence. Both Luther and Bugenhagen clearly concluded that the church's traditional blend of local and extra-local authority was essential, recognizing only that local authority had been obscured by the absolute control exercised by the ordained ecclesiastical hierarchy which represented, for them, an abusive extra-local authority.

Perhaps the issue might be helped by abandoning the term ordination and focussing instead on the whole vocational process. Thus the liturgical act of uniting pastor and community might be seen as only one part of a larger whole that includes training, examination, call/election, and liturgical recognition of one's new role in the community and wider church through a rite of prayer with laying on of hands. The ritual component of the process could then legitimately be repeated if one moved to other communities without calling into question the fact of one's being an already ordained leader in the church. For the other components of the vocational process would not be repeated. The relationship of those other components to the first instance of the liturgical action of prayer with laying on of hands would therefore qualify it as the person's once-for-all point of entry into ordained service in the church. Subsequent ritual acts of recognition (installation, investiture) would then no longer raise the question of whether they were reordinations.

The point of contention between Catholic and Reformation traditions with regard to ordained ministry will remain the ecclesiological issue of how local and extra-local dimensions of the church are symbolized. Perhaps the liturgical witness for ordaining cannot alone bear the burden of creating mutual recognition as is the case, for example, in the sacramental ritual act of baptizing. In baptism it is the liturgical action itself that serves to satisfy the concern for validity, integrity, mutual recognizablity—even at the point where there is not an ordained person performing the ritual act. But in the recognition of ministries the juridical dimension of the church's structure plays a role comparable to the theological/liturgical, and thus clouds the question of whether and how continuity can be mutually affirmed.

Whether the traditional role of the bishop and pope is integral to the liturgy of ordaining is thus the unresolved dilemma. This is also the case in the continuing discussion between Lutherans and Roman Catholics with regard to the role of the priest in the eucharist. The issue cannot be neatly divided into jurisdictional and theological components, as if these functioned independently. In other words, one cannot say that the rite (liturgy) carries the theological gravity of the church's concern for validity or integrity and that the matter of who presides is a purely juridical concern. The role of bishops is precisely a theological concern in these examples. For the medieval Catholic tradition the role of the bishop in ordaining was not a secondary ritual element. But neither was it secondary for Luther and other reformers. What was at issue was how one properly identified who was a true bishop. For the reformers, episcopal succession and succession in apostolic teaching were not necessarily synonymous.

One must conclude, therefore, that the liturgical witness can help in sorting out the concerns, but it cannot solve the troublesome points of division. Yet the mix of ritual experience, theological reflection, and ecclesiastical polity that come together in the vocational process which leads to and includes the ritual act of ordaining may afford the best possible context for working toward solutions.

NOTES

1 The terminology was developed by George H. Williams, *The Radical Reformation* (Philadelphia: Westminster Press, 1962).

2 Paul F. Bradshaw, "The Reformers and the Ordination Rites," *Ordination Rites*, Papers Read at the 1979 Congress of Societas Liturgica, edited by Wiebe Vos and Geoffrey Wainwright (Rotterdam: Liturgical Ecumenical Center Trust, 1980), 96.

3 Emil Sehling, *Die evangelischen Kirchenordnungen des 16. Jahrhunderts*. 15 Vols. (Leipzig : O. R. Riesland, 1902ff. Vols. I–V; Tübingen: J. C. B. Mohr, 1955 ff. Vols. VI–XV). See, VIII, 345.

4 Ibid., 450–451.

5 Martin Luther's German version, "Komm heiliger Geist"; for the text see Philipp Wackernagel *Das deutsche Kirchenlied*, 5 vols. (Hildesheim: Georg Olms, 1964), Vol. III, No. 19, 14.

6 Sehling, VIII, 452; this section of the rite is taken directly from the 1566 Church Order, 204.

7 Ibid., 454: "Dieses seind nun, geliebter bruder im Herrn Christo, die vornembste stück, die ein pfarrherr oder diener der kirchen des Herrn Jhesu Christi in seinem ampt tun und verrichten muss. Da beger ich nun vor dem angesicht Gottes und unsers Herrn Jhesu Christi und seiner heiligen engel, auch dieser ganzen christlichen versamlung von euch zu wissen, ob ihr auch bedacht seid und alhie verheissen wöllet, diesem allem also fleissig und treulich nachzukommen."

8 Ibid.: "Ich erkenne wol, dass es ein schwer ampt ist, darin ich mich begeben will. Dieweil ich aber doch ordentlich hierzu berufen bin und mich auf die gnedige göttliche hülf, die er allen seinen berufenen dienern zusagt, und auf das gebet der gemeinen christlichen kirchen genzlich verlasse, so gelobe und verheisse ich allhier vor dem angesicht Gottes und dieser christlichen gemein, alles was mein ampt erfordert nach allem meinem vermögen mit Gottes hülf treulich u leisten und zu verrichten."

9 For the text of the prayer see Appendix III, p. 267.

10 Sehling, 454–455: "So ordene und bestetige ich nun von wegen der kirchen Gottes euch auf euwere getane zusage zum ordentlichen diener der kirchen und lehrer des heiligen evangelii, im namen Gottes des Vaters und des Sohns und des heiligen Geistes. Amen."

11 For the *Te Deum laudamus* see Wackernagel I, No. 26, 24, for the Latin version; Wackernagel III, No. 31, 19, for the German version.

12 Sehling, VIII, 455: "Form einen pfarherr oder kirchendiener einzuführen und ihm die gemeine zu commendieren, so all bereits zuvor ordinirt und ein zeitlang im predigampt gewesen ist."

13 Ibid., see 419ff. for the prayers from which the superintendent could choose. One can assume that free prayer might also be possible and that those listed are models.

14 Niebergall, 149.

15 Ibid., 159.

16 Ibid., 160.

17 Sehling, I/1, 382: "Gemeine form und weise, auf welche ein neuer kirchendiener ordinirt, und durch den superintendenten seiner ihm verordenten kirchen commendirt und investirt werden sol."

18 Schulz, *Evangelische Ordination*, 52.

19 Sehling, I/1, 208: "Von der investitur, oder einsetzung der priester in die pfarren. Das einsetzen, einweisen der pfarrherr und prediger, sole durch die nehesten superattendenten, einen oder zween geschehen, in facie ecclesiae, auf des kirchspiels kosten, das des pfarrherrs benötigt. Erstlich mit verlesung des sechsten cap. 1. Timo. anzufahen, häc doce, & exhortare, bis ans ende. Zum andern, das der pfarrherr oder prediger dem volk gelobt werde, wie gott Moisi befohl, das er dem Josua thun solt, da er spricht: Lauda eum laude tua, sag viel guts von im, num. 27. cum impositione manuum."

20 Frieder Schulz, "Evangelische Ordination," *Jahrbuch für Liturgik und Hymnologie* 17 (1972): 1–54.

21 Ibid., 3.

22 Ibid., see page 2 for the structural chart.

23 Ibid., 3.

24 As examples Schulz (5, note 13) cited Braunschweig 1569 (Sehling, VI, 189), Oldenburg 1573 (Richter, II, 353), and Lauenburg 1585 (Sehling, V, 408).

25 Schulz, "Evangelische Ordination," 5.

26 Ibid. "Eine Handauflegun, die mit dem: "Ich ordne uns." verbunden ist, kann eigentlich nur als Gestus der mit Hehorsampflicht verbundened Indienstnahme im Rahmen der durch den Landesherrn o.ä. in Ordnung gehaltenen, verfassten Kirche aufgefasst werden."

27 Ibid., 7.

28 Ibid., 9.

29 Ibid., 23.

30 W. Jardine Grisbrooke, "Recent Reforms of Ordination Rites in the Churches," *Studia Liturgica* 13 (1979), 111.

31 Ibid., 116.

32 Ibid., 117.

33 Susan C. Karant-Nunn, *Luther's Pastors: The Reformation in the Ernestine Countryside* (Philadelphia: Transactions of the American Philosophical Society, Vol. 69, part 8, 1979), 65.

34 For a discussion of the problems see Karant-Nunn, Ibid., 60-70.

35 Bradshaw, "The Reformers," 107.

APPENDIX I

Texts of the Medieval Roman Rites

Leonine Sacramentary (Verona)

Source: L. C. Mohlberg, *Sacramentarium Veronense*. Rerum Ecclesiasticarum Documenta, Series Maior, Fontes I (Rome: Herder, 1956), 121–122 (Nos. 952, 953, 954).

Translation: H. Boone Porter, *The Ordination Prayers of the Western Churches* (London: SPCK, 1967), 24–29.

Oremus, dilectissimi, deum patrem omnipotentem, ut super hos famulos suos, quos ad presbyterii munus eligit, caelestia dona multiplicet: quibus quod eius dignatione suscipiunt, eius exsequantur auxilo: per.

Let us pray, dearly beloved, to God the Father Almighty that, upon these his servants, whom he has chosen for the office of presbyter, he may multiply heavenly gifts, with which what they have begun by his favour they may accomplish by his aid; through...

Exaudi nos, deus salutaris noster, et super hos famulos tuos benedictionem sancti spiritus et gratiae sacerdotalis effunde uirtutem; ut quos tuae pietatis aspectibus offerimus consecrandos, perpetua muneris tui largitate prosequaris: per.

Hear us, O God of our salvation, and pour forth the benediction of the Holy Spirit and the power of priestly grace upon these thy servants, that thou mayest accompany with the unfailing richness of thy bounty these whom we set before thy merciful countenance to be consecrated; through...

Domine sancte pater omnipotens aeterne deus, honorum omnium et omnium dignitatum quae tibi militant distributor; per quem proficiunt uniuersa; per quem cuncta firmantur, amplificatis semper in melius naturae rationalibis incrementis per ordinem congrua ratione dispositum. Unde sacerdotales grados et officia leuitarum sacramentis mysticis instituta creuerunt; ut cum pontifices summos regendis populis praefecisses, ad eorum societatis et operis adiumentum sequentis ordinis uiros et secundae dignitatis elegeris. Sic in heremo per septuaginta uirorum prudentium mentes Mose spiritum propagasti; quibus ille adiutoribus usus in populo, innumeras multitudines facile gubernauit. Sic in Eleazaro et Ithamar, filiis Aharon, paternae plenitudinis abundantiam transfudisti, ut ad hostias salutares et frequentiores officii sacramenta sufficeret meritum sacerdotum.

  Ac prouidentia, domine, apostolis filii tui doctores fidei comites addedisti, quibus illi orbem totum secundis

O Lord, Holy Father, Almighty, Everlasting God, bestower of all the honours and of all the worthy ranks which do thee service, thou through whom all things make increase, through whom everything is made firm, by the ever-extended increase to the benefit of rational nature by a succession arranged in due order; whence the priestly ranks and the offices of the Levites arose and were inaugurated with mystical symbols. Thus when thou didst set up high priests to rule over thy people, thou didst choose men of a lesser order and secondary dignity to be their companions and to help them in their labor. Likewise in the desert thou didst spread out the spirit of Moses through the minds of the seventy wise men, so that he, using them as helpers among the people, governed with ease countless multitudes. Likewise also thou didst impart unto Eleazar and Ithamar, the sons of Aaron, the richness of their father's plenty, so that the benefit of priests might be sufficient for the salutary sacrifices and the rites of a more frequent

praedicatoribus impleuerunt. Quapropter infirmitati quoque nostrae, domine, quaesumus, haec adiuuenta largire; qui quanto magis fragiliores sumus, tanto his pluribus indigemus. Da, quaesumus, pater, in hos famulos tuos presbyterii dignitatem. Innoua in uisceribus eorum spiritum sanctitatis. Acceptum a te, deus, secundi meriti munus obtineant, censuramque morum exemplo suae conuersationis insinuent. Sint probi cooperatores ordinis nostri. Eluceat in eis totius forma iustitiae, ut bonam rationem dispensationis sibi creditae reddituri, aeternae beatitudinis praemia consequantur per.

worship. And also, by providence, O Lord, thou didst add, to the Apostles of thy Son, teachers of the faith as companions, and they filled the whole world with these secondary preachers.

Wherefore we beseech thee, O Lord, to grant these assistants to our weakness also, for we who are so much frailer need so many more. Grant we beseech thee, O Father, the dignity of the presbytery unto these thy servants. Renew in their inward parts the Spirit of holiness. May they obtain and receive of thee, O God, the office of second dignity, and by the example of their conversation may they commend a strict way of life. May they be virtuous colleagues of our order. Let the pattern of all righteousness show forth in them, in order that, rendering in time to come a good account of the stewardship committed unto them, they may obtain the rewards of eternal blessedness; through.

The Old Gelasian Sacramentary

Source: L.C. Mohlberg, *Liber Sacramentorum Romanae Aeclesiae Ordinis Anni Circuli* (Sacramentarium Gelasianum). Rerum Ecclesiaticarum Documenta, Series Maior, Fontes IV (Rome: Herder, 1960), 25-26 (Nos. 143-148).

Translation: H. Boone Porter, *The Ordination Prayers*, 50-52.

AD ORDINANDUS PRAESBYTEROS. Oremus dilectissimi...[same as above; the Roman bidding].

Exaudi nos...[same as above; the Roman Collect].

CONSECRATIO. Domine sanctae pater...[same as above; the Roman consecration prayer].

CONSUMMACIO PRAESBYTERI. Sit nobis, fratres, communis oratio, ut hii qui in adiutorium et utilitatem uestrae salutis eleguntur, praesbyteratus benedictionem deuinae indulgentiam muneris consequantur, ut sancti spiritus sacerdotalia dona priulegio uirtutum, ne inparis loco depraehendantur, obteneant: per suum: per.

Let us pray together, brethren, that this man, who is chosen to aid and further your salvation, may by the mercy of divine assistance secure the blessing of the presbyterate, in order that he may obtain by the privilege of virtue the sacerdotal gifts of the Holy Ghost, so that he be not found

Appendix I

ITEM BENEDICTIO.
Sanctificationum omnium auctor, cuius uera consecratio, cuius plena benedictio est; tu, domine, super hos famulos tuos, quos praesbyterii honore dedicamus, manuum tuae benedictionis his infunde, ut grauitate actuum et censura uidendi probent se esse seniores, his instituti disciplinis quas Tito et Timetheo Paulus exposuit: ut in lege tua die ac note, omnipotens, meditantes quod elegerent et credant, quod crediderint doceant, quod docuerint imitentur; iustitiam, constantiam, misericordiam, fortitudinem in se ostendant et exemplo probent, admonitionem confirment: ut purum adque inmaculatum ministerii tui donum custodiant, et per obsequium plebis tue corpus et sanguinem filii tui immaculata benedictine transformentur, et inuiolabile caritate in uirum perfectum, in mensuram aetatis plenitudinis Christi, in die iustitiae aeternae iudicii constantia pura, fide plena spiritu sancto pleni persoluant: per.

wanting in his office; through.

Author of all sanctification, of whom is true consecration, full benediction: do thou, O Lord, spread forth the hand of thy blessing upon this thy servant, N., whom we set apart with the honour of the presbyterate; so that he may show himself to be an elder by the dignity of his acts and the righteousness of his life, taught by these instructions which Paul presented to Titus and Timothy: that meditating day and night upon thy law O thou Almighty, what he readeth, he may believe; what he believeth, he may teach; what he teacheth, he may practise. May he show in himself justice, loyalty, mercy, bravery; may he provide the example and demonstrate the exhortation, in order that he may keep the gift of thy ministry pure and untainted; and with the consent of the people may he transform, by an untainted benediction, the body and blood of thy Son. And in unbroken love, may he reach unto a perfect man, unto the measure and stature of the

The *Missale Francorum*

Source: L.C. Mohlberg, *Missale Francorum*. Rerum Ecclesiasticarum Documenta, Series Maior, Fontes II (Rome: Herder, 1957), 8-10 (Nos. 27-34).

ALLOCUTIO AD POPULUM IN ORDINATIONE PRESBYTERI. Quoniam, dilectissimi fratres, rectores nauem et nauigium deferendis eadem est uel securitates ratio uel timores, communes eorum debet esse sententia, quorum causa cummunes existet. Ne frustra a patribus reminescimur institutum, ut de electione eorum, qui ad regimen altaris adhibendi sunt, consoletur et populos, quia de actu et conuersatione praesenti quod nonnumquam ignorantur a pluribus scitur a paucis, et necesse est, ut facilius quis oboedientiam exhibeat ornato, cui adsensum praebuerit ordinando. Fratris nostri et conpresbiteri conuersatio, quantum nosse mihi uideor, probata ac deo placita est, et digna (ut arbitror) eclesiastici

fullness of Christ, in the day of judgement with a pure conscience, with full faith, full of the Holy Ghost; through...

Translation: H. Boone Porter, *The Ordination Prayers*, 48-53.

ALLOCUTION TO THE PEOPLE AT THE ORDINATION OF A PRESBYTER. Whereas, dearly beloved brethren, those who rule a ship and those engaged in the voyage share the same purpose for reason of safety or of fear, there should be agreement in common among those who have a common cause. Nor is it in vain that we recall the ordinance of the Fathers that the people also be consulted concerning the choice of those who are appointed to the regulation of the altar, since concerning his activity and present conversation what is sometimes unknown to most people is known to a few, and

Appendix I

honoris augmentum. Sed ne unum fortasse uel paucos aut decipiat adsensio, aut fallat affectio, sententia est expectanda multorum. Itaque quid de eius actibus aut moribus noueritis, quid de merito censiatis, deo teste consolemus. Debet hanc fidem habere caritas uestra, quam secundum praeceptum euangelii et deum exhibere debitis et proximo, ut huic testimonium sacerdoti magis pro merito quam pro affectione aliquid tribuatis. Et qui deuotione omnium expectamus, intellegere tacentes non possumus. Scimus tamen, quod est acceptabilius deo, aderit per spiritum sanctum consensus unus omnium animorum. Et ideo electionem uestram debitis uoce pupleca profitere: per dominum.

it is certain that anyone will more readily yield obedience to the ordained man for whom one hath given consent when he was being ordained. Our brothers and fellow presbyters, the conversation of this man, as far as I know, is approved and worthy, I think, of the increase of ecclesiastical honour. But lest either favour lead astray or feelings deceive one perhaps or a few persons, the opinion of many must be sought. And so we ask your counsel regarding what ye may know concerning his actions and conduct, of what ye may judge concerning his merit, with God as witness. Your charity, which according to the teaching of the gospel ye ought to show both to God and to your neighbour, should have this truthfulness, that ye should give testimony to this priest more for merit than for any affection. And we who await the sentence of all, cannot understand those who are silent. We know, however, that what is most acceptable to God, the single consent of the minds of all, will come through the Holy Spirit. And, therefore, your election ye

ORATIO AD PRESBYTEROS ORDINANDOS. Oremus, dilectissimi...[same as above; the Roman bidding].

ITEM ALIA. Exaudi nos... [same as above; the Roman Collect].

CONSECRATIO. Domine, sanctae pater...[same as above; the Roman consecration prayer].

CONSUMMATIO PRESBYTERII. Sit nobis... [same as above; the Gallican bidding].

ITEM BENEDICTIO. Sanctificationum omnium auctor...[same as above; the Gallican blessing].

CONSECRATIO MANUS. Consecrentur manus istae et santificentur per istam unctionem et nostram benedictionem, ut quaecumque sanctificauerint sanctificentur: per dominum.

ITEM ALIA. Unguantur manus istae de oleo sanctificato et crismate sanctificationis:

should declare with a common voice: through...

CONSECRATION OF THE HANDS. May these hands be consecrated and hallowed by this unction and our blessing, so that whatever they bless may be blessed and whatever they hallow may be hallowed; through...

ANOTHER. May these hands be anointed with hallowed oil and the chrism of holiness. As

sicut uncxit Samuhel Dauid in regem et prophetam, ita unguantur er consummentur in nomene dei patris et filii et spiritus sancti, facientes imaginem sanctae crucis saluatoris domini nostri Iesu Christi, qui nos a morte redemit et ad regna caelorum perducit.

Exaudi nos, pie pater, omnipotens aeterne deus, et preasta quid te rogamus et oramus: per.

Samuel anointed David to be a king and prophet, so be they anointed and perfected, in the name of God the Father, and the Son, and the Holy Ghost, making the image of thy holy cross of the Saviour Jesus Christ our Lord, who redeemed us from death and leadeth us to the kingdom of heaven.

Hear us, O Gracious Father, Almighty Everlasting God, and grant what we ask and pray of thee; through...

The Eighth Century Gelasians: The Gellone Sacramentary

Source: A. Dumas, *Liber Sacramentorum Gellonensis*. Corpus Christianorum Series Latina, CLIX (Turnholti: Typographi Brepolis Editores Pontificii, 1981), 388–391 (Nos. 2529–2537).

Translation: H. Boone Porter, *The Ordination Prayers*, 87-89.

ORDO PRESBITERII. Presbiter cum ordinatur, episcopu eum benedicente et manus super caput eius tenente, etiam omnes presbiteri qui presentis sunt super caput eius manus suas iuxta manum episcopi teneant.

ALLOCUTIO AD POPULU AS ORDINAND. PBRU. Quoniam, dilectissimi fratres...[same as above; the Gallican Allocution].

OR AD PBR ORDINANDUM. Oremus, dilectissimi...[same as above; the Roman bidding].

ITEM. Exaudi nos...[same as above; the Roman Collect].

CONSECRATIO PRESBITERI. Domine sancte pater...[same as above; the northern recension of the Roman consecration].

CONSECRATIO PBRI. Sit nobis fratres...[same as above; the Gallican bidding].

ITEM BENEDICTIONE. Deus, santificationum auctur...[same as above; the Gallican blessing].

Hic uestris ei casula. Benedictio patris et fili et spiritus sanctus discendit super te, <et> sis benedictus in ordine sacerdotale et offeras placabilis hostias pro peccatis adque offensionibus populi	Here thou clothest him with the chasuble. The blessing of the Father and of the Son and of the Holy Ghost descend upon thee, and mayest thou be blessed in the priestly order and offer acceptable sacrifices,

omnipotentem deum, cui est honor et gloria in secula seculorum [Per.].	for the sins and offenses of the people, unto Almighty God, to whom be honour and glory.
CONSECRA MANUU. Consecrentur manus isti...[same as above].	

The Pontifical of William Durandus

Source: M. Andrieu, *Le pontifical romain au moyen-âge*, Tome III. "Le pontifical de Guillaume Durand." *Studi e Testi* 88 (1940), 363-373.

XIII. On the Ordination of the Presbyter

1. When the deacons have been ordained, the bishop approaches the seat. Then the tract (or the Alleluia, if it is later than the octave of Pentecost) is sung. Then, before the Gospel is recited, the bishop proceeds to the ordination of the presbyters. In certain churches, however, the presbyters are ordained only after the reading of the Gospel, before the Creed is begun.

2. And so, in the ordination, he proceeds in this way: when the deacons have returned to their seats, the archdeacon speaks in a loud voice saying, "Let those approach who are to be ordained into the order of presbyters." Shortly thereafter, he calls them one by one and by name, as is prescribed in the treatise on subdeacons (although without mentioning title). Then garbed as is customary for deacons—in cloak, alb, cincture, stole and maniple—and holding their chasuble [planeta] folded on their arms and lit candles in their hands, they come before the official who is presiding at the ordination. They do this two by two and gather in a circle before him. Then, when they have all been arranged in this way, the decree is made as above.

3. Then the archdeacon says in a loud voice, as though he were giving a reading: "Our mother, the Catholic Church, requests that you ordain the deacons here present to the rank of presbyter." Then the bishop asks him: "Do you know that they are worthy?" The archdeacon replies: "As much as human frailty can know, that I do know and I bear witness that they are worthy of the responsibilities of this office."

4. Then, being seated, the bishop speaks to the clergy and the people in a simple reading voice. He announces the following in accordance with the statute of the Carthaginian council: "Most beloved brethren, both the helmsman of a ship and the ship's passengers share the same source of security and fear. Their feelings should be shared since a common cause exists for them. And so, it is not without reason that we recall the institution of our fathers: that the people, too, are consulted about the election of those who will be called to a position of authority at the altar. Concerning the life and conversation of the candidate, what is unknown to many is sometimes known by a few. Thus he who consents to the ordination will more readily obey the one ordained. If indeed, the conversation of these deacons who are about to be ordained as presbyters—with God's help—was as upright and as pleasing to God and as worthy as it seems to me, then I believe that it serves as an increase of ecclesiastical honor. But lest consent may deceive or affection blind one or a few, the opinion of the multitude should be awaited. And so, whatever you know about their actions and character, whatever you believe about their merit, speak freely and disclose this and grant them evidence of their priesthood. Do this in accordance with their merits rather than out of mere affection. If, therefore, anyone has anything against them, in God's name and for God's sake let him come forth and speak with confidence. Only let him be mindful of his own condition."

5. After this, the bishop, remaining seated, instructs and advises those who are about to be ordained. He uses the following words: *Admonition.* "O my brothers, O you who are about to be consecrated, be zealous in assuming the office of presbyter worthily. And, once you have assumed it, be zealous in pursuing it commendably. For a priest ought to offer, to bless, to preside, to preach and to baptize. Certainly, such an important step should be anticipated and approached with great

Appendix I 247

fear: this, so that one's character—righteous because of heavenly wisdom—and the daily observation of justice may commend the chosen to it.

Because of this, the Lord, instructing Moses to choose seventy men from all of Israel to help him—men to whom he would distribute the gifts of the Holy Spirit—added: 'Choose those whom you know because they are old people.' If indeed you are distinguished among the seventy old men, if guarding the decalogue of the law through the sevenfold spirit, you are upright and mature both in wisdom and deed. Under the same mystery and the same image in the New Testament, the Lord chose seventy-two men and sent them in pairs before Him to preach. He did this in order that they might teach, both by word and deed, that the ministers of his church ought to be perfect in faith and deed and strengthened with the virtue of innate love, that is, of course, God's and his Son's. And so, if you desire to be such—helpers of Moses and the twelve apostles, which is to say of the catholic bishops who are based upon Moses and the apostles—you may prevail through the grace of God to be chosen worthily.

Surely the holy church is surrounded, adorned and governed by this remarkable variety, with some consecrated in it as bishops, some as priests of a lesser order, deacons and men of diverse orders. And one body of Christ is composed of many members, each with its own value. Therefore, O beloved, preserve those whom the church has chosen to be consecrated to our judgment of our helpers, our brothers; preserve them by your character in the integrity of a chaste and holy life.

Know what you are doing. Imitate what you are treating insofar as, celebrating the mystery of our Lord's death, you may take care that your members die to all vices and desires. Let your doctrine be spiritual medicine for God's people. Let the savor of your life be delight in Christ's church, so that by your preaching and by your example you may build a home (that is to say, a household of God). And do this so that neither might we deserve to be condemned by the Lord on account of your advancement nor you on account of your undertaking such a great office. Rather, do this that we might deserve some slight reward. And may he grant us this through his grace." Response: Amen.

6. After this, the ordinator, without accompaniment of either prayer

or song, places both hands on the head of each candidate, one at a time, each candidate kneeling before him in turn. And, after him, three or more priests there present do the same thing. These priests shall be clothed in a cope or white chasuble [planeta].

7. When this has been done, both the bishop and the presbyters hold their right hands over them, and the bishop recites this prayer over them: *Prayer*: "Beloved, let us pray to God, the Father Almighty, that over these servants...with help. Through... Amen." [*Oremus, dilectissimi*; as above].

8. Then, turning towards the altar, he says: "Let us pray." And the deacon says: "Let us kneel...Arise." And then, turning towards the candidates (who are kneeling), he recites this preface: *Prayer*: "Hear us, we beseech you, Lord, our God, and over...may you attend. Through...In unity. [*Exaudi nos*; as above].

9. Then he says in a moderate voice, with hands joined in front of his breast: *Preface*: "Through all the ages, etc. Truly worthy, etc. Bestower of honors and distributor of all dignities...may rewards follow." Let what follows be spoken clearly in order that it may be heard by those who are standing around. "Through the same...In unity...Amen."

10. Here he turns back the orarium or stole from the left shoulder to the top of the right shoulder of each one in turn. He says to each: "Receive the yoke of the Lord. For his yoke is easy and his burden light. In the name of the Lord. Amen."

11. Afterwards, he places on the back of each one's shoulders, in turn, a chasuble. Let each one wear this chasuble folded above his shoulders hanging down from the upper part. He says to each one: "Receive this priestly garment, by which your charity is known. For the Lord is able to increase charity and perfect work for you." Response: "Thanks be to God."

12. A blessing, which is recited as though read, with everyone kneeling: "God, the author of all sanctification...Filled with the Holy Spirit, let them redeem. Through the same. In unity. Amen." [*Deus sanctificationum*; as above].

13. Then the bishop turns toward the altar and kneels. Before the middle of the altar, he begins in a loud voice: "Alleluia. Come Holy

Appendix I 249

Spirit" (see below on the consecration of the altar) or, if it is later than the octave of Pentecost, the hymn, "Come, Creator Spirit."

14. Then, when the first verse has been sung, he rises and washes his hands. While the preludes are being sung, all of the candidates for ordination kneel before him in turn. He anoints them, not with chrism, but with oil of catechumens. He anoints, at the same time, both hands and thumbs of each of them in the shape of a cross. He does so by producing, with his own anointed right thumb, two lines of ointment: the first, from the right thumb of each to the left index finger; the second, from the right index finger to the left thumb. And while anointing the palms completely, he says to each of them: "Lord, may you deem it worthy to consecrate and sanctify these hands...may they be blessed and sanctified. In the name of our Lord, Jesus Christ." And let each candidate respond: "Amen."

15. Then the bishop closes or joins the hands of each in turn. And then each returns to his place and keeps his hands closed in this way, right over left, until the end of the mass. In certain churches, however, they wash their hands immediately after the Gospel has been read.

16. If there should be need (because of the number of those to be ordained), let the following sequence be sung: "Come, Holy Spirit and send forth from heaven." When everything has been completed in this way, the bishop washes and dries his hands.

17. When this has been done, he passes to each in turn a chalice with wine and water, and a paten set on top of it with a host. They take them between the index and middle fingers of both hands: first the base of the chalice and then the mouth of the paten. He says to each one: "Receive the power to offer sacrifice to God and to celebrate masses both for the living and for the dead. In the name of the Father and of the Son and of the Holy Spirit." Response: "Amen."

18. And when the pope ordains a presbyter as cardinal, he gives him a ring saying: "To the honor of our Lord, Jesus Christ, and of the apostles Peter and Paul, we entrust to you this church with its clergy and people."

19. When this has been completed, the Gospel is read by one of the newly ordained deacons.

20. After this, the hosts are prepared on the altar in accordance with

the number of candidates for ordination (all of whom ought to receive communion). And the mass proceeds in the customary order. Those who have been ordained may, if they wish, have books before them. From these, they may quietly recite the canon and whichever parts from the mass the ordinator recites.

21. The Secret is recited on behalf of those who have been ordained. It is recited under one "Through the Lord" along with the Secret for the mass of that day. "We beseech you, Lord, act through your mysteries that we may worthily offer these gifts to you. Through..."

22. Then, before the "Lamb of God" is sung, a solemn blessing: "May Almighty God bless you through his mercy," and so on, among our blessings. And after the ordinator has received communion, then the ordained priets will receive communion from his hand (as stated above in the *titulus* on Holy Orders).

23. When this has been done, the ordinator begins the response: "I shall no longer call you servants: I shall call you my friends because you have learned everything which I have done in your midst. Alleluia. Receive the Holy Spirit, the Paraclete, among you. He is the one whom the Father will send to you. Alleluia." Verse: "You are my friends, if you will do what I command you. Receive. Glory be to the Father and to the Son and to the Holy Spirit. He...."

24. And while the response is being sung, they, standing in front of the altar before the bishop, confess the faith which they will preach, saying, "I believe in one God..." and so on.

25. When this has been done, the bishop places hands over the heads of each of them in turn. As he does this, they shall bow their heads slightly. He says to each of them: "Receive the Holy Spirit. Whose sins you forgive, they shall be forgiven. Whose sins you retain, they shall be retained."

26. Then, pulling forth and unfolding the chasuble (which each of them wears folded on his shoulders), he vests each of them successively in it. He does this in such a way that the candidate's hands may always remain folded. And he says to each one: "May the Lord clothe you in the stole of innocence."

27. And then each one approaches the bishop again, one at a time.

Appendix I

They place their hands, still joined, between the hands of the bishop and he says to each of them: "Do you promise obedience and reverence to me and to my successors?" And the candidate responds: "I promise." He does this unless he is subject to another. Likewise the bishop, holding the hands of the candidate between his own, kisses each candidate, saying: "May the peace of the Lord be with you always." And the candidate responds, "Amen."

28. When this has been completed and everyone has returned to his place, he says to them: *Instruction*: "Dearest brothers, because the task which you are about to undertake is rather dangerous, I urge you to learn carefully and honorably the order of the whole mass, and the consecration and breaking of the host, and communion. Learn this from other priests who already know it before you proceed to celebrate mass."

29. After this, the bishop turns toward the altar and the communion song is sung. And the postcommunion, the one on behalf of those who have been ordained, is sung under one "Through the Lord" with the postcommunion of the mass. *Postcommunion*: "Lord, graciously lift up with your continuing aid those whom you restore with your sacraments, in order that we may receive the fruit of your redemption both in these mysteries and in the conduct of our lives. Through...." Response: "Amen." Then, "Let us bless the Lord" is said or "Go. The mass is ended," if time allows.

30. When this has been done, he turns with his mitre and staff toward those who have been ordained. He urges them, all together, to live well and to consider carefully the order which they have undertaken. He urges them, too, to pray for him and for others that he wishes. He enjoins masses upon them and other things which he has seen to be advantageous. He asks that they undertake these things devoutly and answer that they will do them.

31. Finally, they kneel while he blesses them. He says in a clear voice: "May the blessing of God Almighty, of the Father and of the Son and of the Holy Spirit, descend upon you. May it do so in order that you be blessed in this priestly order and that you may offer pleasing sacrifices for the sins and offenses of the people of God Almighty. For to him is the honor and the glory for ever and ever." Response: "Amen."

Finally, they enter the sacristy and wash their hands there. They rub them with the white of the bread and the water of ablution, or in a pool.

APPENDIX II

Text of the 1529 Hamburg Order

Source: Emil Sehling, *Die evangelischen Kirchenordnungen des sechzehnten Jahrhunderts*. (Leipzig: O.R. Riesland, 1902). Volume 5; 502–503.

"How such servants of the Word shall be initiated [*annehmen*] into the church."

Such elected servants of the Word shall be announced on the previous Sunday from the pulpit when they are to assume what has been described earlier [the different pastoral offices outlined in the preceding section of the Church Order]. They shall receive a spiritual ordination at Sunday worship before the congregation, whether they have been anointed or not. They may call it *ordinati ad ministerium spiritus non literae* (II Cor.3:6), which is to say, those people who are ordained to preach the gospel of Christ. Just as others receive a secular order, this one is God's order. It is as if he were ordained to be a major civil servant, etc.: as long as his duties [*Amt*] continue, so shall his order [*orden*], the order into which he is ordained. It is not to be construed in this spiritual order into which one is ordained for Word and Sacrament (and it would be a mockery) that we do anything but that which is contained in I Cor. 4. Indelible character is a fiction.

Anointing and tonsuring are no help in this office—only God's gifts count, given to a person by God. He shall be an honest, just, capable man who shall be strong enough to teach God's word, to resist the enemy, as Saint Paul has described such gifts in I Timothy 3. Some who take orders and call themselves ordained belong to that group which Saint Paul calls the unordained and shuns when they will not convert. Among the early Christians ordination was accomplished with prayer and the laying on of hands, as we see in the book of Acts and in Paul's epistles. Accordingly, we will do it succinctly and in a Christian way.

When the epistle has been read a preacher or chaplain shall enter the pulpit and announce:

> Dear friends in Christ, you know that we have prayed that God for Christ's sake

would send us a good superintendent (pastor, or chaplain, or preacher). Those who have been entrusted have done their duty and chosen, N., whom they have, with as much judgment and understanding as humanly possible, judged to be honest, just, capable, and not envious. He is blameless to himself and to those around him. He has the strength to teach the Word of God the Lord to the consciences, to stop the mouths of those who would contradict, as Saint Paul teaches in Timothy and Titus, and Christ teaches in the faithful and wise servant (Matthew 24:45ff.) Pray, therefore, that God, through Jesus Christ, would give him grace to carry out his office and lead us to salvation.

Remember the example that Christ has given us in Luke 6: On the morning on which he wished to teach and choose his twelve disciples for the office of preaching, he prayed to God on the previous night alone on the mountain. If God commands this matter according to our prayers, then it cannot fail, even if we were possibly to choose a Judas. But this, N., shall be presented before this altar with song, prayer, and the laying on of hands so that he may be commended to the grace of God, and so that this congregation may know that this person has been commended by us to such an office. I admonish all of you—councilmen, deacons, citizens, and common folk, young and old—to pray while the children's choir sings the Alleluia.

The children in the choir then shall sing the Alleluia, *Veni Sancte Spiritus*, etc. While this is being sung, pastors from all churches shall kneel before the altar, with the ordinand in the middle, in silent prayer. The following Collect will be read when all pastors have assembled and knelt before the altar. For that reason, the church bells on those days shall be rung one half hour earlier, so that the pastors may leave their pulpits at an earlier time. All this, so that they may join in the prayer after the sermon preceding the ordination.

When a superintendent is to be ordained or installed [*verordnet*] to his office before the congregation, it shall take place at St. Peters Church, and the pastor there shall read or chant the Collect as a second Collect. When a pastor or an adjutor is to be ordained, it shall take place in his own church and the superintendent shall chant the Collect. When a chaplain is to be ordained, the pastor of his church shall read the Collect, and only the superintendent shall attend, not the other pastors. But for the priest [*prester*] of Holy Spirit hospice, the pastor of St. Nicholas Church shall read the Collect and, with his chaplains, accompany him into the hospice of the Holy Spirit and present him to the paupers. The third chaplain of St. Jacob shall be introduced in the same way: the pastor shall accompany him with the other chaplains after mass into the hospital of St.George. The superintendent and pastors shall be present at all ordinations, along with the chaplains of the respective churches, when they are not hindered in other duties of their office.

When the Alleluia is finished, all preachers shall rise and lay on hands on the head of the ordinand. The one who stands nearest the altar, facing the candidate who has his back to the congregation, shall lay his hands on as well and read this Collect or prayer:

> Let us pray: Almighty, eternal Father, you have taught us through our master Jesus Christ that the harvest is great but the workers are few, therefore pray the Lord of the harvest, that he may send into his harvest laborers who will be good workers. That is, preachers who by your grace admonish with hearty prayer to improve. We ask you in your boundless mercy that you would look with favor upon this, your servant, our elected preacher, that he may be diligent with your Word, preaching Jesus Christ for our salvation, instructing our consciences, comforting us, and punishing, warning, and admonishing us with forbearance and teaching; that he may preach the pure, holy gospel without deadly human doctrine; that he may abide with us and bring from among all of us the fruits of salvation, through the same, our Lord Jesus Christ. Amen.

Then the people shall sing *Nun bitten wir den heiligen Geist*. The pastors shall kneel and entrust these things to God through Jesus Christ. They shall then rise during the song and go straight out of the church to their own pulpits. After the song they shall preach, etc.

Special clothing or finery is not needed for this action. But this prescribed acceptance has two important factors. First, that we commend this action to God in prayer. Second, that the congregation may see and acknowledge that the one who stands before them has been chosen as preacher and pastor [*Seelsorger*]. This ordination occurs before God and before the people for their salvation.

APPENDIX III

Texts of the Hesse Orders

The 1566 Kirchenordnung

Source: Emil Sehling, *Die evangelischen Kirchenordnungen des 16. Jahrhunderts.* (Tübingen: J.C.B. Mohr, 1955), Volume VIII, 203-207

"How Preachers Shall Be Ordained"

After the ordinands have been found to be able, they shall be ordained in this manner on the following day [after their examination] in Marburg before the congregation. When everything customarily done on the church day is completed, except the prayer of dismissal, the superintendent shall stand in that place at Marburg where it is customary to celebrate the Lord's Supper. The other servants of the Word and the elders of the congregation, together with the ordinands, shall be seated. Then the superintendent shall disclose to the congregation that one person or several have been called, selected, presented, and examined in an orderly way, have been found to be qualified through examination, and that they wish to proceed with the help of God into the preaching office of their own region.

Because it is important to the entire congregation, indeed all the faithful, that the Church shall be well represented, and that shepherds and teachers might not be qualified or able to work faithfully in such high office unless it were given to them by God, the superintendent shall seriously admonish the congregation that they should desire to hear God's Word concerning the office of the preacher. They should further pray seriously to God for his grace and help, that they may faithfully carry out their office and might remain steadfast and pious in it.

Then the superintendent shall read from the Holy Scriptures and say:

> Listen, beloved in the Lord, how the office of the shepherds and elders who work with the Word shall be, from the teaching of our Lord Jesus Christ, the great shepherd, and his apostle Matthew. In the twenty-eighth chapter (verses 18-20) Christ commands his disciples and all servants of the Church who follow

him, thus: "All authority in heaven and on earth has been given to me. Go therefore and make disciples of all nations, baptizing them in the name of the Father, and of the Son, and of the Holy Spirit, teaching them to observe all that I have commanded you; and lo, I am with you always, to the close of the age."

The Apostle Paul writes to Titus (1:5-9), [the text of the passage follows]. The same Apostle writes in II Timothy 3:(14) to 4:5, [here, only verse 5 is included in the text of the Order]: "As for you, always be steady, endure suffering, do the work of an evangelist, fulfill your ministry."

After all of this the superintendent shall address the ordinands, who stand at the side of the altar where the Holy Supper is celebrated:

1. My beloved in the Lord, you have heard what your office is, that it is not human teaching, but from the command of our Lord Jesus Christ and his holy apostles, how it is explained in Holy Scripture and especially in the epistles of Paul to Timothy and Titus. But so that all may better understand, and that you yourselves might intentionally observe this and be mindful of this in your lives, I will summarize it briefly and specifically.

The one who is ordained as pastor or teacher in God's Church must purely and faithfully present and exposit the entire teaching of the Christian church included in the books of the prophets and apostles of the Old and New Testaments, which is briefly sumarized in the three creeds, Apostolic, Nicene, and of St. Athanasius. That person must not be frightened by any fear or danger or human favor from that same form and apostolic teaching. He shall explain and confirm the teaching of God's Word and law and Gospels, not only before the people but at home in his own house.

He shall cast off all unspiritual loose talk, angry words, foolish and useless questions (II Timothy 2:16). And when some people might themselves spread and defend a false teaching or, deceived by others, embrace a false teaching, then you must contradict them from the basis of Holy Scripture, overthrow the teaching, and with gentleness bring those who are in error back to the right path. It may also happen that you will admonish people of different classes and occupations, and they must accept that teaching as the Word of God.

And further, with those who lead a sinful life and cause all kinds of trouble, you must sometimes be gentle and act with generosity, and at other times be firm and serious, sometimes privately and sometimes publicly punish and scold and use arguments taken from God's Word. And last, you shall lift up, strengthen, and comfort the sick, the troubled and fearful, and all those who need comfort.

2. You shall dispense the sacraments of the Christian Church, Baptism and the Lord's Supper. You have heard from God's Word that they have been instituted

Appendix III

by the Lord Jesus Christ (Matthew 28:19; I Cor.11:23) and what is given in those holy sacraments to the faithful. You shall explain often the right use of the same, and actively educate and command your congregation and see vigorously that they (the sacraments) are neither desecrated nor misused by anyone.

3. You shall particularly exert yourselves and see to it that through your teaching your listeners are awakened and moved to bear spiritual fruit, which is appropriate as they recognize pure teaching and correct uses of the sacraments, and that those fruits may be apparent to all, so that the name of God may be honored and praised among the people (II Timothy 3:10ff.). So that this might happen, you shall have assistance from the other teachers and elders in that congregation (Acts 14:23; Titus 1:5). You should live peaceably with them as your beloved brothers (I Timothy 5:19) and always consult on the improvement, use, and growth of the Church. Whatever business there is, you shall carry it out with the same energy. If they give good advice or a proposal, you shall decide on it and pursue it energetically and faithfully, so that nothing is avoided or neglected which would maintain good discipline and which might be useful and helpful for the general education and correct administration of the Church. The Church's salvation and welfare are not only maintained solely by pure doctrine, but by wise government as well.

4. So that everything is administered correctly and fruitfully, it is necessary that you teach not only with words, but also with works and deeds. You must be honest and upright toward all, manage your household well, not be a drunkard nor a penny pincher (I Timothy 3:3f.), so that you may do all things with economy and modesty. In all, you must be an example in your behavior, in your love, spirit, faith, word and in your modesty. Persist in reading, in admonishing, in teaching. Do not neglect the gifts you have been given. Expect such things and proceed, that your growth in all things may be manifest. Be attentive to yourselves and your doctrine, be steadfast in all these things (I Timothy 4:12-14, 16). You shall not pay attention nor be hindered in your office, nor doubt God's help when you hear the gossip of evil people and those who despise the Word of God, as well as their tricks and trumped up annoyances. When you are able to ignore this you make yourselves blessed and those who hear you.

This is, then, my beloved in the Lord, the office of preacher and elder who work with the Word, the most superior offices according to God's teaching and that of our Lord Jesus Christ, and the exposition of the apostles. Is it the desire of each of you, before the face of God and our Lord Jesus Christ and his chosen angels (I Timothy 5:21) and this Christian congregation, to promise and keep this constantly and faithfully?

Then the ordinands answer individually that they recognize this is a difficult office in which they wish to betake themselves, but, because they have been called to this and rely entirely on the prayers of the whole Church and the gracious help of a generous God, they promise to do all that is in their power.

The superintendent shall admonish the congregation with a few brief words to call on Almighty God for help and presence in the name of Jesus Christ, and he shall speak this prayer with a loud voice [the prayer is that of the 1539 Erfurt edition of the Cassel Church Order; it was also used in the ordination of superintendents; see Sehling, VIII, 197]:

> O Almighty, gracious God, heavenly Father, when your dear Son, our Lord Jesus Christ, was raised to your right hand in his heavenly being, he at once began to provide for us here on earth apostles, evangelists, prophets, shepherds, and teachers. These are his chosen ones, who gather and teach, who through the command of his dear apostles are chosen and installed. They will dispense faithfully his Holy Gospel and Sacrament, and will provide and accomplish all pastoral care and shepherding. We ask you through the same, our great shepherd and the bishop of our souls, your dear Son, that to these who have been chosen from your people for such service, you might richly impart your Holy Spirit, which will illumine them at all times, lead and strengthen them, so that they may accomplish your lofty and holy service with real understanding and zeal. And that they might seek, find, and bring to your dear Son all who are estranged from him or who have been led against him; that they might educate and improve all who are brought to him and who are still in his congregation. In this, preserve them from all of their own errors and irritations, from all false slander and detraction, as well as from the powerful impediments to their service. All of this so that they may serve you and your dear church joyously, persistently, purposefully, and blessedly, that your name might be ever more blessed and your kingdom spread on every side and be even more splendid. Through the same, your dear Son our Lord Jesus Christ. Amen.

After the prayer the superintendent and the other servants of the Word shall impose hands on the ordinands, who shall come up with all deference and kneel. Following this the superintendent shall say this prayer in a loud voice:

> O Lord God, heavenly Father, you alone make able workers of the Church and give power and strength, we ask you from our hearts that you would enlighten the heart of this your servant with the Holy Spirit. Likewise, guide and direct him with your mighty hand, so that he may faithfully carry out his office to the

Appendix III 261

honor of your name and to the edification of all faithful people in the Church of your Son; through the same, Christ our Lord. Amen.

Finally, he addresses the ordinands who stand before him: "Now I commend to all of you and to each of you the Church. You are set over it as shepherds and teachers, so that you may faithfully and energetically direct, lead, and keep God's flock, purchased by Christ with his own blood, commended and placed before you by the Holy Spirit (Acts 20:28). Each of you attend, that you are examples to the faithful in word, in behavior, in spirit, in faith and in purity (I Timothy 4:12), as you have been admonished already."

Then the superintendent shall speak to the congregation about the office of listener towards teachers of the Church, what may be found concerning this in Holy Scriptures. The passages may be used as in the ordination of a superintendent, from I Thess. 5:12ff., and Hebrews 13:17, from these and other passages the superintendent may make other arguments and explanations, as he sees useful, which should happen with greatest vigor when one is ordained in the Church and congregation where he is to be installed as preacher.

The entire congregation shall sing Psalm 19, "The heavens are telling the glory of God," or some other Christian story. After the song the superintendent shall speak a blessing over the entire congregation and dismiss them.

The superintendent shall enter in his church book, which he should have ready, the year, month, day, and place of the ordination performed by him. Additionally, the ordinands' full names, places of birth, and the congregation to which they have been called [should be recorded].

[Installation]

1. For the one who has been examined by the examiners and ordained and supplied with documents by the superintendent, the superintendent shall bring him, accompanied by a well-regarded, God-fearing pastor, to the place where he shall be installed as pastor. When the congregation of that place has gathered for worship, the

superintendent shall arrange everything as may be necessary,

2. Before the sermon he shall announce to the entire congregation that he, together with his associates, has a written command regarding their future pastor, and has come in order to faithfully carry out that command.

3. Following this, the usual appointed preaching text for the day shall be read, after which shall follow Titus 1:5-9 concerning the office of preaching [the text of the passage follows], and after this from I Thess. 5:12ff., on the office of the listener [the text of the passage follows].

4. Then he shall clarify all that is in the texts in the following orderly way: the first part of the sermon shall be an exposition of the first text. In the second part he shall speak of the second two texts, which is to say, what God expects of the office of pastor and of the listeners.

5. After the sermon and exposition of the texts, the pastor shall conduct the new preacher to the place where the Holy Supper is celebrated, shall admonish the entire congregation and exhort the new preacher that he should carry out the office to which he now belongs with energy.

6. The ordained pastor shall then answer that he will, with the help of God, do all that is appropriate for him in his office.

7. Then the pastor who was brought with the superintendent shall commend the newly ordained pastor as an equal to others in the Church, such as the elders, the deacons, and the entire congregation, and he shall remind them of the duties toward their pastor.

8. When this has been accomplished in an orderly way, the above mentioned pastor from the city shall complete all the remaining things to be done in the church service in the customary manner.

The 1574 Hesse Agenda

Source: Sehling, VIII, 450–457.

"Form for the Ordination of a Pastor [*Pfarrherr*] or Minister [*Kirchendiener*]"

Appendix III

When neccessity demands the choice of a new pastor to a parish vacated either through death or the departure of a pastor, the neighboring pastor will serve the vacant parish until they are supplied properly, proclaiming God's word, distributing the sacraments, and performing all necessary services. The neighboring pastor will, at the end of his sermon, when he explains the things for which they will pray, seriously remind the congregation to pray for another Christian and faithful pastor [*Seelsorger*]. He will insist on it, so that they may give urgent notice to their area's superintendent and seek his advice as to how they once again might contact and retain a pious and learned man as a pastor.

Because the clergy roster belongs to the prince, the superintendent shall seek a pious and learned man who has either already been in pastoral office, or one who has studied at those places where God's word is purely translated and taught. He must have a good record and be able to demonstrate not only his erudition and cleverness, but testify to his life and conduct up until that time (such testimonials shall preferably be from the theological faculty at Marburg or another evangelical university). This person shall be examined by the superintendent and by pastors whom he may consult. They shall hear a sermon by the candidate, and if it is adequate they shall send him to the vacant parish where he may also preach. If the congregation finds no fault in his doctrine and conduct and cannot show any other reason that they would not want him as pastor, the superintendent shall appoint him as pastor and certify him, on the condition that nothing be undertaken or decided in cities or localities without the prior knowledge and approval of the prince.

When the roster does not belong to the prince but rather to another lord or nobleman, the parishoners shall inquire of the one in charge of the roster so that they might recommend and present a person to the superintendent as soon as possible. The candidate shall be evaluated by the superintendent and his adjuncts on the basis of presented testimonials, examination, and evaluation of a sermon. If the candidate is found to be upright and capable, and the parishoners can show no good reason that they would not wish to have him as pastor, he shall be accepted, introduced and certified.

The keepers of the roster shall be reminded that they must not be distracted by appearance, favoritism, gifts or presents, etc. The Church of God shall not be poorly cared for, and the keepers must remember that they must keep the Church supplied with enough workers. In God's eyes they are as responsible as the superintendent is for the parishoners. They must leave the superintendent and his adjuncts free and encourage only those who are adequate for the preaching office. Because there are scholars who are obliged to serve in Hesse, as well as other practiced and deserving men, they might very well be preferred because of their education and experience. They shall be commended in a Christian and obliging way to the superintendent's recollection and favor. These scholars shall not push their laws too strictly in the congregation of the Church of God, but shall use them in moderation and fairness for the edification and promulgation of the holy, divine Name. When there is a person chosen and accepted in the above way who has not yet been in the pastoral office, he shall be ordained for this congregation in the following manner, declared pastor, and introduced and certified by the superintendent or his designee.

1. First, the superintendent or the pastor designated in place of him, or also another pastor called in for this purpose (because there are two or three neighboring pastors invited to such an event as witnesses), shall preach a sermon. The sermon should be of one half or three quarter hour's length, discuss the offices of preacher and listener, and give a summary of Christian evangelical doctrine. To this end the teachers and listeners shall direct all of their energies and judgments. Other appropriate arguments may be used. At the end of this sermon the preacher will seriously remind the local congregation and all others who attend that they must pray devotedly to God for the new pastor, who is to be certified as a minister. As in all other occupations, but especially in this high and difficult office, nothing may be made fruitful without God's grace and the help of the Holy Spirit. As the Lord has said (John 15:5), "For apart from me, you can do nothing." And John the Baptist says (John 3:27): "No one can receive anything except what is given him from heaven."

2. After the sermon the superintendent (or his substitute) shall stand before the altar with the witnessing pastors on each side of him. The

Appendix III 265

superintendent and those next to him shall face the congregation, the ordinand shall face the superintendent. The entire congregation shall sing, "Come Holy Spirit."

3. When "Come Holy Spirit" has been sung, the superintendent (or his substitute or whoever on his account is responsible for the ordination) shall speak to the congregation:

> Beloved in the Lord, your pastor has entered into his rest in the Lord (or, for various reasons has been called away to preach the word of God in another place). For that reason another Christian teacher and pastor is called, who will instruct you in God's Word, admonish you to faith, love, and all other Christian virtues. He will be an example to you in Christian conduct and will direct you as is necessary. This congregation asks necessarily and according to the means of God's Word and our gracious prince's order that (name), here present, be called. It asks that he shall henceforth care for you and your children by means of the proclamation of God's Word and the dispensing of the Holy Sacraments. At this time he will be ordained according to old Christian practice with the laying on of hands. He will be certified and publicly commended to this congregation. For that reason we desire to read and explain to him concerning the office of a true preacher and faithful pastor, how he shall conduct himself in a Christian and godly way. We shall commend him to this congregation when we have reminded him and bound him to be energetic and faithful in his office, and called and prayed for God's Spirit and grace.
> So hear now, beloved in the Lord...[the remaining part of section three repeats verbatim the correpsonding material in the 1566 Church Order; see the preceding rite in this appendix].

4. After all of this the superintendent (or his substitute) shall address the ordinand:

> Dear brother in the Lord, you have now heard what your office is to be. It is not one from human thoughts but from the command and ordering of our Lord Jesus Christ and his holy apostles. It is presented and explained also in the epistles of the Apostle Paul to Timothy and Titus. But so that all may better understand, and so that you yourself might diligently observe and keep it fresh in your memory, I shall summarize it.
>
> 1. One who is ordered to be pastor or teacher in God's Church must present in a pure and unfalsified way all of the doctrine of the Christian Church, which is in the books of the Old and New Testaments, the writing of the prophets and the apostles, briefly summarized in the three creeds, Apostolic, Nicene, and

Athanasian, similarly in the Augsburg Confession and its Apology. According to that form and measure he will construct and present his sermons, teaching, care and admonition, etc. He shall not be turned away by any advantage, fear or danger. He shall cast away all unspiritual loose talk, quarrelsome words, and foolish and useless questions. And those who seek to spread either self-concocted or acquired false teaching he shall refute and disprove with clear and inerrant proof from the Holy Scriptures. He shall demonstrate their error and with gentleness bring those who are in error on to the right path. He shall be faithful to all persons in their own class and office. He shall remind them and admonish them, shall punish all secret and public sins. He shall encounter all prevailing irritations in appropriate seriousness with specialized and public admonitions from God's Word. He shall strengthen and comfort all the sick, troubled, clouded and fearful hearts and consciences.

2. He shall unhesitatingly and faithfully dispense the sacraments of the holy Christian Church according to the instruction of God's Word. He shall often explain and instruct the people on by whom they were instituted, what is offered and given, what their use and fruits are. And he shall look carefully to it that they are neither desecrated nor misused by anyone.

3. Not only will he always pray with great devotion and seriousness for all needs of the Christian Church and especially for the congregation entrusted to him, but, together with his adjuncts and seniors see to it that all live according to pure divine doctrine in a Christian and honest way, and that Church propriety and discipline, according to God's Word and the princely command, shall be maintained.

4. He shall pursue catechism and children's instruction with great energy and teach the principal articles of Christian faith to both young and old. He shall visit the sick, accompany to the grave those who have died in the Lord, and give them Christian burial. He shall commend himself to the poor, the asylums, the hospitals and schools. He will take great care not only that the property and annual income will be faithfully maintained, distributed and computed, that nothing from them will be misused or diverted, but also he will see to it that all persons in charge of these are kept faithfully in Christian decency and honesty. He shall see that the youth are raised and shown all good skills and Christian virtues.

5. He shall show himself to be Christian, honest and upright to all, just as he teaches others (I Tim. 3:2ff.), he must manage his wife, children, and household, not addicted to much wine, not greedy for gain. He shall strive for equity and modesty in all things. He shall avoid all things foreign to his office, shall obey his superintendent. In short, he shall be an example to the faithful in conduct, in love, in spirit, in faith, in word, in purity. He shall be diligent in reading, with preaching, with teaching. He shall not neglect the gifts which were given to him, he shall practice them, devote himself to them so that all may see his

Appendix III 267

progress. He shall take heed to himself and to his teaching, and be faithful in these things with all steadfastness. He shall pay no attention to the gossip of evil people and those who despise God's Word, nor shall he be hindered in his office by them. He shall not doubt God's help. When he does all of these things he will save both himself and his hearers.

These are the principal tenets, dear brother in Christ, which a pastor or servant in the Church of our Lord Jesus Christ must do in his office. I now ask you before God and Jesus Christ, the holy angels, and this Christian congregation, if you are resolute and promise faithfully and energetically to carry this out.

The ordinand answers:

I recognize that this is a difficult office to which I wish to commit myself. But because I have been rightly called and rely entirely on the prayers of the Christian Church for God's gracious help, which he promises to all of his called servants, I swear and promise here before God faithfully to accomplish with God's help all that my office demands, with all my power.

5. The superintendent then admonishes the congregation to pray and speaks this prayer:

Almighty and gracious God, Heavenly Father, when your dear Son, our Lord Jesus Christ, was raised to your right hand in heaven, he sent to us here on earth apostles, evangelists, prophets, shepherds and teachers. These are his chosen ones, who gather and teach, who choose and install elders in the congregations as commanded by the apostles. They preach his holy gospel purely and without error. They faithfully dispense the blessed sacraments and accomplish all pastoral care and shepherd's work. We ask you through the same Lord Jesus Christ, our great shepherd and the bishop of our souls, that you would richly grant your Holy Spirit to this chosen and called servant. It is your Spirit that enlightens, directs and strengthens, so that this servant might fruitfully carry out this, your high and holy service, with right understanding and zeal; that he may seek, find and bring to your dear Son all who may be estranged from him, all who have been seduced from him; that he may teach and correct all who commit themselves to him and remain faithfully in his congregation. Preserve him from sin and anger, from false gossip and lies and from all powerful hindrances to his service. All of this, so that he might faithfully and pleasingly serve your dear Church, that your name might always be blessed and your kingdom increased. Through the same, your dear Son, Jesus Christ our Lord. Amen.

6. After this prayer, hands shall be laid on the ordinand, who kneels before the altar, and the superintendent (or substitute) shall say: "I declare and certify you, in God's Church, upon your promise, a servant of the Church and a teacher of the holy Gospels, in the name of the Father and of the Son and of the Holy Spirit. Amen."

Then he will again admonish all to pray and will speak this prayer in a loud voice:

> Lord God, heavenly Father, it is you alone who creates and sends worthy servants to your Church. It is you who gives them power for such office. We humbly ask you that you would enlighten the heart of this your servant with the Holy Spirit in the name of our Lord Jesus Christ; that you would guide him with your mighty hand so that he may faithfully carry out his commended office to the honor of your name and to the edification of all the faithful in the Church of your beloved Son, through the same, your beloved Son, Jesus Christ. Amen.

7. Finally the superintendent shall say to the ordinand and then to the congregation:

> And now I commend to you, dear brother in Christ, this Church and congregation, over which you are set as shepherd and teacher. You shall feed this flock of God, which has been purchased with Christ's blood, which has been commended to you by the Holy Spirit. May you nurture it faithfully and diligently, govern it and preserve it in eternal salvation. And take care that you are not forced to do it, but are willing; that you do nothing for shameful gain, but from the depths of your heart; that you do not lord it over your people, but are an example for your flock.
>
> And to the congregation I commend on behalf of God and also our gracious prince and superior, this servant before you, that you may recognize him, keep him as pastor, love and value him for his work and effort; that you might be peaceable with him, follow and obey him; that you might always recall (Heb.13:17) that he keeps watch over your souls, as men who will give account. Let him do this joyfully and not sadly. Behave toward one another as God has commanded in his Word, as it is fitting for a Christian pastor and congregation. Do all of this so that it may go well for you before the judgment seat of our Lord Jesus Christ, before which we must all appear, so that we may redeem the unfading crown to which God, the eternal Father of our Lord Jesus Christ, graciously desires to give us, for the sake of his only beloved Son, our mediator and petitioner, who lives and reigns with the Father and the Holy Spirit, one almighty and eternal God, to whom be praise and honor forever. Amen.
>
> The Lord bless you, that you may bring forth fruit. Amen.

Appendix III 269

On closing, the congregation shall sing the *Te Deum laudamus*, in German, or Latin when there are schools nearby, or *Danksgeben wir alle, Gott unserem Herrn, Christo* etc., or another such song of praise.

"Form for ordaining and installing a pastor or minister who has already been ordained and served a time in a congregation."

When someone has been ordained and served for a time in a congregation, and for some reason is called to another place, he shall be introduced, commended and presented to a congregation in the following way:

1. First, the superintendent, or whoever is designated, or even the new pastor himself, shall preach upon the office of pastor and listener. At the end of that, he shall admonish the congregation concerning the needs of the Christian Church, and for the new pastor or chaplain that God might grant his grace to carry out those duties.

2. After the sermon, the *Veni Sancte Spiritus* shall be sung, in German or Latin. The superintendent and the new pastor shall go up before the altar. The superintendent shall, when the song is finished, present a short reminder to the people and recall how the pastor was selected, how his good qualities were evaluated, and how he was called. He shall declare that all should hope and intend the new pastor would serve faithfully and diligently in the proclamation of God's Word and the dispensing of the sacraments. For that reason it will be appropriate for the congregation to give him fitting obedience in matters pertaining to their salvation; how he likewise is obligated to undertake seriously and diligently according to God's guidance, all things necessary for their salvation. After that, he shall admonish them to pray, and shall speak one of the appointed prayers [from a series of Collects; see Sehling, VIII, 419-420]. He shall say further: Hear the Holy Gospel, described to us by the holy evangelist John (John 20:21-23), "The Lord said to his disciples, as the Father has sent me, even so I send you. And when he

had said this he breathed on them, and said to them, 'Receive the Holy Spirit. If you forgive the sins of any, they are forgiven; if you retain the sins of any, they are retained.'"

The superintendent, depending on the time and the Church, and for reminder may read the following epistle: Thus writes St. Paul in the first letter to Timothy (3:1–7), [the text of the passage follows]. Thus writes St. Paul to the elders of the congregation at Ephesus (Acts 20:28–31), [the text of the passage follows]. Now let us pray, and speak with me:

> Gracious God, heavenly Father, you have spoken to us through the lips of your Son, Jesus Christ: the harvest is great, but the workers are few, pray to the Lord of the harvest that he may send workers to the harvest. At your holy command we ask you from our hearts, that you would generously impart your Holy Spirit to this your servant, to us, and to all who are called to your Word, that we may be, with the great crowd, your true servants, confessors; that we may be faithful and strong against the devil, the world, and the flesh, so that your name may be blessed, your kingdom increased, your will accomplished. We pray that you would finally lead to an end the abomination of the papacy and the Mohammedans and other mobs that slander your name, destroy your kingdom and resist your will. Graciously hear our prayer (as you have called, instructed and comforted us), as we believe and trust, through your Son, our Lord Jesus Christ, who lives and reigns with you and the Holy Spirit forever. Amen.

5. Finally, the superintendent shall commend the congregation to the new pastor, and likewise the pastor to the congregation, with the words: "Now I commend you, dear brother in Christ...etc." [the text of the commendation above is repeated here]. The *Te Deum, laudamus* or another Christian song of praise shall be sung in closing.

APPENDIX IV

Text of the Württemberg Order

Source: A. L. Richter, *Die evangelischen Kirchenordnungen des sechzehnten Jahrhunderts. 2 Vols. Nieuwkoop: B. Degraaf, 1967 (Weimar, 1846, First edition);* II, 202–203.

"The manner in which a new minister [*kirchendiener*] may be commended, incorporated and installed by the superintendent of his church."

As soon as a person is judged to be accepted as a minister of the church and found acceptable to a parish, the superintendent, accompanied by a judiciary of that place and a neighboring pastor as witness to the procedure, shall bring the future pastor to the new parish.

When people have gathered in the church they shall begin by singing, "Now Let Us Pray to the Holy Spirit." When that has been sung, the superintendent or his adjunct shall rise and preach on the ministry of the Word or another appropriate proposition: by whom the ministry was instituted, its usefulness, etc. In that way he shall admonish the people with the sermon. The Creed shall be sung.

The superintendent or his adjunct shall rise during the singing and call forward the new pastor or deacon, who shall kneel before him for prayer. When the song is completed the superintendent shall admonish the people, mentioning how this pastor or deacon was chosen and recognized as capable, how he was called with the hope that he would accept them, etc. In that way he shall admonish them to pray that the Lord might grant grace and prosperity, speaking the following prayer with a bright, clear and understandable voice and say, "Let us pray" [Prayer from the 1547 Church Order]:

> Almighty God, Heavenly Father you have instituted the worthy office of preaching through your beloved Son, Jesus Christ, so that poor humanity might be comforted and helped. You have also stated and promised that those who believe and are baptized will be blessed. Because we know that our corrupt and awful flesh is troublesome and dangerous, we pray your special help and gracious assistance to protect this dear and worthy treasure from the greatly depraved and

wrathful enemy, which we would not be capable of doing in our miserable, weak, and earthly vessels. We ask you in your boundless grace and mercy, that you would not leave or abandon us, but would hold us in your divine hand. We especially pray for your Servant, N., who has been sworn to preach the Holy Gospel, that he may remain steadfast against all onslaughts of the Devil, steadfast in your healing, useful and necessary command until the end of the earth in your sacred kingdom. We pray that we may never be deprived of your heavenly comfort, through Jesus Christ your Son, our Lord, who with you and the Holy Spirit lives and reigns, one God forever. Amen.

Hear the Holy Gospel, recorded by the Apostle John. The Lord said to his Apostles: "As my heavenly Father has sent me... ." The superintendent may also read the following epistle, according to opportunity and the time allocated, to strengthen recollection. Thus writes Saint Paul in the first letter to Timothy, the third chapter: "The saying is sure, if anyone aspires to the office of bishop, he desires a noble task...etc." Saint Paul exhorts the elders of the congregation at Ephesus, "So care for yourselves and for your flock."

Then let us pray and speak with me [Prayer from the 1547 Church Order]:

> O merciful God, heavenly Lord and Father, you have comforted us in a fatherly way through the apostle Paul, saying that it pleases you to save us through the scandalous preaching of the cross to those who believe. We ask you earnestly for that now, that you would give your servant, N., called to your office of preaching, your divine grace and Holy Spirit. In the power of this, he will be strengthened against all temptations of the devil. With your healing and unerring Word, may he feed your flock, dearly purchased with the blood of our Lord Jesus Christ, your Son. All of this, to the praise and glory of your holy name, and the promotion of your kingdom, through Jesus Christ your dear Son. Amen.

Or the following prayer may be said, "Merciful God, heavenly Father..." [Luther's Prayer]. We [then] pray with our hearts the Lord's Prayer that we may accomplish all of this. When there are schoolboys present the Lord's Prayer may be sung...etc.

After the praying or singing of the Lord's Prayer, the superintendent, facing the altar and with his back to the people, shall, according to Christian usage, as was done ceremonially by our Lord Jesus Christ, lay his right hand on the bare head of the new pastor or deacon and say

Appendix IV

[From the 1547 Church Order]:

> Dear brother, we have gathered in the Holy Spirit, have called out and prayed to God our Heavenly Father through Jesus Christ our Lord and Savior on your account. We do not doubt that He has heard us according to his divine promise, and that He will grant our petitions. Accordingly, by command of the Almighty and by command of our gracious Prince and Lord, who is the right and God-given magistrate, I ordain, confirm and certify you as servant and pastor of this congregation. All of this with the earnest command that you would energeticallly and faithfully administer this with all honesty and without anger, as you must give account on that day before the judgment seat of our Lord Jesus Christ, the true judge, in the name of the Father and of the Son and of the Holy Spirit. Amen.

The congregation shall then sing the *Te Deum laudamus* or *Grates nunc omnes* in German. The superintendent closes with a blessing, etc.

BIBLIOGRAPHY

Primary Sources

Andrieu, M. *Les Ordines Romani du haut moyen-âge.* Vol.I. Louvain: Spicilegium Sacrum Lovaniense, Fasc.11, 1931; Vol.III, Fasc.24, 1951; Vol.IV, Fasc.28, 1956.

Andrieu, M. *Le pontifical romain au moyen-âge.* Tome I. "Le pontifical romain du XIIIe siècle." *Studi i Testi* 86 (1938). Pp. 134-137.

Andrieu, M. *Le pontifical romain au moyen-âge.* Tome II. "Le pontifical de la curie romaine au XIIIe siècle." *Studi i Testi* 87 (1939). Pp. 341-350.

Andrieu, M. *Le pontifical romain au moyen-âge.* Tome III. "Le pontifical de Guillaume Durand." *Studi i Testi* 88 (1940). Pp. 363-373.

Botte, Bernard. *La tradition apostolique de saint Hippolyte.* Liturgiewissenschaftliche Quellen und Forschungen, Heft 39. Münster:1966.

Buchwald, G. *Ungedruckte Predigten Joh. Bugenhagens aus den Jahren 1524 bis 1529.* Leipzig, 1910.

Deshusses, Jean. *Le sacramentaire grègorien.* Spicilegium Friburgense, Vol. 16. Fribourg: 1979. Pp. 95-96; 602-603.

Die Bekenntnisschriften der evangelisch-lutherischen Kirche. Göttingen: Vandenhoeck, 1959.

Dumas, A. *Liber Sacramentorum Gellonensis.* Corpus Christianorum Series Latina, CLIX. Turnholti: Typographi Brepolis Editores Pontificii, 1981. Pp. 388-391.

Friedensburg, Walter, ed. *Nuntiaturberichte aus Deutschland Erste Abteilung 1533-1559, Erste Band, Nuntiaturen des Vergeri 1533-1536*. Gotha, 1892; reprint, Frankfurt: Minerva G.M.B.H., 1968.

Luther, Martin. *D. Martin Luthers Werke*. Kritische Gesamtausgabe. Weimar, 1883-.

Luther, Martin. *Luther's Works*. Edited by Jaroslav Pelikan, Vols. 1-30, and Helmut T. Lehmann, Vols. 31-55. Philadelphia: Fortress Press.

Mohlberg, L.C. *Sacramentarium Veronense*. Rerum Ecclesiasticarum Documenta, Series Major, Fontes I. Rome: Herder, 1956. Pp. 121-122.

Mohlberg, L.C. *Liber Sacramentorum Romanae Aeclesiae Ordinis Anni Circuli* (Sacramentarium Gelasianum). Rerum Ecclesiasticarum Documenta, Series Major, Fontes IV. Rome: Herder, 1957. Pp.25-26.

Mohlberg, L.C. *Missale Francorum*. Rerum Ecclesiasticarum Documenta, Series Major, Fontes II. Rome: Herder, 1957. Pp. 8-10.

Munier, Charles. *Les Statuta Ecclesiae Antiqua*. Paris: Presses Universitaires de France, 1960.

Richter, A.L. *Die evangelischen Kirchenordnungen des sechzehnten Jahrhunderts*. 2 vols. Nieuwkoop: B.Degraaf, 1967 (Weimar, 1846, First ed.).

Sehling, Emil. *Die evangelischen Kirchenordnungen des 16. Jahrhunderts*. 15 Vols. Leipzig: O. R. Riesland, 1902ff. Vols.I-V; Tübingen: J. C. B. Mohr, 1955. Vols. VI-XV.

Tappert, Theodore, ed. *The Book of Concord*. Philadelphia: Fortress Press, 1959.

Vogel, C. and Elze, R. "Le pontifical romano-germanique du dixieme siècle." Le Texte I. *Studi i Testi* 226 (1963).

Secondary Sources

Bläser, Peter. *Amt und Eucharistie*. Paderborn: Bonifacius-Druckerei, 1973.

Bradshaw, Paul F. "The Reformers and the Ordination Rites." In: *Ordination Rites*. Papers Read at the 1979 Congress of Societas Liturgica, 94–107. Edited by Wiebe Vos and Geoffrey Wainwright. Rotterdam: Liturgical Ecumenical Center Trust, 1980.

Brunotte, Wilhelm. *Das geistliche Amt bei Luther*. Berlin: Lutherisches Verlaghaus, 1959.

Brunner, Peter. "Salvation and the Office of Ministry." *The Lutheran Quarterly* XV, 2 (1963), 99–117.

Brunner, Peter. *Nikolaus von Amsdorf als Bischof von Naumburg*. Gütersloh: Verlaghaus Gerd Mohn, 1961.

Buchwald, G. "Wann hat Luther die erste Ordination vollzogen." *Theologische Studien und Kritiken* (1896).

Buchwald, G., ed. *Wittenberger Ordiniertenbuch I*. Leipzig, 1894.

Burgsmüller, A. and Frieling, R. *Amt und Ordination im Verständnis evangelischer Kirchen und ökumenischer Gespräche*. Dokumentation, Arnoldshainer Konferenz. Gütersloh: Gerd Mohn, 1974.

Carlson, Edgar M. "The Doctrine of Ministry in the Confessions." *The Lutheran Quarterly* 15 (1963): 118-131.

Drews, Paul. "Vorwort zum Ordinationsformular in der Weimarer Ausgabe." WA 38, 401-433.

Drews, Paul. *Die Ordination, Prüfung und Lehrverpflichtung der Ordinanden in Wittenberg 1535.* Giessen: Otto Kindt, 1904.

Dykmans, Marc. *Le Pontifical romain. Studi e Testi* 311 (Rome: Vatican City, 1985).

Ellard, G. *Ordination Anointings in the Western Church Before 1000 A.D.* Cambridge, Mass.: The Medieval Academy of America, 1933.

Estes, J. M. "Church Order and the Christian Magistrate According to Johannes Brenz." *Archiv für Reformationsgeschichte* 59 (1/1968): 5-24.

Ewing, W. A. "What Is Ordination Into the Ministry?" *The Lutheran Quarterly* 16 (1964): 211-221.

Fagerberg, Holsten. "Amt, Ämter, Amtverständnis." In *Theologische Realenzyklopedie.* Vol. II, 5, pp. 553-574. Edited by Gerhard Krause and Gerhard Müller. Berlin: de Gruyter, 1978.

Fischer, L. *Die kirchlichen Quatember.* Munich: 1914.

Fischer, Robert H. "Another Look at Luther's Doctrine of the Ministry." *The Lutheran Quarterly* 18 (1966): 260-271.

Gerrish, Brian A. "Priesthood and Ministry in the Theology of Luther." *Church History* 34 (1965): 404-422.

Green, Lowell. "Change in Luther's Doctrine of Ministry." *The Lutheran Quarterly* 18 (1966): 173-183

Gritsch, Eric. "The Church as Institution: From Doctrinal Pluriformity to Magisterial Mutuality." *Journal of Ecumenical Studies* 16 (1970): 448–456.

Gritsch, Eric. "The Function and Structure of Gospelling: An Essay on 'Ministry' According to the Augsburg Confession." *Sixteenth Century Journal* XI, 3 (1980): 37–45.

Gritsch, Eric. "Lutheran Teaching Authority: Past and Present." In *Lutherans and Catholics in Dialogue VI*, pp. 138-148. Edited by Paul C. Empie and T. Austin Murphy. Minnesota: Augsburg Publishing House, 1978.

Grützmacher, R.H. "Beitrage zur Geschichte der Ordination in der evangelischen Kirche." *Neue Kirchliche Zeitschrift* 23 (1912).

Gy, Pierre Marie. "La theologie des prieres anciennes pour l'ordination des eveques et des pretres." *Revue des sciences philosophique et theologiques* 58 (1974): 599–617.

Hannemann, Manfred. *The Diffusion of the Reformation in Southwestern Germany, 1518–1534.* Chicago: University of Chicago Department of Geography Research Paper Number 167, 1975.

Harjunpa, Toivo. "Communion and Ordination." *Una Sancta* 24 (1976): 30–35.

Heinecken, Martin J. "What Does Ordination Confer?" *The Lutheran Quarterly* 18 (1966): 120–135.

Heinecken, Martin J. "The Ministry, a Functional Office." *The Lutheran Quarterly* XX (1947): 432–441.

Heintze, Gerhard. "Allgemeines Priestertum und besonderes Amt." *Evangelische Theologie* 23 (1963): 617–646.

Heubach, J. "Die Ordination zum Amt der Kirche." In *Arbeiten zur Geschichte und Theologie des Luthertums*. Band 2. Berlin: 1956.

Höfling, J.W.F. *Grundsätze evangelisch-lutherischer Kirchenverfassung*. Erlangen: 1835.

Jenson, Robert. "Ministries Lay and Ordained." *Partners* (III, No. 5, October 1981): 11-15.

Jöst, W. "Amt und Ordination—unüberholbare Strukturen?" *Kerygma und Dogma* 17 (1971): 75-85.

Josefson, Ruben. "The Ministry as an Office in the Church." In *This is the Church*. Edited by Anders Nygren. Philadelphia: Muhlenberg Press, 1952.

Jungmann, Josef. "Die Dezemberordinationen des Papstbuches und ihr Messformular." *Zeitschrift für katholische Theologie* 56 (1932): 599-604.

Kalb, Friedrich. *Theology of Lutheranism in 17th Century Lutheranism*. Translated by H. P. A. Hamann. St. Louis: Concordia, 1965.

Karant-Nunn, Susan C. *Luther's Pastors: The Reformation in the Ernestine Countryside*. Philadelphia: Transactions of the American Philosophical Society, Vol. 69, part 8, 1979.

Kleinheyer, Bruno. *Die Priesterweihe in römischen Ritus*. Trier: Paulinus-Verlag, 1962.

Kleinheyer, Bruno. "Studien zur Nichtrömischen-Westlichen Ordinationsliturgie." *Archiv für Liturgiewissenschaft* 23 (1981): 313-366.

Kolde, T. "Zur Geschichte der Ordination und der Kirchenzucht." *Theologischen Studien und Kritiken* (1894).

Le Goff, J. "Les Gestes symboliques dans la vie sociale, les gestes de la vassalite." In *Simboli e Simbologia Nell'Alto Medievo,* 679-779. Spoleto: Settimane di Studio del centro Italiano di Studi sull'alto Medioevo, 1976.

Lieberg, Helmut. *Amt und Ordination bei Luther und Melanchthon.* Göttingen: Vandenhoeck und Ruprecht, 1962.

Lindbeck, George. "The Sacramentality of the Ministry." In *Oecumenica,* 282-301. Edited by Friedrich Kantzenbach and Vilmos Vajta. Gütersloh: Gerd Mohn, 1967.

Lindbeck, George. "The Lutheran Doctrine of the Ministry: Catholic and Reformed." *Theological Studies* 30 (1969): 588-612.

Lindbeck, George. "'Rite Vocatus.' Der theologische Hintergrund zu CA 14." In *Confessio Augustana und Confutatio.* Edited by E. Iserloh. Münster Westfalen: Aschendorf, 1980.

Manns, Peter. *Martin Luther: An Illustrated Biography.* New York: Crossroad, 1983.

Michels, T. "Beiträge zur Geschichte des Bischofsweihetages im christlichen Altertum und in Mittelalter." *Liturgiewissenschaftliche Forschungen* 10 (1927): 20-30.

Moreton, Bernard. *The Eighth-Century Gelasian Sacramentary.* Oxford: Oxford University Press, 1976.

Mumm, Richard and Krems, Gerhard, eds. *Ordination und kirchliches Amt.* Paderborn: Bonifacius-Druckerei, 1976.

Niebergall, Alfred. "Die Anfänge der Ordination in Hessen," 141-160. In *Reformatio und Confessio.* Berlin: Lutherisches Verlaghaus, 1965.

Ockeley, A. *Die Kirchenordnungen von Ziegenhain und Kassel 1539.* Marburg: 1939.

Piepkorn, Arthur C. "*Ius Divinum* and *adiaphoron* in Relation to Structural Problems in the Church: The Position of the Lutheran Symbolical Books." In *Lutherans and Catholics in Dialogue V*, 119-127. Edited by Paul C. Empie and T. Austin Murphy. Philadelphia: Fortress Press, 1981.

Piepkorn, Arthur C. "The Sacred Ministry and Holy Ordination in the Symbolical Books of the Lutheran Church." *Lutherans and Catholics in Dialogue IV*, 101-119. Minneapolis: Augsburg Publishing House, 1979.

Piepkorn, Arthur C. "A Lutheran View of the Validity of Orders." In *Lutherans and Catholics in Dialogue IV*, 209-226. Edited by Paul Empie and T. Austin Murphy. Minneapolis: Augsburg Publishing House, 1979.

Porter, H. B. *The Ordination Prayers of the Ancient Western Church.* Alcuin Club Collections, XLIX. London: SPCK, 1967.

Prenter, Regin. "Die göttliche Einsetzung des Predigtamtes und das allgemeine Priestetum bei Luther." *Theologische Literaturzeitung* 86 (1961): 322-332.

Prenter, Regin. "Das kirchliche Amt als königliche Vertretung Christi und als priesterliche Vertretung der Gemeinde," In *Oecumenica*, 254-281. Edited by Friedrich Kantzenbach and Vilmos Vajta. Gütersloh: Gerd Mohn, 1967.

Quere, Ralph W. "The Spirit and the Gifts Are Ours: Imparting or Imploring the Spirit in Ordination Rites?" *The Lutheran Quarterly* 27 (1975): 322-346.

Reiss, John C. *The Time and Place of Sacred Ordination*. The Catholic University of America Law Studies, Number 343. Washington, D.C.: The Catholic University of America Press, 1953.

Reumann, John. "Ordained Minister and Layman in Lutheranism." In *Lutherans and Catholics in Dialogue*, IV, 227–282. Edited by Paul C. Empie and T. Austin Murphy. Minneapolis: Augsburg Publishing House, 1979.

Rietschel, Georg. *Luther und die Ordination*. Wittenberg: R. Herrose, 1889.

Rietschel, Georg. "Luthers Ordinationsformular in seiner ursprünglichen Gestalt." *Theologische Studien und Kritiken* (1895).

Schoenleber, Richard. "The Sovereign Word: The Office of the Ministry and Ordination in the Theology of Martin Luther." Ann Arbor, Michigan: University Microfilm International, 1983.

Scholz, A. "Bugenhagens Kirchenordnungen in ihrem Verhältnis zueinander." Archiv für Reformationsgeschichte 10 (1912/13): 1–50.

Schmidt, W. *Die Homberger Synode und ihre Vorgeschichte*. Festschrift zur Vierhundertjahrfeier der Homberger Synode, 1926.

Schulz, Frieder. "Evangelische Ordination." *Jahrbuch für Liturgik und Hymnologie* 17 (1972): 1–54.

Schulz, Frieder. "Luther's Liturgische Reformen." *Archiv für Liturgiewissenschaft*, Heft 3 (1983): 249–275.

Schütte, Heinz. *Amt, Ordination und Sukzession*. Düsseldorf: Patmos-Verlag, 1974.

Senn, Frank. "Martin Luther's Revision of the Eucharistic Canon in the Formula Missae of 1523." *Concordia Theological Monthly* 44 (1973): 101–118.

Spinks, Bryan. "Luther's Other Major Liturgical Reforms: 2, The Ordination of Ministers of the Word." *Liturgical Review* IX, 1 (1979): 20–32.

Spitz, Lewis W. "Luther's Ecclesiology and His Concept of the Prince as *Notbischof.*" *Church History* 22 (1953): 113–141.

Stahl, F. J. *Die Kirchenverfassung nach Lehre und Recht der Protestanten.* Erlangen: 1862.

Storck, Hans. "Das allgemeine Priestertum bei Luther." *Theologische Existenz Heute* 37 n.s. (1953).

Tüchel, Klaus. "Luthers Auffassung vom geitstliche Amt." *Luther Jahrbuch* 25 (1958): 61–98.

Vajta, Vilmos. *Die Theologie des Gottesdienstes bei Luther.* Stockholm: 1952. English Translation, *Luther On Worship.* Philadelphia: Muhlenberg Press, 1958.

Vetter, P. "Das älteste Ordinationsformular der lutherischen Kirche." *Archiv für Reformationsgeschichte* 12 (1915).

Vogel, C. *Introduction aux sources de l'histoire du culte chretien au moyen-âge.* Spoleto: Centro Italiano di Studi sull'Alto Medioevo. 1975. English Translation: *Medieval Liturgy: An Introduction to the Sources.* Translated by William G. Storey and Niels Krogh Rasmussen. Washington, D.C.: The Pastoral Press, 1986.

Wingren, Gustaf. *Luthers Lehre vom Beruf. Forschungen zur Geschichte und Lehre des Protestantismus, X.* Edited by Ernst Wolf. Munich: Kaiser, 1952.

Auxiliary Sources

von Allmen, J.J. "Ministry and Ordination According to Reformed Theology." *Scottish Journal of Theology* 25 (1972): 75–88.

Bradshaw, Paul F. *The Anglican Ordinal*. Alcuin Club Collection, LIII. London: Society for the Preservation of Christian Knowledge, 1971.

von Campenhausen, Hans. *Ecclesiastical Authority and Spiritual Power*. Translated by J. A. Baker. Stanford: Stanford University Press, 1969.

Cooke, Bernard. *Ministry to Word and Sacrament: History and Theology*. Philadelphia: Fortress Press, 1976.

Courvoisier, J. *La notion d'Eglise chez Bucer dans son developpement historique*. Paris: F. Alcan, 1933.

Elert, Werner. *The Structure of Lutheranism*. Translated by Walter A. Hansen. St. Louis: Concordia, 1962.

Fagerberg, Holsten. *Bekenntnis, Kirche und Amt in der deutschen konfessionellen Theologie des 19. Jahrhunderts*. Uppsala: Almquist & Wiksell, 1952.

Fagerberg, Holsten. *A New Look at the Lutheran Confessions*. Translated by Gene J. Lund. St. Louis: Concordia Publishing House, 1972.

Fink, Peter. "The Sacrament of Orders: Some Liturgical Reflections." *Worship* 56 (1982): 482-502.

Galtier, P. "Imposition des mains." *Dictionnaire de theologie catholique* VII/2. Paris: Librarie Letouzey et Ane, 1927.

Gritsch, Eric W. and Jenson, Robert W. *Lutheranism*. Philadelphia: Fortress Press, 1976.

Jenson, Robert W. *Visible Words*. Philadelphia: Fortress Press, 1978.

Lehmann, Karl. "Gottesdienst als Ausdruck des Glaubens." *Liturgisches Jahrbuch* 30 (1980): 197–214.

Maurer, Wilhelm. *Historischer Kommentar zur Confessio Augustana*. 2 vols. Gütersloh: Gerd Mohn, 1976–1978.

Niehbuhr, H. Richard and Williams, Daniel D. Eds. *The Ministry in Historical Perspective*. New York: Harper, 1956.

Nygren, Anders. "Vom geistlichen Amt." *Zeitschrift für systematische Theologie* 12 (1935): 36–44.

Pauck, Wilhelm. *Heritage of the Reformation*. Illinois: Free Press, 1961.

Pauck, Wilhelm. "The Ministry in the Time of the Continental Reformation." In *The Ministry in Historical Perspective*, 110–148. Edited by H. Richard Niebuhr and Daniel D. Williams. New York: Harper, 1956.

Schillebeeckx, Edward. *Ministry*. New York: Crossroad, 1981.

Schlink, Edmund. *The Theology of the Lutheran Confessions*. Translated by Paul F. Koehneke and Herbert J. Bouman. Philadelphia: Muhlenberg Press, 1961.

Schlink, Edmund. *The Coming Christ and the Coming Church*. Philadelphia: Fortress Press, 1967.

Schmid, Heinrich. *The Doctrinal Theology of the Evangelical Lutheran Church*. Trans. by C. A. Hay and H. E. Jacobs. Philadelphia: 1876.

Vogel, Cyrille. "L'imposition des mains dans les rites d'ordination en Orient et Occident." *La Maison–Dieu* 102 (1970): 57–72.

Wainwright, Geoffey. *Doxology. The Praise of God in Worship, Doctrine and Life.* New York: Oxford University Press, 1980.

INDEX

Absolute ordination, 50
Anabaptists, 149, 160, 174, 207
Anointing, 24, 29–30, 49, 56, 113, 114, 120, 221
Apology to the Augsburg Confession, 9, 204
Apostolic Tradition, of Hippolytus, 18
Apostolic succession, 228, 230
Authority, ministerial, 9; to appoint, 147
Augsburg Confession, 6, 9, 60, 204, 218

Baptism, 49, 53–55, 58, 114, 132
Benedicite, 24
Bishop, 3, 5, 8, 18, 29, 32, 60, 65, 69, 91, 115, 116, 149, 158
Blessing, 120, 124, 128–129, 155
Book of Concord, 6
Brunotte, Wilhelm, 10
Bucer, Martin, 149–151, 175, 216–217
Bugenhagen, Johannes, 63, 68–69, 87, 88, 93, 131–132, 151, 186, 201, 211, 219, 221, 229; ordination rite of, 161–162;

Call, 57, 58, 65, 68, 69, 111, 119, 227, 229
Character, 56, 65
Charge to ordinands, 127–128, 154
Chrism, 57
Clergy, 3, 8, 49, 51, 131
Common priesthood, 11
Confirm, 58, 60, 69, 89, 97, 98, 119, 123, 165, 186
Congregational prayer, 2, 56, 90, 95, 109–111, 167, 205, 208, 223
Collects, 3, 90–91, 114, 154
Concelebration, 32
Consecration (see also anointing), 49, 51, 58–59, 62, 69, 157–158; episcopal, 56–57, 60, 97, 153

Day, for ordination, 18–19, 90, 94, 97 108, 153, 162, 211
Deacon, 3, 5, 18, 20, 21, 28, 62, 87, 90, 109, 150, 167, 181–182
Declaratory formula, 30
De iure divino, 95, 228
Divine institution, 11
Doctrines of ministry, 7, 9, 11
Doctrinal writings, 4, 5, 45
Durandus, William, 3, 17, 28, 33, 95 158, 160, 220

Ecclesiology, 2, 50, 58
Elders, 150, 177, 179–180
Electoral decree of 1535, 66–67
Episcopal consecration, 56, 63, 66, 68, 70, 87, 94, 109, 124, 153, 228
Ember Days, 19, 20, 28, 32, 221
Enthronement, 157
Enthusiasts, 93–95, 174, 207
Episcopal Ministry, 6, 154
Eucharist, 64
Evangelical process for ordaining, 64, 66, 87, 98, 131, 164
Exhortations, 31, 109, 117–118, 154, 173–175, 204, 208

Fasting, 20
Formulas, 90, 118, 152, 166
Functional view of ministry, 11

Gelasian Sacramentary, 19, 33
Gregorian Sacramentary, 19
Gift of the Spirit, 113, 124, 152, 166, 169

Hamburg, 1529 rite of, 5, 93–98
Hesse, 1526 rite of, 5; 1566 Church Order, 170–182; 1574 rite of, 203–209
Hierarchy, 202

Hildesheim, 1544 rite of, 161–162
Hindrances, to ordination, 24
Hippolytus, 18, 32
Höfling, J.W.F., 9
Holy Spirit, gift of, 113, 124, 152, 166
Hymn, for the Spirit, 129 (see also *Veni Sancte Spiritus*, *Veni Creator Spiritus*)
Homberg Church Order of 1526, 87-92

Indelible Character, 1
Installation, 4, 58–59, 62–63, 94, 97 132, 164, 179, 183, 185–186, 209–212, 214, 229
Intercession, 3
Iure Divino, 110
Iure humano, 50

Jurisdiction, 92, 135 note 22, 147

Kasseler Kirchenordnung, 1539, 149
Kirchenordnung, definition of, 4, 7, 88
Kyrie, 20, 21

Laity, 3, 6, 8, 49, 132
Lambert, Franz, 88, 131, 149
Laying on of hands, 2, 18, 26, 29, 30 50, 60, 93, 96, 112, 119–125, 152 205, 207, 214, 215, 218, 220, 224
Leitourgia, 2
Lex orandi, lex credendi, 2, 6–7, 33 124
Lieberg, Hellmut, 10
Lord's Prayer, 125, 130, 152, 155, 166
Luther, Martin, views on ministry, 45; reforms of the Mass, 46; ordination of, 48; on priesthood, 52; on the act of ordaining, 54–56; 1535 ordination rite of, 98–133; influence of rite, 203

Magistrates, 132, 226
Mass, 22, 31
Melanchthon, Philip, 4, 9, 67, 88, 98, 218
Ministerium Verbi, 2, 160, 161, 201 202
Ministry of the word, 52, 54, 164
Missale Francorum, 23

Nikolaus von Amsdorf, 116, 125, 128, 129, 153–161

Obedience, oath of, 26, 30, 31, 119 149, 176
Office of Ministry, 49, 51, 55, 56, 115
Ordaining, liturgical act of, 2; distinct from installing, 4, 62, 97, 185, 209, 212
Ordering, 8
Ordinand, promise of, 205–206
Ordination prayers, 19, 96, 125–127, 151–152, 173, 177, 180, 184, 218
Ordination, rite as evidence, 45; as a sacrament, 50, 218; distinct from consecration 58; definition of, 62; centralization of 217
Ordines Romani, 19

Pastor, 3
Pastoral role, 52, 54
Patronal privilege, 63, 132
Patrizzi-Piccolmini, Agostino, 32
Philip of Hesse, 88, 148
Pietism, 9
Pontifical, 26, 27, 158, 160
Pontificale Romano-Germanicum, 26
Prayers, of ordination, 3, 18, 19, 27

Index

Preaching, 62, 202
Presbyter, 3, 5, 6, 18, 20, 28
Presidential Prayer, 2, 96, 205, 218
Priest, 8, 51, 52, 55, 186
Priesthood, external versus spiritual, 51–53; sacrificial, 199; distinct from office, 49, 51, 55, 56
Priesthood of all believers 53, 55, 110
Prince, role of, 89, 117, 149, 185, 228
Private Mass, 50, 57
Promise, of ordinand (see vow, obedience)

Reordination, 48, 202, 212, 229
Rietschel, Georg, 9, 57, 59, 71, 97
Roman rite, 5
Rörer, Georg, 5, 62, 67, 87

Sacrament, ordination as, 1, 50, 151, 218
Sacramentaries, 23, 24, 25
Sacrifice of the Mass, 31, 54, 207
Sacrificial priesthood, 49, 51, 54, 202
Schumann, Benedict, 126, 128, 155
Scripture, texts in ordination rites:
  Acts 6:1-6, p. 179
  Acts 13, p. 61
  Acts 14:23, p. 179
  Acts 20, pp. 114, 116, 153, 179, 184, 207, 210, 217
  Matthew 9, p. 96
  Matthew 24:42-47, pp. 20, 95
  Matthew 28:18-20, pp. 172, 176, 178, 180, 204, 217
  John 4:47, p. 61
  John 8:30-39, p. 20
  John 20:21, pp. 168, 169, 184, 207, 210, 217, 221
  Luke 6, p. 95
  I Peter 2:9, p. 51
  I Peter 5:2-4, pp. 127, 168
  I Thessalonians 5:12; p. 178
  I Timothy 3:1-7, pp. 20, 95, 115, 169, 170, 172, 173, 178, 184, 207, 210, 217
  I Timothy 3:8-13, pp. 20, 93, 95, 114, 153
  I Timothy 6, p. 213
  II Timothy 3:14-4:5, pp. 178, 204
  Titus 1:1-9, pp. 20, 93, 178, 204

Smaldcald Articles, 70
Spirit, gift of, 11, 184; invocation of, 114
Stahl, F.J., 9
Status, ordination as, 2, 52
Statuta Ecclesia Antiqua, 23
Storck, Hans, 10
Superintendent, 68, 147, 149, 171, 185, 211

Teaching, 116
Te Deum, 156, 167, 184, 205, 206–207
Time, for ordination, 24
Traditio casulae, 24
Traditio instrumentorum, 27, 29, 30, 91, 120, 221
Threefold Office, 131
Tonsure, 120

Vajta, Vilmos, 10, 46
Validity, 202, 224
Veni Creator Spiritus, 29, 113, 221
Veni Sancte Spiritus, 29, 95, 111–114, 154, 162, 204, 206, 207, 221
Verona Sacramentary, 19, 33
Vestments, 21, 24, 27, 29, 30, 221
Visitations, 96, 116, 147, 182, 185
Visitors, 89
Vocation, 60, 95, 111
Vollzugsformel, 152, 186, 205, 215–218
Vow, 118, 149, 176, 180, 205, 209, 216, 221

Wolfenbüttel, 1569 rites of, 182–185
Württemberg, ordination rites 1547 and 1559, 162–170

Ziegenhainer Zuchtordnung, 1539, 149

RENAISSANCE AND BAROQUE
STUDIES AND TEXTS

This series deals with various aspects of the European Renaissance and Baroque. Studies on the history, literature, philosophy, and the visual arts of these periods are welcome. The series also will consider translations of important works, especially from Latin into English. These translations should, however, include a substantial introduction and notes. Books in the series will include original monographs as well as revised or reconceived dissertations. The series editor is:

>Eckhard Bernstein
>Department of Modern Languages
>   and Literatures
>College of the Holy Cross
>Worcester, MA 01610